Dictionary Three

J. Neale

Dd Ee Ff Gg Hh Ii Jj Kk Ll Mm Nn Oo Pp Qq Rr Ss Tt Uu Vv Ww Xx Yy Zz

CONTENTS

Parts of Speech are given as follows

n	noun		interj	interjection
v	verb		conj	conjuction
adj	adjective	adv — adverb		
pron	pronoun		[pl] = plural	
prep	preposition		[abbr] = abbreviation	

First published in 1989 by Holmes McDougall Ltd, Edinburgh
This edition published 1991 by
Collins Educational *An imprint of* Harper Collins *Publishers*
77-85 Fulham Palace Road
London W6 8JB

Reprinted 1993, 1996

ISBN 0 00 316136 6

Designed and illustrated by Dorothy Hamilton. Printed in Hong Kong

Aa

abandon	*v*	*1* to give up altogether *2* to leave and not return
abate	*v*	to become less
abattoir	*n*	a slaughterhouse for cattle and sheep
abbess	*n*	a woman who is the head of a convent or abbey
abbey	*n*	*1* a church and other buildings where monks or nuns live *2* a great church such as Westminster Abbey
abbot	*n*	a man who is head of an abbey or monastery
abbreviate	*v*	to make shorter
abdicate	*v*	to give up a position of power, such as a throne
abdomen	*n*	the part of the body containing the stomach
abduct	*v*	to carry off by force; to kidnap
abide	*v*	to stay or live
ability	*n*	skill or power to do things
ablaze	*adj*	on fire
able	*adj*	having talent, skill or power to do things
abnormal	*adj*	not normal; unusual; strange
aboard	*adv, prep*	on or into a ship, bus, aircraft, train etc.
abolish	*v*	to stop or to do away with
abominable	*adj*	most unpleasant; disgusting
Aborigines	*n*	the first or earliest inhabitants of a country, such as the first Australians
abound	*v*	to exist in large numbers
about	*adv*	more or less
about	*prep*	around; nearby
above	*prep*	overhead; higher than something
abrasion	*n*	a place where the surface of the skin is grazed by scraping or rubbing
abreast	*adv*	side by side
abridge	*v*	to make shorter by using fewer words
abroad	*adv*	in a foreign country
abrupt	*adj*	*1* sudden and unexpected *2* rude; impolite
abscess	*n*	a pus-filled swelling on or in the body
absence	*n*	being away
absent	*adj*	not present; away
absolutely	*adv*	completely
absorb	*v*	to soak up or drink in
abstain	*v*	to avoid doing
absurd	*adj*	silly; ridiculous
abundance	*n*	a great quantity
abundant	*adj*	more than enough; plentiful
abuse	*v*	*1* to say unkind or rude things *2* to put to wrong use
abuse	*n*	*1* rude or unkind words *2* wrong use
abyss	*n*	a very deep hole or gorge in the earth
academy	*n*	a school or college; a place of learning
accelerate	*v*	to move faster
accent	*n*	*1* a way of speech or pronouncing a language *2* greater force given to a word or part of a word
accept	*v*	*1* to receive something that is offered *2* to agree to
access	*n*	entrance
accident	*n*	a mishap; something happening by chance
accommodate	*v*	to provide someone with a place in which to live
accommodation	*n*	a place to live
accompany	*v*	*1* to go with, such as on a journey *2* to play an instrument while someone sings or plays
accomplish	*v*	to succeed in doing

account *n*
1 a record of money received, paid or owed
2 a description or report of an event

account *v* to explain; to give reasons for

accumulate *v* to collect; to pile up

accurate *adj* exactly right

accuse *v* to blame someone with doing wrong

ace *n*
1 the name for 'one' in cards
2 a service in tennis that cannot be returned
3 a person of great skill

acetylene *n* a gas that burns with a hot, bright flame

ache *n* a continuous pain

ache *v* to have or suffer a dull, continuous pain

achieve *v* to do or finish something successfully

acid *adj* sour; bitter

acid *n* a sour or corrosive substance

acknowledge *v*
1 to admit that something is true
2 to say that you have received something

acorn *n* the fruit of the oak tree

acquaint *v* to make something known to a person

acquaintance *n* a person who is known to someone

acquire *v* to obtain; to gain

acquit *v* to give a decision that a person is not guilty

acre *n* a measure of land about 4,047 square metres

acrobat *n* someone who does balancing tricks, often in a circus

across *prep* from one side to the other

act *n*
1 a thing done
2 a law made by Parliament
3 a main division in a stage play

act *v*
1 to do
2 to play a part in; to pretend

action *n* movement

abbey

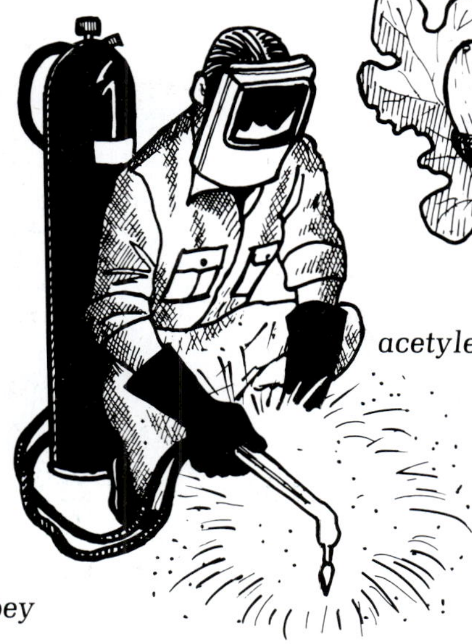
acetylene

acorn

acrobat

active *adj* lively; busy; full of energy

actor *n* a person who acts in plays, in films or on T.V. (fem: actress)

actual *adj* real; existing in fact

acute *adj* sharp; quick at understanding

adapt *v* to alter something for another use

add *v* to put things together to make more

adder *n* a small, poisonous snake

addict *n* someone who is unable to give up a harmful habit, such as drugs

address *n* the place where a person lives and to where mail is sent

address *v*
1 to make a speech
2 to write directions on a letter

adenoids *n* small growth between the back of the nose and throat

adequate *adj* enough; sufficient

adhere *v* to stick to something

adhesive *adj* sticky

adjacent *adj* very close to; next to

adjective *n* a word that describes what something or somebody is like

adjourn *v* to put off; to postpone

adjust *v* to arrange; to put in order

admiral *n* a very high rank in the navy

admire *v* to think well of something or somebody

admission *n*
1 being allowed to enter
2 saying that something is true

admit *v*
1 to let in
2 to own up as true; to confess

adolescent *n* a girl or boy in the period of life between being a child and being a grown-up

adopt *v*
1 to take someone else's child into a family
2 to choose

adore *v* to love very much; to worship

adorn *v* to decorate

adrift *adj* boats etc. floating to and fro without control

adult *n* fully grown person or animal

advance *v* to move or come forward

advantage *n* something that may help one to be successful

advent *n* an arrival; a coming

adventure *n* an exciting or daring experience

adverb *n* a word that tells us how, when or where something happens

advertise *v* to make known to the public, as in a newspaper or on T.V. etc.

advertisement *n* a notice for something for sale, services offered etc.

advice *n* something said to you to help you decide what to do

advise *v* to give advice

aerial *n* a wire, rods or framework put up to receive or send out radio and television signals

aerial

advertisement

aerodrome	*n*		a small airport
aeronautics	*n*		the science of flight
aeroplane	*n*		a flying vehicle, heavier than air, that has wings and at least one engine
aerosol	*n*		a small container from which liquid is sprayed in a fine mist
affair	*n*		a thing or business that has been done or has to be done
affect	*v*		to produce a change or result
affection	*n*		love; great liking
affectionate	*adj*		showing love and fondness
afford	*v*	*1*	to be able to buy or give
		2	to spare
afloat	*adj*		on water; at sea; on board a boat or ship
afraid	*adj*		frightened
after	*adv*		behind
afternoon	*n*		the part of the day between morning and evening
afterwards	*adv*		later
again	*adv*		once more; another time
against	*prep*	*1*	next to; resting on
		2	in opposition to
age	*n*	*1*	the length or time a person or animal has lived
		2	a length of time in history, such as the Iron Age
agent	*n*		someone working on behalf of someone else
aggravate	*v*		to make worse; to annoy
agile	*adj*		nimble; quick
agitate	*v*		to stir up; to shake
ago	*adj*		back in time past; previously
agony	*n*		great pain or suffering
agree	*v*		to consent; to say yes to
agriculture	*n*		farming
aground	*adj*		stranded on the bottom of shallow water
ahead	*adv*		in front

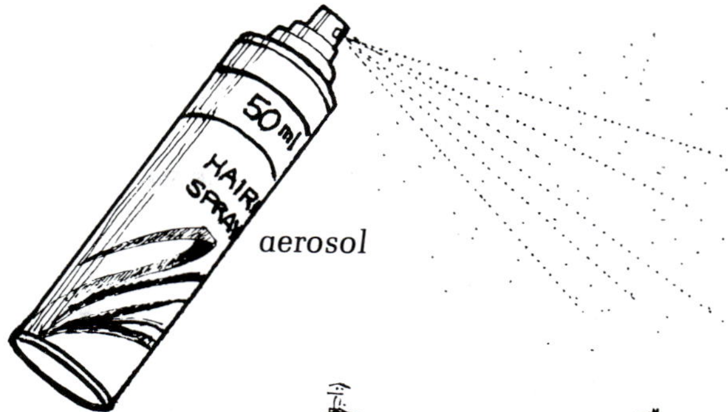

aerosol

aircraft carrier

aid	*v*		to help
aid	*n*		help that is given
aim	*v*		to point or direct towards some object
air	*n*		the mixture of gases we breathe
airborne	*adj*	*1*	carried by the air, such as seeds
		2	in flight, such as aircraft
aircraft	*n*		a flying machine of any type
aircraft carrier	*n*		a large warship carrying aircraft which land and take off on its large flat surface
airhostess	*n*		a woman who looks after passengers on an aircraft
airline	*n*		a business that owns and flies aircraft for carrying passengers and cargo
airmail	*n*		letters, cards and packages sent by air
airport	*n*		a place where aircraft land and take off
airtight	*adj*		not allowing air to pass in or out

aisle *n* a passage between rows of seats in a church, cinema or theatre

alarm *n* *1* a warning of danger such as a bell, siren etc. sounding *2* sudden fear

alarm *v* *1* to warn of danger *2* to startle

album *n* a book used for collecting stamps, photographs etc.

alcohol *n* a spirit found in wines, beers, whisky etc.

alcove *n* a recess in a wall

alder *n* a type of birch tree

alert *adj* watchful and ready

alert *v* to warn

algae *n* a group of plants that live in or near water and are usually very small

algebra *n* a branch of mathematics in which symbols and letters are used instead of numbers

alias *n* a false name

alien *n* a foreigner

alien *adj* belonging to another country or race; foreign

alight *adj* on fire; in flames

alike *adj* similar

alive *adj* living

all *adj* each, every; the whole of something

Allah *n* the Muslim name for God

alley *n* a short, narrow passage between buildings

alligator *n* a reptile similar to a crocodile that lives in the hot, wet parts of China and Americas

allocate *v* to share out

allow *v* to let someone do something; to permit

alloy *n* a mixture of metals

ally *n* a friend, or country that helps another

almost *adv* very nearly

alone *adv* by yourself; only

aloud *adv* in a voice that can be heard

alpha *n* the first letter of the Greek alphabet

alphabet *n* the letters of a language arranged in order

also *adv* as well as; in addition to something

altar *n* the communion table in a Christian church

alter *v* to change

alternative *n* offering the choice between two things

although *conj* even if; otherwise

altitude *n* height above sea level

altogether *adv* completely; entirely

aluminium *n* a light, easily shaped, silver-white metal

always *adv* at all times

amateur *n* someone whose pastime is done for pleasure, not money

amaze *v* to astonish; to surprise

aisle

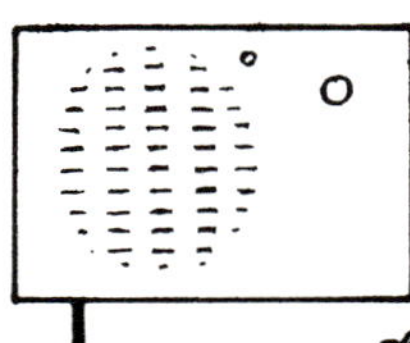

alarm

alligator

alpha

ambassador *n*	someone who represents one country in another country
ambition *n*	strong desire for success
ambulance *n*	a vehicle for carrying sick or injured people
ambush *v*	to lie in wait then attack
amen *n*	the final word of a hymn or prayer, meaning 'so be it'
amend *v*	to make changes; to put right
amethyst *n*	a semi-precious stone, purple in colour
ammonia *n*	a strong chemical, often used for cleaning
ammunition *n*	bullets, bombs, shells for firearms
among *prep*	in the middle of; surrounded by
amount *n*	a quantity or sum
amphibian *n*	an animal that lives both in water and on land
ample *adj*	enough or more than is necessary
amputate *v*	to cut off a limb
amuse *v*	to make someone smile or laugh
anaesthetic *n*	a drug used so that people do not feel pain during an operation
anagram *n*	a word formed from the letters of another word
anatomy *n*	knowledge of how our bodies are built
ancestor *n*	a person now dead from whom another is descended
anchor *n*	a heavy metal hook used to keep a boat or ship from moving
ancient *adj*	very old; belonging to olden times
and *conj*	also; as well as; too
angel *n*	a messenger from God

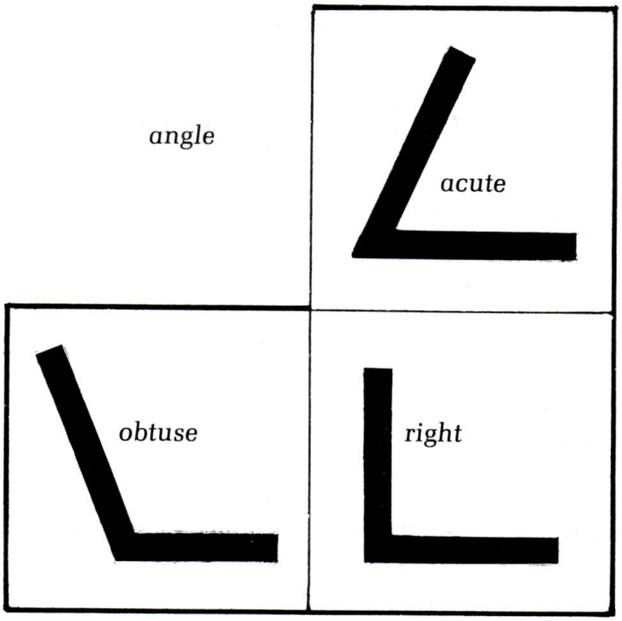

anger *n*	bad temper; rage
angle *n*	a corner; the space between two straight lines or surfaces that meet
angler *n*	a fisherman, with rod and line
angry *adj*	filled with anger; enraged
animal *n*	anything alive that is not a plant
ankle *n*	the joint between the leg and the foot
anniversary *n*	the date of an annual celebration or event
announce *v*	to make known
annoy *v*	to make someone cross or angry
annual *adj*	happening every year
anonymous *adj*	nameless; unknown
anorak *n*	a short, waterproof jacket with a hood
anorexia *n*	a dangerous condition in which there is no wish for food

another *adj* one more; a different one
answer *v* to reply to a question
answer *n* the solution to a problem
ant *n* a small, busy insect
antarctic *n* the south polar region
antelope *n* an animal like a deer, with horns
antenna *n* *1* the feeler of a fish or insect *2* a kind of aerial
anthem *n* a song of praise
antibiotic *n* a drug which helps to fight harmful bacteria
anticipate *v* to look forward to; to expect
anticyclone *n* a mass of air which often causes settled weather, either hot or cold
antifreeze *n* a chemical substance used to lower the freezing point of water in a car radiator
antique *adj* very old and often valuable
antiseptic *n* a chemical substance that kills bacteria
antler *n* the branched horn of a stag
antonym *n* a word opposite in meaning to another word
anvil *n* a blacksmith's iron block
anxiety *n* uneasiness of mind
anxious *adj* troubled; worried
any *adj, adv, pron* some; one out of many
anybody *pron* any person; no matter who
apart *adv* aside; separately
apartheid *n* the keeping separate of races of different colours, especially in South Africa
apartment *n* a flat; a set of rooms in a building
ape *n* a large monkey-like animal with no tail
apex *n* a pointed tip or peak
apologise *v* to say you are sorry for doing or saying something
apparatus *n* the equipment needed for work or experiments
appeal *v* to ask for help or sympathy
appear *v* *1* to come into sight *2* to seem
appetite *n* the desire for food
applaud *v* to show approval by clapping
apple *n* a roundish fruit, red, green or yellow in colour
apply *v* to ask for something
appoint *v* to choose someone to do a particular job
appointment *n* an arrangement to meet someone
approach *v* to move towards
approve *v* to be pleased with; to give permission
approximate *adj* very near; almost correct
apricot *n* a soft, orange-coloured stone-fruit
apron *n* clothing worn to protect clothes
aqualung *n* a diver's breathing apparatus carried on the back
aquarium *n* a tank for live fish
aqueduct *n* a pipe, bridge, or canal, that carries a water supply across a valley

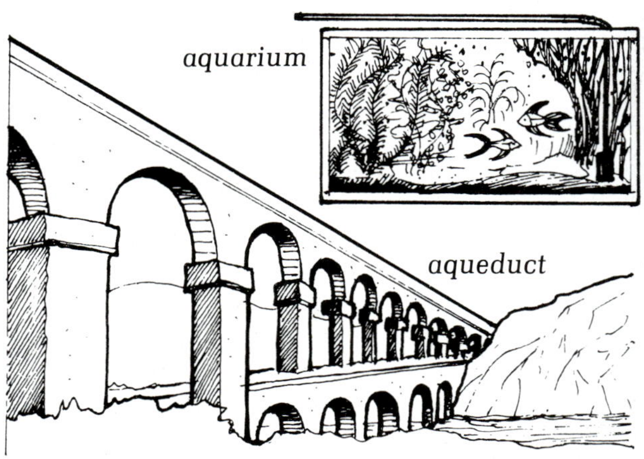

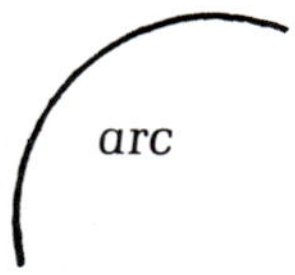

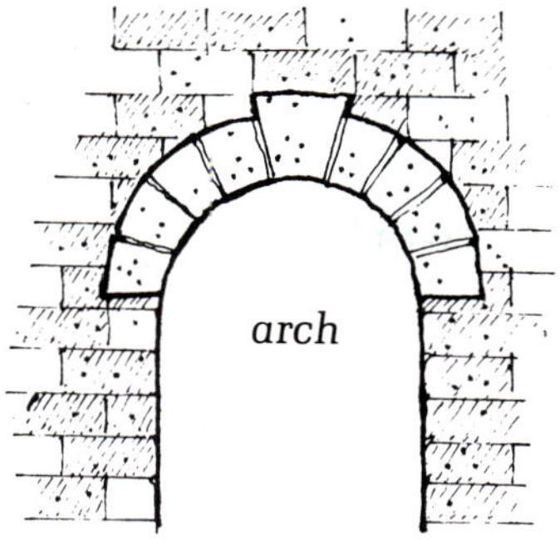

arc *n*		a curved line; part of a circle
arch *n*		the curved top of a doorway, tunnel or bridge
archaeology *n*		the study of history through the things that people have made and built
archbishop *n*		a chief bishop
archer *n*		a person who shoots with a bow and arrow
architect *n*		a person who plans and designs new buildings
arctic *n*		the north polar region
area *n*	1	any flat surface
	2	a region
	3	an amount of space measured in squares
argue *v*		to disagree with someone, often in a noisy way
arid *adj*		dry; parched
arise *v*		to get up
arithmetic *n*		working with numbers
ark *n*	1	a chest or box
	2	a large ship, especially the one built by Noah
arm *n*		the part of your body from the shoulder to the hand
arm *v*		to supply with weapons
armchair *n*		a chair with an arm on each side of the seat
armada *n*		a fleet of warships
armour *n*		protective covering worn in battle
arms *n*		weapons; firearms
army *n*		a large number of trained soldiers
around *adv, prep*		on all sides; in a circle
arrange *v*	1	to put in proper order
	2	to make plans
arrest *v*		to capture or to take prisoner
arrive *v*		to reach a place after a journey
arrow *n*		a pointed stick with feathers at one end, shot from a bow
arson *n*		the crime of setting fire to property
art *n*		the study of, or the making of, beautiful things, especially in painting, music, pottery etc.
artery *n*		a blood vessel that carries blood from the heart to the rest of the body
article *n*	1	a single thing, an object
	2	a piece of writing in a newspaper or magazine
artificial *adj*		not real or natural
artillery *n*		large guns
artist *n*		someone who paints, carves, sings, etc skilfully
ascend *v*		to rise; to climb up
ash *n*	1	a tall tree with greyish bark and tough white wood
	2	the black powder left after a fire

ashamed *adj* very sorry for having done something wrong or silly
ashore *adv* on the seashore; on land
aside *adv* to or at one side
ask *v* to question someone
asleep *adv* not awake
asparagus *n* a green vegetable sold in bunches
asphalt *n* a kind of pitch used in road building and roofing
ass *n* a donkey
assemble *v* to meet; to gather together
assembly *n* a meeting
asset *n* something of value
assist *v* to help
assistant *n* a person who helps another, as in a job
association *n* a group of people or organizations that work together
assortment *n* a mixture of different kinds
aster *n* a star-like flower
asterisk *n* a star-like mark (*)
astern *adv* in or at the back part (stern) of a ship
asthma *n* a disease that makes breathing difficult
astonish *v* to surprise greatly; to amaze
astronaut *n* a traveller in space
astronomy *n* the study of the stars and their movements
athlete *n* a person who is active in sports
atlas *n* a book of maps
atmosphere *n* the air around the earth
atoll a coral island with a central lagoon, or lake
atom *n* a tiny particle
attach *v* to join together
attack *v* to move forward and fight
attempt *v* to try to do something
attend *v* *1* to be present at
2 to give thought to
attic *n* a room in the roof of a house
attitude *n* the way a person thinks, acts or feels
attract *v* to draw towards
attractive *adj* charming; very pleasant
auction *n* a sale in which each thing is sold to the person who will give the most money for it
audience *n* people listening to or watching a performance, show etc.
audition *n* a hearing given to an actor, a singer etc. for a test
aunt *n* *1* a sister of your mother or father
2 the wife of your uncle
author *n* a writer of books
authority *n* *1* power over other people
2 an expert
autobiography *n* the life story of a person written by herself or himself
autograph *n* a person's name written by herself or himself
automatic *adj* working by itself
automation *n* the using of machines controlled by computers etc.

attic
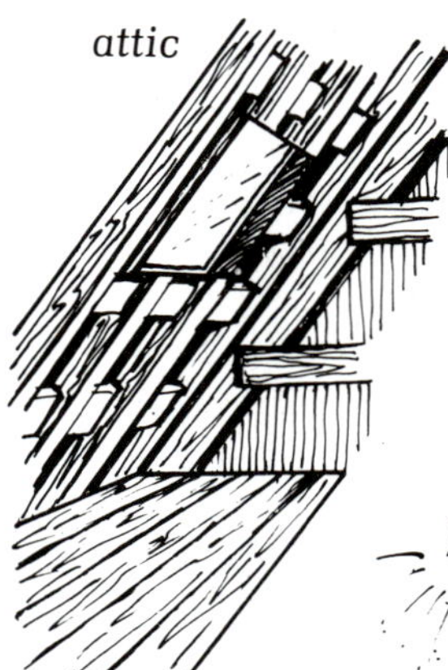

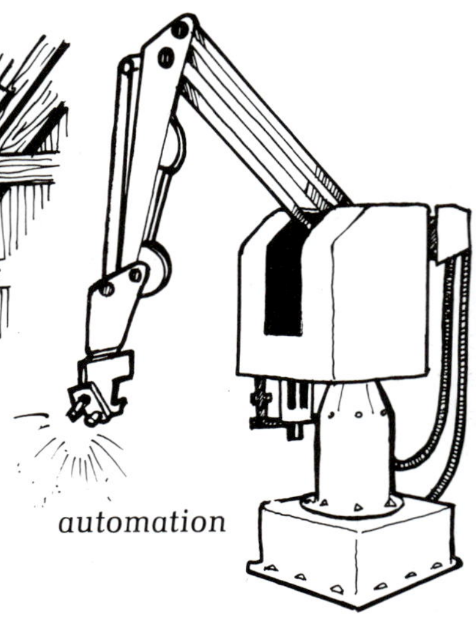
automation

aviary

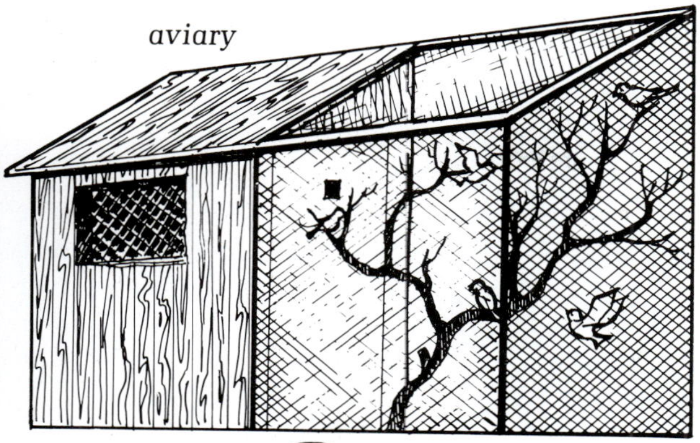

axle

autumn *n*		the season of the year between summer and winter
avalanche *n*		a heavy fall of snow and rocks down a mountain side
avenue *n*		a road or street, often lined with trees
average *adj*		normal; usual; everyday
aviary *n*		a bird-house
aviation *n*		the art or science of flying aircraft
avoid *v*		to keep clear of; to keep away from
await *v*		to wait for
awake *adj*		not asleep
award *n*		a prize of honour
away *adv*	*1*	further off
	2	absent
awful *adj*		very bad; terrible; dreadful
awhile *adv*		for a short time
awkward *adj*		clumsy
axe *n*		a sharp tool for cutting
axle *n*		the rod on which a wheel turns
ayatollah *n*		a Muslim religious leader
azure *adj*		sky-blue

Bb

baboon *n*		a kind of large African monkey
baby *n*		a very young child
babysitter *n*		someone who looks after young children
bachelor *n*		a man who is not married
back *n*	*1*	the part of your body that is opposite to the front part
	2	the rear part of anything
back *adj*		opposite to front
back *v*	*1*	to help
	2	to go backwards
backbone *n*		the spine; a line of little bones down the back of your body
backgammon *n*		a board game for two players
backward *adj*	*1*	towards the back
	2	not very clever
backwards *adv*		facing the wrong way
bacon *n*		salted or smoked meat from the back and sides of a pig
bacteria *n*		very tiny living things, some of which cause disease
bad *adj*	*1*	not good; wicked
	2	rotten; decayed
badge *n*		a special sign or mark worn by members of a club or society, or to show that they have a special job
badger *n*		a burrowing, nocturnal, grey-coated animal
badminton *n*		a game similar to tennis, played on a court with a racket and a shuttlecock
baffle *v*		to puzzle someone completely
bag *n*		a pouch or container made of paper, fabric, plastic etc. and having an opening in the top
baggage *n*		luggage to hold what you need when you go on a trip
baggy *adj*		hanging loose

Bb

bagpipes *n*	a musical instrument with a windbag and pipes
bail *n*	one of a pair of wooden crosspieces on the top of cricket stumps
bail *v*	to scoop water out of a boat etc.
bait *n*	food put on hook to tempt fish, or food used to tempt an animal into a trap
bake *v*	to cook in an oven
baker *n*	a person who makes bread and cakes
balance *n*	*1* an instrument for weighing things *2* steadiness
balance *v*	*1* to keep steady *2* to make things equal
balcony *n*	a platform attached to an outside wall or window of a building
bald *adj*	having little or no hair on the head
bale *n*	a large bundle of goods or material e.g. hay, wool etc.
ball *n*	something round, like a sphere
ballad *n*	a simple song or poem telling a story
ballerina *n*	a female ballet dancer
ballet *n*	a story or play told in the form of graceful dancing
balloon *n*	a bag of thin material filled with air or gas
ballot *n*	a system of secret voting
ballpoint *n*	a pen having a small ball that rolls ink onto the paper
balsa *n*	the very light, strong wood of a South American tree
bamboo *n*	very tall grass, growing in tropical lands
ban *v*	to forbid
banana *n*	a long, curved tropical fruit with a thick yellow skin
band *n*	*1* a narrow strip used for holding things together *2* a group of musicians playing together
bandage *n*	a narrow strip of cloth or other material used to cover wounds
bandit *n*	a robber
bang *n*	a sudden, loud noise
bang *v*	to strike noisily
banish *v*	to drive away; to send into exile
banister *n*	the handrail guarding the edge of stairs or a landing
banjo *n*	a musical instrument with four or five strings
bank *n*	*1* a place where money is kept and paid out *2* land along the side of a river or lake *3* a mound of earth, sand, snow etc.
bank *v*	to fly an aircraft at an angle when turning
bankrupt *n*	someone who is unable to pay debts
banner *n*	a flag
banquet *n*	a feast or dinner party, with speeches
bantam *n*	a small fowl
baptism *n*	the Christian ceremony of touching or covering a person with water to show that he has become a member of the church
bar *n*	*1* a rod, often of metal *2* a counter where drinks are sold
barbecue *v*	to cook over an open fire
barbed wire *n*	wire with sharp spikes, used for fences

barber *n* — a person who cuts men's and boys' hair

bare *adj* — *1* naked; not covered
2 empty

bargain *n* — something bought cheaply and is good value for money

bargain *v* — to argue about price or terms

barge *n* — a flat-bottomed boat used on rivers and canals

bark *n* — *1* the outside skin or cover of a tree trunk or branch
2 the sharp cry of a dog, fox etc.

barley *n* — a grain that is used for food

barn *n* — a farm building used for storing crops or sheltering animals

barometer *n* — an instrument that measures air pressure, and shows changes in the weather

barracks *n* — buildings that soldiers live in

barrel *n* — *1* the tube of a gun
2 a metal or wooden cask

barricade *n* — a barrier quickly put up to block a street etc.

barrier *n* — something standing in the way

barrister *n* — a lawyer who can defend or prosecute people in any court

base *n* — the part that something rests or stands on; the lowest part

baseball *n* — a game played with bat and ball on a field with four bases

basement *n* — the floor below ground level in a building

basic *adj* — simple, but important

basin *n* — a round bowl

basket *n* — a container usually made of cane, grasses etc.

basketball *n* — a game played with a large ball on a court with two nets

bass *n* — a fish that can be eaten

bat *n* — *1* a piece of wood for hitting a ball e.g. cricket bat
2 a small mouse-like flying animal

batch *n* — a number of things of the same kind

bath *n* — a large container for washing the whole body

bathe *v* — *1* to have a bath
2 to go swimming

bathroom *n* — a room with a bath, basin, and toilet

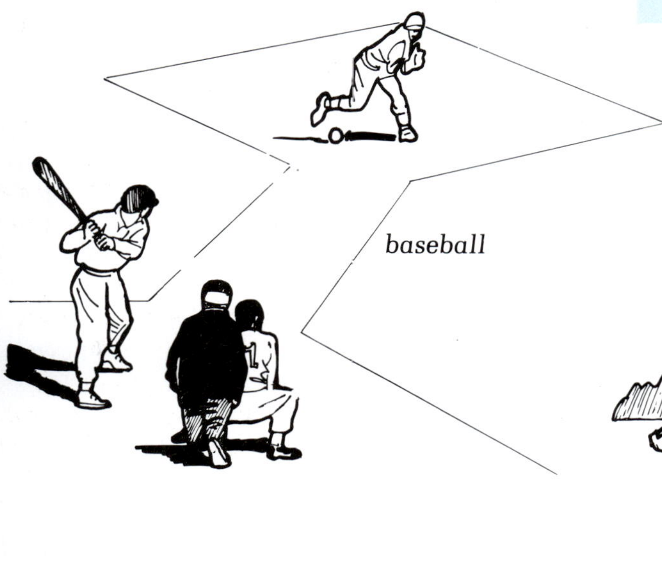

Bb

battalion *n*		a part of a regiment of soldiers
batter *v*		to hit very hard
batter *n*		a mixture of flour, eggs and milk, beaten together and cooked
battery *n*		a container for storing electricity
battle *n*		a fight between enemies
bawl *v*		to shout or cry out loudly
bay *n*		part of the sea shore that makes a wide curve inward
be *v*		to live, to exist
beach *n*		the shore of an ocean or lake, either sandy or covered with pebbles
beacon *n*		a light or fire used as a warning signal
bead *n*		a small, pierced ball of glass, metal or other material in a necklace
beagle *n*		a small, smooth-haired dog
beak *n*		the hard, pointed part of a bird's mouth
beam *n*	*1*	a ray of light
	2	a long piece of wood or metal
bean *n*		a plant with long pods containing seeds which are eaten
bear *n*		a very big, furry animal
bear *v*	*1*	to put up with
	2	to give birth to
beard *n*		the hair on a man's face
beast *n*		a four-footed animal
beat *v*	*1*	to hit hard and often
	2	to defeat another person or group
beat *n*	*1*	a usual route taken by a police officer on duty
	2	a regular sound
beautiful *adj*		lovely, very pretty
beauty *n*		a person or thing pleasing to the sight or hearing
beaver *n*		a soft, furry animal that lives in water as well as on land
because *conj*		as a result of; for the reason that
become *v*		to grow to be
bed *n*	*1*	a piece of furniture used to sleep or rest on
	2	a patch of ground in a garden for flowers or vegetables to grow
	3	the bottom of the sea, river, lake etc.
bedroom *n*		a room to sleep in
bee *n*		a four-winged, honey-making insect
beech *n*		a large tree with a smooth, grey bark
beef *n*		meat from cattle
beehive *n*		a small box where bees are kept
beer *n*		a strong drink made from malted barley and hops
beet *n*		a vegetable with a sweet, fleshy root
beetle *n*		an insect with a hard, shiny back to protect its wings
before *prep*	*1*	in front of
	2	earlier than
beg *v*		to ask for help, food or money
beggar *n*		a poor person who lives by begging for food or money
begin *v*		to start to do something
beginner *n*		someone who is just starting to learn something
behave *v*		to show good or bad manners in front of others
behaviour *n*		the way someone behaves
behind *prep*		at the back of
behind *adv*		not on time
beige *n*		a light brown colour

belfry *n* a bell tower

believe *v* to think that something is true

bell *n* a hollow object that makes a musical sound when struck

bellow *v* to roar, to shout in an angry way

belly *n* the stomach

belong *v*
1 to be owned by
2 to be a member of

below *prep, adv* underneath; lower than; beneath

belt *n* a strip of leather or other material worn around your waist

bench *n*
1 a long, wooden seat
2 a work table

bend *v*
1 to curve something
2 to lean over

bend *n* something that is bent, such as a curved part of a road or stream

beneath *prep, adv* lower than, under

berry *n* a small, juicy fruit enclosing seeds

beside *prep* by the side of

besides *adv* also, as well

best *adj* the very finest

better *adj*
1 recovering, or having recovered, from an illness
2 finer, worth more

between *prep*
1 in the middle of
2 shared by two people

beware *v* to be on your guard against; to watch out for

bewilder *v* to puzzle; to confuse

beyond *prep*
1 on the farther side of
2 too far for

Bible *n* the sacred book of the Christian religion

bicycle *n* a two-wheeled vehicle powered by the rider

bid *v* to offer to pay a price at an auction

big *adj* large; important

bike *n* a short name for a bicyle

bill *n*
1 a bird's beak
2 an account of money that you owe

billion *n* a very large number, one thousand million

bin *n* a container such as a dustbin or breadbin

bind *v* to tie together with string, rope, thread etc.

bingo *n* a game of chance played on numbered squares

binoculars *n* two very small telescopes fastened side by side, used to make things far away look closer

biography *n* the written story of a person's life

biology *n* the study of living things

birch *n* a tree with smooth bark, often white, which peels off like paper

belfry

binoculars

Bb

bird *n*		a feathered animal that lays eggs and has wings and two legs
birth *n*		being born
biscuit *n*		a small, flat, thin, hard-baked cake
bishop *n*		a high-ranking member of the clergy
bison *n*		a North American wild animal, a buffalo
bit *n*	*1*	a small piece of something
	2	the metal part of a horse's bridle, held in its mouth
bite *v*		to take hold of, or cut off, with your teeth
bitter *adj*		having a sharp, sour taste
black *n*		the darkest of all colours; the opposite of white
blackberry *n*		the fruit of the bramble
blackbird *n*		a song-bird of the thrush family
blackboard *n*		a board on which things can be written in chalk
blackcurrant *n*		a fruit that grows on a garden shrub
blackmail *n*		the crime of demanding money from someone in return for keeping something secret
blacksmith *n*		a person who works with iron and makes shoes for horses

bloodhound

blade *n*		the flat, cutting part of a knife or sword
blame *v*		to find fault with; to hold responsible
blancmange *n*		a jelly-like pudding made mainly from milk, cornflour and sugar
blank *adj*		empty, not written on
blanket *n*		a warm covering for a bed
blast *n*	*1*	a rush of air
	2	an explosion
	3	a loud sound
blast-off *n*		the sending off of rockets and missiles
blaze *n*		a bright fire throwing out flames
bleach *n*		something that makes an object white by taking out its colour
bleat *v*		to make a noise like a sheep, goat etc.
bleed *v*		to lose blood
blend *v*		to mix two or more substances together
bless *v*		to wish happiness or health
blind *adj*		unable to see
blind *n*		a window cover
blink *v*		to drop and raise your eyelids quickly
blister *n*		a watery swelling under the skin
blizzard *n*		a heavy snowstorm with strong winds
block *n*	*1*	a solid piece
	2	a row of buildings
block *v*		to get in the way of
blond *adj*		having fair hair and a light skin (fem: blonde)
blood *n*		the red liquid pumped around your body by your heart
bloodhound *n*		a large dog with a keen sense of smell

bloom *n*		a flower, blossom
blossom *n*		a flower, usually of a fruit tree
blot *n*		a stain, a smudge or mark
blouse *n*		a kind of loose shirt, usually worn by women
blow *n*		a hard knock
blow *v*		to make the air move
blubber *n*		the fat of whales and some other sea animals
blue *n*		the colour of a cloudless sky
bluebell *n*		a flower with small blue petals, shaped like a bell
blunder *v*		to make a bad mistake
blunt *adj*	*1*	not sharp
	2	saying what you think, not being polite
blur *v*		to make something hazy and not easy to see
blush *v*		to go red in the face because you are shy, excited or ashamed
boa *n*		a large snake
boar *n*	*1*	a wild animal like a pig
	2	a male pig
board *n*		a long, thin piece of wood
board *v*	*1*	to enter a ship, train or bus
	2	to live somewhere, paying for food and a room
boast *v*		to brag; to praise yourself
boat *n*		a small vessel or ship
bob *v*		to move quickly up or down
body *n*	*1*	the whole of any animal or thing
	2	the main part of anything
	3	a group of people
bodyguard *n*		someone who protects another person
bog *n*		soft wet ground; a marsh
boil *n*		a small, painful swelling on the skin
boil *v*	*1*	to heat liquid until it bubbles and steams
	2	to cook something in boiling water
bold *adj*		brave; daring
bolt *n*	*1*	a sliding bar used to fasten a door or gate
	2	a metal pin with a screw at one end that goes into a nut to fasten things
bomb *n*		a container filled with explosive
bone *n*		one of the hard white pieces that make up a skeleton
bonfire *n*		a large, open-air fire
bonnet *n*	*1*	a head-covering usually worn by small children
	2	the covering of a car engine
book *n*		written or printed sheets bound together
book *v*		to reserve a ticket or a place
boom *n*		a deep, rumbling sound
boomerang *n*		a curved stick that can turn in the air and come back to the thrower
boot *n*	*1*	footwear reaching above the ankles
	2	a place for luggage in a car
border *n*	*1*	the part near the edge of something
	2	the line or frontier where two countries meet

Bb

bore *n* someone who makes you tired by talking too much about dull things
bore *v* to drill a hole
borrow *v* to get something from someone else which you use and then give back
boss *n* someone in charge
botany *n* the study of plants and how they grow
both *adj, pron* the two together
bother *v* to cause trouble; to annoy
bottle *n* a container, usually made of glass, in which liquid is kept
bottom *n* the lowest part
bough *n* a branch of a tree
boulder *n* a large rock rounded by the action of water etc.
bounce *v* to spring up again like a ball that is dropped on the ground
boundary *n* a line dividing one area from another
bouquet *n* a bunch of flowers
boutique *n* a shop, usually selling modern clothes
bow *v* to bend the body forwards
bow *n* the front part of a ship
bow *n*
1 a weapon for shooting arrows
2 a stringed rod used to play stringed instruments such as the violin, cello etc.
3 a ribbon tied in loops
bowl *n*
1 a deep dish or basin
2 a ball for rolling in the game of bowls
bowls *n* an outdoor or indoor game in which a bowler tries to bowl a big ball as near as possible to the 'jack', a smaller ball
box *n* a container, usually with a cover
box *v* to fight, wearing gloves, in a boxing ring
boy *n* a male child
bracelet *n* a piece of jewellery worn on the wrist
brag *v* to boast, to show off
braille *n* raised letters that a blind person can read by touching them
brain *n* the grey matter in the head of people and animals, which controls thought and feeling
brake *n* a device for slowing down movement
bramble *n* a prickly shrub bearing blackberries
bran *n* the outer covering of wheat and other grains
branch *n*
1 a bough of a tree, growing out of its trunk
2 one of a group of stores or banks, but not the chief one
brand *n* a certain make of a product
brand *v* to burn the owner's symbol on the hide of cattle
brandy *n* a strong spirit distilled from wine
brass *n* a yellow metal, made by melting copper and zinc together
brave *adj* full of courage
brawl *n* a noisy quarrel turning into a fight
bray *v* to make the sound that a donkey makes
bread *n* a food made from flour, water and yeast baked in an oven
breadth *n* the distance from side to side

break *v*		to split, to smash into pieces
break *n*		a break, a pause
breaker *n*		a large wave that rolls onto the shore
breakfast *n*		the first meal of the day
bream *n*		a freshwater fish with a thick, flat body
breast *n*		the upper part of the body; the chest
breath *n*		air taken in and pushed out by the lungs
breathalyser *n*		an instrument for measuring the amount of alcohol in the blood
breathe *v*		to draw air into or push it out of your lungs
breed *n*		a kind or class of animal (or plant) usually developed by man
breed *v*		to produce young; to rear
breeze *n*		a gentle wind
brew *v*		to make a drink by soaking and boiling
bribe *n*		money or a gift offered to gain a favour
brick *n*		a block of hard-baked clay used for building
bride *n*		a woman on her wedding day
bridegroom *n*		a man on his wedding day
bridesmaid *n*		a bride's attendant
bridge *n*	*1*	a structure to carry traffic over a road, railway or water
	2	a card game
	3	a platform on a ship for navigating etc.
bridle *n*		the part of a harness fitting over a horse's head
brief *adj*		lasting for a short time
bright *adj*	*1*	shining
	2	clever, intelligent
brighten *v*		to make or become bright

brilliant *adj*	*1*	shining brightly
	2	very clever
brim *n*	*1*	the edge of a cup or bowl
	2	the edge of a hat
bring *v*		to fetch; to carry
brink *n*		the edge of something, such as a cliff or steep place
brisk *adj*		quick, rapid
bristle *n*		a short, stiff hair
brittle *adj*		easily snapped or broken
broad *adj*		very wide
broadcast *v*		to spread news, especially by radio or television
broccoli *n*		a large green vegetable
brochure *n*		a small, thin book such as a holiday brochure
brontosaurus *n*		a huge dinosaur which had a long neck, small head and thick tail
bronze *n*		a metal made by melting copper and tin together
brooch *n*		a piece of jewellery fastened to clothing by a pin
brood *n*		a number of young birds produced at one hatch
brood *v*		to worry over something in a quiet moody way

brontosaurus

Bb

brook *n* a small stream
broom *n* 1 a yellow-flowered shrub
2 a sweeping brush with stiff bristles
brother *n* a man or boy who has the same parents as you do
brow *n* the forehead
brown *n* the colour of coffee or chocolate
brownie *n* a junior girl guide
bruise *n* a mark on the skin caused by a fall or a blow
brunette *n* a girl or woman with dark brown hair
brush *n* an implement for sweeping, scrubbing or painting
bubble *n* a very thin balloon of liquid filled with air
buck *n* a male deer, goat, rabbit etc
bucket *n* a container, with a handle for carrying water etc.
buckle *n* a clasp on a belt or shoe
bud *n* a leaf or flower not fully open
budge *v* to move slightly
budgerigar *n* a small, brightly coloured bird kept often as a pet
buffalo *n* a large, wild, North American animal; a bison
buffer *n* anything that softens a blow
bug *n* 1 a small, blood-sucking insect
2 a hidden listening device
bugle *n* a small trumpet
build *v* to make by putting different parts together
building *n* a structure with roof and walls
bulb *n* 1 an electric lamp
2 the roundish underground stems of some plants like onions, daffodils etc.
bulge *v* to swell outwards
bulky *adj* large and sometimes, clumsy
bull *n* the male of cattle; a male elephant
bulldog *n* a heavy dog with a flattened face
bulldozer *n* a powerful tractor that moves soil and rocks
bullet *n* a piece of metal fired from a rifle or revolver
bullion *n* gold or silver in the form of bars
bully *n* someone who frightens and hurts a smaller and weaker person
bump *n* 1 a dull thud
2 a swelling or lump
bump *v* to knock into or against
bumper *n* a bar fixed on the front or back of a car for protection
bun *n* a small, round cake
bunch *n* a number of things of the same kind together, such as grapes, bananas etc.
bundle *n* a number of things tied or wrapped together
bungalow *n* a house that has all its rooms on the ground floor
bunk *n* a box-like bed; a sleeping berth on a ship
buoy *n* a large, anchored float used to guide ships
burden *n* a heavy load
burglar *n* someone who breaks into a house to steal
burial *n* a funeral; the burying of anything
burn *n* a mark caused by fire or heat
burn *v* to destroy or damage something by fire
burrow *n* a hole in the ground made by an animal as a home and shelter

burst *v* to break open or fly into pieces suddenly

bury *v* to put something in the ground

bus *n* a large motor vehicle with seats for passengers

bush *n* a shrub; a small tree with many branches

business *n* a trade, work, shop, factory etc.

busy *adj* having a lot to do

but *conj*
1 though
2 except

butcher *n* a person who cuts up and sells meat

butler *n* a male servant in a large house

butter *n* a soft, yellow food made from fats contained in cream

buttercup *n* a small yellow flower with yellow petals

butterfly *n* an insect with large colourful wings

button *n* a small disc or knob for fastening clothes

buy *v* to get something you want by paying money for it

buzz *n* the humming sound made by a flying bee

bypass *n* a road going around a busy town to avoid the traffic

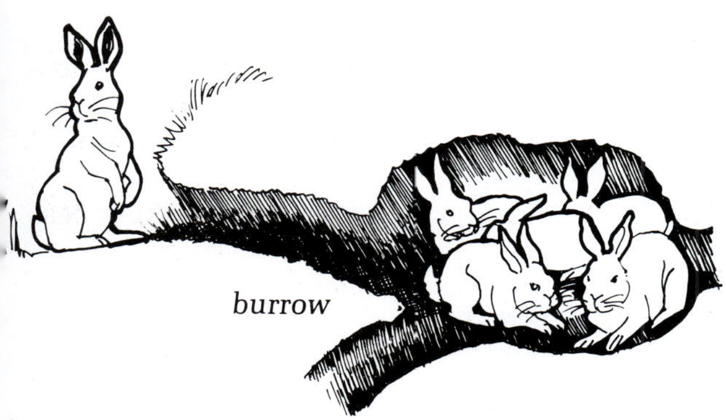

Cc

cab *n*
1 a taxi
2 the part of a lorry or locomotive where the driver sits

cabbage *n* a large, round green vegetable

cabin *n*
1 a small hut
2 a room in a ship or aircraft

cabinet *n*
1 a cupboard having drawers and shelves
2 a group of ministers of parliament who help the prime minister to govern

cable *n*
1 a strong wire or rope
2 covered electric or telephone wires

cackle *n* the screeching noise made by a hen

cactus *n* a very prickly desert plant

caddie *n* a person who carries clubs etc. for a golfer

cadet *n* a person in training to be an officer in the armed forces or to be a police officer

café *n* a place where food and drink are sold

cage *n* a box with wires or bars used to hold a bird or an animal

calculate *v* to count or reckon with figures; to work out

calculator *n* a machine which can add, subtract, multiply, divide etc.

calendar *n* a list of all the days, weeks and months of the year

calf *n* a young cow, elephant or whale

call *v*
1 to shout, cry out
2 to speak on the telephone
3 to pay a short visit

Cc

calm *adj* 1 quiet, still, without wind
2 not excited

camel *n* a desert animal with one or two humps on its back

camera *n* a device for taking photographs or films

camouflage *v* to disguise something by making it merge into its background

camp *v* to stay and sleep in tents

camp *n* a place where people stay in tents

can *n* a metal container

can *v* to be able

canal *n* a waterway dug across land

canary *n* a yellow songbird often kept as a pet

cancel *v* 1 to stop something that has been arranged
2 to cross out

cancer *n* an illness caused by a harmful growth in the body

candle *n* a stick of wax with a wick in it, burned to give light

cane *n* the hard, springy stem of certain tall grasses, such as bamboo

canine *adj* to do with dogs

canister *n* a small box or container

cannibal *n* a human being who eats human flesh

cannon *n* a large gun

canoe *n* a very light, narrow boat, moved with paddles

canteen *n* a dining room in a factory, office-building etc.

canter *n* an easy gallop on horseback

canvas *n* a strong cloth used for shoes, tents and sails

canyon *n* a deep, narrow gorge or valley

cap *n* 1 a soft hat with a peak
2 a cover or top

camp

canyon

canister

capable *adj* able to do something well

capacity *n* the amount that can be held in something

cape *n* 1 a cloak, an overcoat without sleeves
2 a piece of land that juts out into the sea

capital *n* 1 the chief city of a country
2 a large letter used to begin a sentence or name

capsize *v* to overturn

capsule *n* 1 a pill
2 part of a spacecraft

captain *n* 1 the officer in charge of a ship
2 an officer in the army
3 the leader of a sports team
4 the pilot of an air-liner

captive *n* a prisoner

capture *v* to take someone prisoner

car *n* a vehicle on wheels for carrying people

caravan *n* a home on wheels, usually pulled by a car

carcass *n* the body of a dead animal

card *n* a piece of stiff paper

cardboard *n* a thick, stiff paper, used for making boxes

cardigan *n* a knitted woollen jacket

cardinal *n* a senior priest in the Roman Catholic church

care *n*
1 attention
2 worry, trouble

care *v*
1 to look after, to tend
2 to mind, be worried or anxious about
3 to like

career *n* the job or jobs a person has during his working life

careful *adj* cautious, taking care

careless *adj* thoughtless, not taking care

caretaker *n* someone who looks after a building such as a school

cargo *n* goods carried by a ship or plane

caribou *n* a North American reindeer

carmine *n* a purple-red colour

carnation *n* a large, brightly coloured flower, related to the garden pink

carnival *n* an event with amusements, merrymaking etc.

carol *n* a religious song at Christmas

carpenter *n* a person who works with wood

carpet *n* a thick floor covering of woven or knitted material

carriage *n* a wheeled vehicle, often pulled by horses

carrot *n* an orange-coloured root vegetable

carry *v* to take something from one place to another

cart *n* a two-wheeled vehicle, usually pulled by a horse

cartoon *n*
1 a funny drawing
2 a film made with drawings

carve *v*
1 to cut meat into slices
2 to cut wood or stone into a shape

case *n* a box in which to keep things

cash *n* money in the form of coins or notes

casserole *n* a dish in which food is both cooked and served

cassette *n* a container for holding magnetic recording tape

cast *v*
1 to throw
2 to choose actors for a play, film etc.

cast *n*
1 a plaster support, used to protect broken bones while they are mending
2 the actors in a play, film etc.

castle *n* a strongly-built building with thick walls to be defended against attack

cat *n*
1 a small furry animal kept as a pet
2 a member of the cat family such as lions, tigers etc.

catalogue *n* a list of things, usually in alphabetical order or other order, such as books in a library

catch *v*
1 to seize and hold something
2 to be in time for

Cc

Cc

caterpillar *n* the grub of a butterfly or moth
cathedral *n* the main church of an area (diocese)
catkins *n* the hanging, fluffy flowers of the willow and hazel
cattle *n* cows, bulls, calves etc.
cauliflower *n* a vegetable with green leaves around a large white head of underdeveloped flowers
cause *v* to make something happen
cause *n* a reason
caution *n* care
caution *v* to warn
cautious *adj* careful; watching for danger
cavalry *n* soldiers on horseback
cave *n* a hollow place in the earth
cease *v* to stop, to come to an end
cedar *n* an evergreen tree with spreading branches and cones
ceiling *n* the inside top surface of a room
celebrate *v* to hold a party or other festivity in honour of an important event
celery *n* a vegetable with greenish-white stems
cell *n* *1* a small room in a prison *2* a very small unit of living matter in animals and plants
cellar *n* an underground storeroom
cello *n* a stringed musical instrument like a large violin
Celsius *adj* the scale on which temperature is measured on a thermometer
cement *n* a grey powder used for making concrete
cemetery *n* a burial ground for the dead
census *n* a counting of all the people in a country
cent *n* a coin used in many countries
centenary *n* a hundredth anniversary
centimetre *n* a metric measure of length; cm is the symbol. 100cm = 1m
centipede *n* a small creature with a long body and many legs
central *adj* at or near the middle
centre *n* the middle point or part
century *n* *1* one hundred years *2* a score of 100 runs in cricket
cereal *n* grain crops such as wheat, oats, maize etc. used as food
ceremony *n* a formal celebration, sometimes happy, sometimes sad
certain *adj* sure; without any doubt
certificate *n* an official statement or document proving that something is true
chaffinch *n* a small song-bird
chain *n* a length of joined links
chair *n* a seat with a back, for one person
chalet *n* a wooden house with a steep roof built on the Swiss style
chalk *n* *1* soft, white limestone *2* a white material used for writing on a blackboard
challenge *v* to dare someone to try to beat you in a game or contest
champagne a sparkling white wine from France
champion *n* a person or animal unbeaten in competition
chance *n* *1* luck *2* an opportunity
change *v* *1* to alter *2* to put one thing in place of another

Cc

change *n*	*1* the money you get back when you pay too much *2* an alteration; difference
channel *n*	*1* a long, narrow stretch of water *2* a band of frequencies given to a radio or TV station
chapel *n*	a small church, or part of a large church
chapter *n*	a section of a book
character *n*	*1* the things that make you the person you are *2* a person in a book, film or play
charcoal *n*	partly burnt wood
charge *v*	*1* to rush at *2* to ask a certain price for something *3* to accuse or blame someone
charge *n*	*1* an attack *2* a price *3* responsible for
chariot *n*	a horse-drawn cart used for fighting and racing in ancient times
charity *n*	help and kindness shown to people
charm *n*	*1* a magic spell *2* an object that is supposed to bring good fortune *3* a pleasant manner
charm *v*	to delight someone
chart *n*	*1* a sea map for sailors, showing sea depth, position of buoys, rocks, shoals etc. *2* a diagram giving information, such as a weather chart
chase *v*	to run after; to pursue
chat *n*	a friendly talk between two people
chat *v*	to talk in an easy, friendly way
chauffeur *n*	a person paid to drive a car
cheap *adj*	not costing much
cheat *v*	to be dishonest; to deceive
check *v*	*1* to make sure that something is right *2* to stop or hold back for a short time
cheek *n*	*1* the side of your face below each eye *2* impudence
cheer *v*	*1* to shout applause and encouragement *2* to try to make someone feel happier
cheerful *adj*	bright and smiling; happy
cheese *n*	a food made from the curds of milk
chef *n*	a head cook in a hotel or restaurant
chemist *n*	*1* a person skilled in chemistry *2* a person who is qualified to make and sell medicines
chemistry *n*	a branch of science that is about what substances are made of and how they work together
cheque *n*	a written order to a bank to pay money to someone
cherry *n*	a small, round fruit with a stonelike seed
chess *n*	a game for two people played with black and white pieces on a board of 64 squares
chest *n*	*1* the part of your body around your ribs *2* a large, strong box
chestnut *n*	a large tree with prickly fruits containing shiny, red-brown nuts
chew *v*	to crush food in your mouth with your teeth

Cc

chick *n*		a newly-hatched bird
chicken *n*		a young hen
chicken-pox *n*		a disease that causes red, itchy spots on the skin
chief *n*		a ruler or leader
chief *adj*		most important
child *n*		a young boy or girl
chill *n*		a shivery cold
chill *v*		to cool
chime *n*		the music of bells
chime *v*		to ring out tunefully
chimney *n*		a tube-like passage in a building that allows smoke from a fire to escape
chimpanzee *n*		a large African ape
chin *n*		the part of the face below the mouth
china *n*		fine clay baked and glazed, made into plates, cups etc.
chink *n*		a narrow opening
chip *n*	*1*	a small piece broken off something
	2	a tiny electronic device, usually made of silicon
chips *n (pl)*		slices of fried potato
chipolata *n*		a small sausage
chirp *n*		the small squeak of some birds and insects
chisel *n*		a tool for cutting and shaping wood, stone etc.
chlorophyll *n*		the green colouring matter found in plants' cells
chocolate *n*		a food or drink made from cocoa
choice *n*	*1*	the picking of something
	2	the thing chosen
choir *n*		a group of people trained to sing together
choke *v*		to suffocate, not to be able to breathe properly
choose *v*		to pick; to decide between
chop *n*		a small piece of meat joined to a bone
chop *v*		to cut into pieces, often with an axe
chorus *n*	*1*	a group of people singing together
	2	the part of a song that is repeated
christen *v*		to give a name to and receive into the Christian Church
Christian *n*		a believer in and follower of the teachings of Jesus Christ
Christmas *n*		the festival on 25th December celebrating Christ's birth
chuckle *v*		to laugh quietly to yourself
chunk *n*		a thick lump or slice
church *n*		a building in which people worship God
churn *n*		a container for making butter
cider *n*		an alcoholic drink made from apple juice
cigar *n*		rolled tobacco leaves, for smoking
cigarette *n*		shredded tobacco leaf, rolled in a thin paper tube for smoking
cinder *n*		a piece of partly burnt coal or wood
cinema *n*		a theatre where moving pictures are shown
cinnamon *n*		a spice used to flavour food
circle *n*		a perfectly round ring
circumference *n*		the distance round a circle
circus *n*		a travelling show of animals, clowns, acrobats etc.
citizen *n*		a member of a nation, by birth or by choice
city *n*		a large or important town
claim *v*		to say that you have a right to something
clamber *v*		to climb using your hands and feet

clamp *n* a device that holds parts together firmly

clan *n* a tribe united under a chieftan

clap *v* to slap your hands together

clarinet *n* a musical wind instrument, shaped like a tube

clasp *v* to hold tightly

clasp *n* a fastening, such as a buckle or brooch

class *n* a group of the same kind of people, like children taught together

clatter *v* to rattle noisily

claw *n* a pointed nail on an animal's foot

clay *n* a smooth, sticky kind of earth that goes hard when baked

clean *adj* free from dirt, neat and tidy

clear *adj*
1 easy to see through
2 easy to understand

clergy *n (pl)* ministers, priests etc.

clerk *n* a person who works in an office

clever *adj* quick at learning and understanding

click *n* a sharp, little sound

cliff *n* a very steep, high rock face, especially where land meets sea

climate *n* the kind of weather that a place usually has

climb *v*
1 to go up by using the hands and feet
2 to rise steeply, as an aeroplane

cling *v* to hold fast to

clinic *n* a place where medical treatment is given

clip *v* to trim with scissors or shears

clip *n* a fastener

cloak *n* a loose coat without sleeves

clock *n* a machine for telling the time

clog *v* to block up

clog *n* a wooden-soled shoe

close *v*
1 to shut
2 to draw nearer
3 to come to an end

close *adj* nearby

cloth *n* woven material of threads such as wool, nylon, cotton etc.

clothes *n* the garments we wear

cloud *n* great clusters of tiny water droplets in the sky

clover *n* a small green plant with leaves in three or sometimes four parts

clown *n* a circus performer who makes people laugh

club *n*
1 a group that people can join and do things together
2 a heavy stick with which to hit things
3 a long stick with a special head for hitting a ball, as in golf

Cc

cluck *v* to make a noise like a hen

clue *n* some small thing that helps in solving a mystery, puzzle etc.

clump *n* a number of flowers or trees growing together

clumsy *adj* awkward in moving about and doing things

cluster *n* a bunch; a group

clutch *v* to grasp at; to hold tightly

coach *n*
1 a large, covered rail or road carriage
2 someone who trains sports teams, athletes etc.

coal *n* a hard, black mineral used as fuel

coarse *adj* rough; not fine

coast *n* the land along the edge of the sea

coat *n*
1 an outer garment, with long sleeves, usually worn for warmth
2 an animal's fur, wool, hair etc.

coax *v* to persuade gently, using kind words

cobbler *n* someone who mends shoes etc.

cobra *n* a poisonous snake that can expand its neck into a hood

cobweb *n* a fine web made by a spider

cock *n* a male bird

cockerel *n* a young cock bird

cocoa *n* chocolate powder made from the seeds of the cacao tree

coconut *n* the large nut of the coco palm tree

cod *n* a large seafish eaten as food

code *n*
1 signs or secret words used to make a secret message
2 a set of rules, such as the Highway Code

coffee *n* a drink made from the roasted seeds of the coffee plant

coffin *n* a box in which a dead person is buried

coil *n* a wire or rope wound round and round in a spiral

coin *n* a piece of metal money

coincidence *n* two or more things happening by chance at the same time

cold *adj* being without warmth

cold *n* an illness causing you to sneeze and cough

collage *n* a picture made by pasting on different things such as string, paper, wool, lentils, pasta etc.

collapse *v* to fall down; to give way

collar *n*
1 the part of a garment that fits around the neck
2 a leather band worn around an animal's neck

collect *v* to gather together

college *n* a school for higher education

collide *v* to bump hard into something

collie *n* a large, shaggy dog with a long pointed nose

colliery *n* a coal-mine

colonel *n* a senior army officer who usually commands a regiment

4	1	5	2	3
N	2	W	4	S
3	H	6	T	5
M	2	F	O	R
A	5	L	3	O

code 1

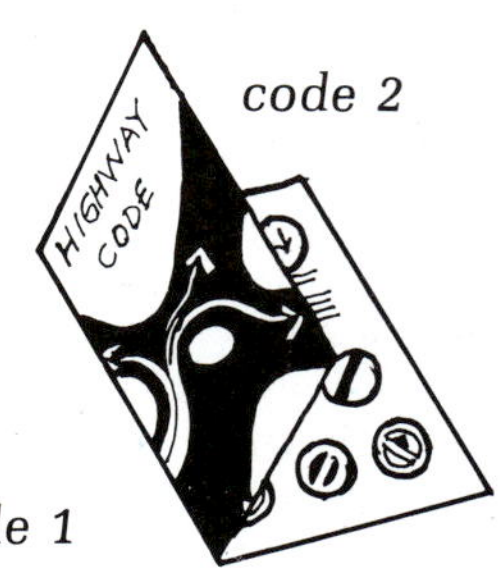

code 2

colony *n* 1 a settlement of people in a new land
2 a group of animals of the same kind, living together, such as an ant colony

colour *n* red, blue and yellow, or any combination of these

colt *n* a young male horse

column *n* 1 a tall, round pillar
2 a list of numbers, one below the other
3 one of the sections, running from top to bottom, of a newspaper page

comb *n* a piece of plastic or metal with teeth, used to smooth your hair

combat *n* a battle, a fight

combine *v* to join together

come *v* to move towards; to arrive

comedian *n* an actor who tells jokes or does amusing things

comedy *n* a funny play, film or event

comet *n* a star-like body in the sky, with a long, glowing tail

comfort *v* to help someone by kind actions and words

comfortable *adj* cosy; at ease; happy

comic *n* 1 a comedian
2 a children's paper with strip pictures

comical *adj* funny, amusing

comma *n* a punctuation mark, denoting a short pause (,)

command *v* to order someone to do something

commandment *n* one of the laws called the Ten Commandments, found in the Bible

commando *n* a soldier highly trained to make quick attacks into enemy areas

commence *v* to begin

commentator

comment *n* an opinion or other remark about someone or something

commentator *n* someone who comments in written or spoken words such as a sports commentator

commerce *n* trade, business, buying and selling

commit *v* 1 to do something, usually wrong, such as a crime
2 to hand over; to entrust

committee *n* a group of people chosen to do special business

common *adj* 1 happening or found in many places; not rare
2 rude in manner

commotion *n* a noisy disturbance

communicate *v* to pass on information or feelings to other people

community *n* a group of people living in a neighbourhood

commuter *n* a person who travels some distance daily to and from work

compact *adj* packed closely together

companion *n* a friend who goes somewhere or shares time with you

company *n* 1 a business firm
2 a group or gathering of people

compare *v* to look at things and see the difference

compartment *n* a separate section of something

compass *n* an instrument that shows direction and used for finding the way

compasses *n (pl)* an instrument used for drawing circles

compel *v* to force; to make

compete *v* to take part in a contest or competition

competition *n* a contest in which a number of people take part to see who is the best

complain *v* to find fault with or object to something

complete *adj* whole; with everything there

complete *v* to finish

complexion *n* the colour and appearance of the skin on your face

complicated *adj* difficult; not simple

compliment *n* words of praise, something nice you say to someone

compose *v* to make up or put together something

composer *n* someone who writes music

computer *n* an electronic calculating machine that can store and recall information and make calculations very quickly

conceal *v* to hide; to keep secret

conceited *adj* having too high an opinion of yourself

concentrate *v* to give careful attention to one thing only

concert *n* a musical entertainment

concise *adj* brief but full of meaning

conclude *v* to finish; to end

concrete *n* a mixture of cement, gravel, sand and water used in building

condition *n* the state something is in

conduct *v*
1 to lead
2 to direct a choir, band, orchestra, etc.

conduct *n* behaviour

conductor *n*
1 a person who beats time and directs a choir, orchestra etc.
2 the person who collects fares on a bus

cone *n*
1 the woody fruit of an evergreen tree
2 an object with a circular base and a point at the top

conference *n* a meeting for discussion

confess *v* to admit, usually to tell that you have done something wrong

confetti *n* tiny peices of coloured paper thrown over a newly married couple at a wedding

confident *adj* bold; sure of yourself

confuse *v*
1 to mix up someone
2 to mistake one thing for another

confusion *n* a mix-up

congratulate *v* to express your happiness to someone over his or her success

congregation *n* a gathering of people, usually for religious worship

conifer *n* a cone-bearing tree, usually evergreen

connect *v* to join one thing to another

conquer *v* to overcome; to beat in battle

conscience *n* a feeling that tells you whether something is right or wrong

conscious *adj* awake and aware of everything around

consent *v* to agree to something; to give permission

consider *v* to think about; to turn over in your mind

considerate *adj* kind, thoughtful to others

Cc

consonant *n*		any letter of the alphabet except a, e, i, o, u, which are vowels
constable *n*		a police-officer
constant *adj*	1	unchanging
	2	happening all the time
constellation *n*		a group of stars, often having a name such as 'Andromeda'
construct *v*		to build, to put together
construction *n*		something built or put together
consult *v*		to seek information or advice
contact *v*		to get in touch with
contain *v*		to hold something
container *n*		a box, jar, tin, barrel etc. used to hold something
contented *adj*		pleased, satisfied
contents *n (pl)*		the things you find in a book or a container
continent *n*		one of the very large land masses of the Earth's surface
continual *adj*		always happening; frequent
continue *v*	1	to keep on doing something
	2	to start again after stopping
continuous *adj*		happening without stopping
contribute *v*		to pay or give something
control *v*	1	to have power over
	2	to keep in check
conundrum *n*		a riddle; a puzzle
convenient *adj*		handy, saving trouble
convent *n*		a place where nuns live
conversation *n*		a talk between two or more people
convict *n*		someone who has been sent to prison
convince *v*		to persuade someone
cook *n*		a person who prepares food
cook *v*		to prepare food for eating by using heat
cool *adj*	1	slightly cold
	2	calm, not excited
copper *n*		a reddish-brown metal
copy *v*		to make something look exactly like something else
coral *n*		a hard, pink or white substance, made up of skeletons of tiny ocean creatures
cord *n*		strong, thick string, or rope
corduroy *n*		a strong, velvety material that has ridges
core *n*		the centre; the middle part
cork *n*	1	the light, tough bark of the cork-oak tree
	2	a bottle stopper
corkscrew *n*		a tool for taking corks out of bottles
cormorant *n*		a diving sea-bird
corn *n*	1	the seeds of wheat, oats, barley etc.
	2	the seeds of maize (corn-on-the-cob)
	3	a painful hard growth on the toe
corner *n*		the place where two walls, lines, streets etc. meet
cornet *n*		a brass musical instrument similar to the trumpet
coronation *n*		the ceremony when a King or Queen is crowned
corpse *n*		a dead body
correct *adj*		right; true; with no mistakes
correct *v*		to put right any mistakes
corridor *n*		a long passage in a building
cosmonaut *n*		a Russian astronaut
cost *n*		the price of anything
costly *adj*		expensive
costume *n*		clothes worn by actors in a play
cosy *adj*		warm, snug; comfortable
cot *n*		a small bed, usually with high sides, for a baby

Cc

cottage *n* a small house, usually in the country

cotton *n*
1 fibre from the seeds of the cotton plant
2 thread or cloth woven from cotton fibre

couch *n* a long, soft seat

cough *n* a sudden and noisy rush of air from the lungs

council *n* a group of people elected to make decisions

count *v*
1 to add numbers
2 to depend on

countdown *n* the time just before the firing of a missile or rocket

country *n*
1 land away from towns
2 the whole land where people live; a nation

county *n* a part of the country with its own local government

couple *n* a pair; two of a kind

coupon *n* a ticket that can be exchanged for something

courage *n* bravery

course *n*
1 the direction that something takes when it is moving
2 a part of a meal
3 a series of lessons
4 an area for a sport, such as golf

court *n*
1 a place where justice is given
2 a place where some game is played, such as tennis

courteous *adj* polite, well mannered

cousin *n* the child of your aunt or uncle

cover *n* something put on top of another thing, usually to protect or hide it

cover *v* to spread one thing over another

cow *n*
1 a farm animal kept for its milk
2 a female of the ox family, or a female elephant, whale or seal.

coward *n* someone without courage

cowboy *n* a person who looks after cattle

crab *n* a shellfish with a hard shell, several legs and two strong claws

crack *n*
1 a split
2 a sharp sound

crack *v*
1 to break open
2 to make a sharp sound

cracker *n*
1 a thin, crisp biscuit
2 a paper toy which bangs when its ends are pulled

cradle *n* a rocking bed for a baby

craft *n*
1 the skill of making things with your hands
2 a ship or an aircraft

crafty *adj* sly, cunning

crag *n* a steep, rugged rock

cram *v* to stuff into a small space

cramp *n* a sudden tightening of a muscle

crane *n*
1 a machine that lifts and moves heavy things
2 a large wading bird with a long beak and long legs

crash *n*
1 the loud noise of something being smashed
2 a collision

crate *n* a large wooden case for holding goods

crater *n* the opening of a volcano

craving *n* a great longing for something

crawl *n*
1 a very slow pace
2 an overarm swimming stroke

crawl *v* to creep on hands and knees

Cc

crayon *n* a kind of colouring stick used for drawing
crazy *adj* mad, foolish
creak *n* a harsh, squeaky sound
cream *n* the fatty part of the milk from which butter and other foods are made
crease *n* a mark or line made by folding
create *v* to make something; to bring into being
creature *n* a living person or animal
credit *n* *1* honour
2 time allowed for the payment of goods
creek *n* *1* a narrow inlet on the coast
2 a small stream
creep *v* *1* to move along close to the ground
2 to move quietly on tiptoe
cremate *v* to burn to ashes
crêpe paper *n* thin, crinkly paper used for making decorations
crest *n* *1* a tuft of feathers on the head of a bird
2 the highest point
crew *n* the people who work on a ship, aircraft etc.
crib *n* a baby's bed
cricket *n* *1* an outdoor game played with bats and a ball by two teams of eleven players
2 a small, jumping, chirping insect
crime *n* something done that is against the law
criminal *n* someone guilty of a crime
crimson *n* a deep purplish-red colour
cripple *n* a person unable to use one or more of his limbs, especially the legs
crisp *adj* dry and hard, but easily broken
crisps *n (pl)* thin slices of potato cooked in very hot fat and sold in packets
croak *v* to make a deep, hoarse sound like a frog
crockery *n* cups, plates, saucers etc. made of baked clay
crocodile *n* a large, four-footed reptile with a scaly skin and sharp teeth, found in the rivers and lakes of some warm countries
crocus *n* a small, spring flower
crook *n* a cheat, a thief; a criminal
crooked *adj* not straight; twisted
crop *n* the plants gathered from a farm, field, garden etc.
cross *n* a mark shaped like + or ×
cross *adj* annoyed
cross *v* to go from one side to another
crouch *v* to bend low
crow *n* a large, black bird with a harsh cry
crowd *n* a great number of people gathered together
crown *n* the headdress of a King or Queen
cruel *adj* very unkind, causing pain
cruise *n* a sea voyage for pleasure
cruiser *n* a large, fast warship
crumb *n* a tiny piece of bread, biscuit, cake etc.
crumble *v* to fall or break into small pieces
crumpet *n* a soft cake eaten toasted, with butter

crumpet

Cc

crumple *v*		to crush something and make wrinkles in it
crunch *v*		to crush something with the teeth
crush *v*		to squeeze hard
crust *n*		a hard outer covering, such as a pie-crust
crutch *n*		something that helps a lame person to walk
cry *v*	*1*	to shout out loudly
	2	to shed tears
crystal *n*		a glassy stone with many flat sides
cub *n*	*1*	a young fox, bear, lion, tiger etc.
	2	a junior scout
cube *n*		a solid object with six equal squares, sides or faces
cuckoo *n*		a bird that lays its eggs in the nests of other birds
cucumber *n*		a long, thin, green vegetable used in salads
cuddle *v*		to hug someone
cue *n*	*1*	a long wooden rod for playing snooker, pool etc.
	2	an action or words that signals the next person to speak or act in a play, film etc.
cuff *n*		the end of the sleeve
cuff *v*		to hit with the open hand
culprit *n*		someone who has done something wrong
cunning *adj*		crafty, sly, clever
cup *n*		a small drinking vessel usually with a handle
cupboard		a piece of furniture used for storing things
curator *n*		a person in charge of a museum, art gallery etc.
curb *v*		to hold back, to control
curd *n*		the thickened part of milk
curdle *v*		to go sour

crutch

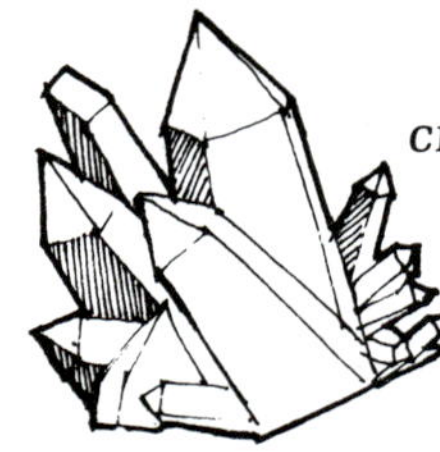
crystal

cub

cucumber

curve

cutlery

cure *v*		to heal, to make well
curiosity *n*		a desire to know
curious *adj*	*1*	wanting to know
	2	unusual, strange, odd
curl *n*		a twisted lock of hair
curl *v*		to twist in a spiral
currant *n*		a small, seedless dried grape
currency *n*		the money that is used in a country
current *n*	*1*	a stream of air or water flowing quickly
	2	a flow of electricity along a wire or cable

curry *n* a hot, spicy food, originally from India and Pakistan
curse *n* an evil wish
curse *v* 1 to swear; to use bad language
2 to wish evil on someone
curtain *n* a cloth hanging in front of a window or a theatre stage
curve *n* a smooth bend
cushion *n* a stuffed bag or soft pillow used on a chair or a settee
custard *n* a thick sweet, yellow sauce made by mixing custard powder with boiling milk
custom *n* a habit; a certain way of doing something
customer *n* someone who buys
customs *n (pl)* taxes on certain goods brought in from another country
cut *n* an opening made with a sharp object
cut *v* to open, slit or divide with a knife, scissors or other sharp object
cutlery *n* knives, forks, spoons etc. used at table
cycle *n* a bicycle, tricycle or motor cycle
cyclist *n* someone riding a cycle
cyclone *n* a violent storm with strong winds
cygnet *n* a young swan
cylinder *n* 1 a hollow or solid object that is shaped like a tube
2 the part of an engine in which the piston moves
cymbals *n (pl)* brass plates used by a drummer to make a clashing sound

Dd

dachshund

dab *v* to touch lightly
dachshund *n* a small dog with a long body and short legs
dad/daddy *n* father
daffodil *n* a yellow or white spring flower, grown from a bulb
daft *adj* silly; foolish
dagger *n* a short, two-edged knife, used as a weapon
daily *adj* every day
dainty *adj* small and delicate; pretty
dairy *n* a place where milk is kept, and cheese, butter and yoghurt are made.
daisy *n* a common wild flower with a yellow centre surrounded by white petals
Dalmatian *n* a large white dog with black spots
dale *n* a valley
dam *n* a thick wall built to hold back the water of a river
damage *v* to cause injury or do harm to something
damage *n* injury, breakage, harm
damp *adj* moist; slightly wet
damson *n* a small, dark-red kind of plum
dance *v* to move feet and body in time to music
dandelion *n* a wild flower with bright yellow petals
dandruff *n* small white pieces of dead skin that fall from the scalp
danger *n* something that is likely to harm you
dangerous *adj* not safe; risky

Cc Dd

Dd

dangle *v*		to hang or swing loosely
dare *v*	*1*	to risk, to take a chance
	2	to challenge someone
dark *adj*	*1*	without light; gloomy
	2	not light in colour
darling *n*		a person who is very dear to you
darn *v*		to mend a hole in cloth
dart *n*		a small, sharp pointed arrow thrown by hand
dart *v*		to dash forward quickly
dash *v*		to rush suddenly
dash *n*	*1*	a rush or quick movement
	2	a small line (—) used in writing
data *n (pl)*		facts; information
date *n*	*1*	the day, month and year
	2	the brown, sticky fruit that grows on a date palm
daughter *n*		a person's female child
dawdle *v*		to waste time; to go slowly
dawn *n*		sunrise, daybreak
day *n*	*1*	the time between sunrise and sunset
	2	a period of 24 hours, from one midnight to the next
daze *v*		to confuse, to bewilder
dazzle *v*		to blind or confuse someone by shining a bright light in his or her eyes
dead *adj*		no longer alive
deaf *adj*		not able to hear
deal *v*	*1*	to do business
	2	to hand out
deal *n*		a business agreement
dealer *n*		a person who buys and sells something
dear *adj*	*1*	greatly loved
	2	costing a lot
death *n*		the end of life
debate *v*		to discuss the reasons for and against something

debt *n*		something you owe someone
decade *n*		ten years
decay *v*		to rot, to go bad
deceased *n/adj*		dead
decent *adj*		nice, well-mannered, kind
decide *v*		to make up your mind
deciduous *adj*		trees that shed their leaves each year
decimal *adj*		based on the number 10
decision *n*		something that is decided or settled
deck *n*		a floor on a ship
declare *v*		to announce; to say something in public
decorate *v*	*1*	to make something look nicer
	2	to paint or paper a room
	3	to give someone a medal awarded as an honour
decrease *v*		to grow smaller, to become less
deed *n*		something which is done, usually good or bad or brave
deep *adj*		going a long way down or inside
deer *n*		a quick, graceful animal; the male deer has antlers
defeat *v*		to beat someone in a game or battle
defend *v*		to guard from attack, to protect
define *v*		to make clear the meaning of something
definite *adj*		certain, without doubt
definition *n*		the meaning of a word
defy *n*		to refuse to obey; to challenge
degree *n*	*1*	a mark on a thermometer showing how hot or cold it is
	2	a qualification given by a university or polytechnic

delay *v*	to put off till a later time
deliberate *adj*	done on purpose
delicious *adj*	very enjoyable to taste and eat
delightful *adj*	very pleasing
deliver *v*	to hand over
delta *n*	a triangle of land formed at the mouth of some rivers
demand *v*	to ask firmly for something
democracy *n*	a country in which the government is chosen by the people
demon *n*	an evil spirit
demonstrate *v*	to show clearly
den *n*	a hidden home of a wild animal
denim *n*	a strong cotton cloth used especially for jeans
dense *adj*	*1* closely-packed *2* stupid
dent *n*	a small hollow made by a blow
dental *adj*	having to do with teeth
dentist *n*	a person qualified and skilled in the care of teeth
deny *v*	to say that something is not true
deodorant *n*	a substance that prevents or takes away unpleasant smells
depart *v*	to leave, to go away
department *n*	a separate part, or section
depend on *v*	to rely on, to trust
deport *v*	to expel from a country
deposit *n*	*1* a sum of money put down in advance of a larger payment *2* money placed in a bank
deposit *v*	*1* to put something down *2* to put into a bank *3* to give in part payment of something
depot *n*	*1* a storehouse *2* a garage for buses
depress *v*	*1* to press down *2* to make sad
depth *n*	the distance downwards or inwards
deputy *n*	someone who can take the place of another person
descend *v*	to go down or come down
describe *v*	to say what something or somebody is like
desert *n*	a large area of dry land where very few plants grow
desert *v*	to leave behind, to run away from
deserve *v*	to be worthy of something
design *v*	to draw or plan out
desire *v*	to want very much, to wish for
desk *n*	a piece of furniture, like a table, for writing on.
despair *n*	a feeling of being without hope
desperate *adj*	almost without hope
despise *v*	to hate very much
dessert *n*	pudding, fruit, cake etc. served at the end of a meal
destination *n*	the place you are travelling to
destroy *v*	to ruin completely
detach *v*	to unfasten, to disconnect
detail *n*	a very small part of something
detain *v*	to hold someone up; to keep back
detect *v*	to discover, to find out
detective *n*	a person who investigates crimes
detergent *n*	a liquid or powder used for cleaning dishes or clothes
detest *v*	to hate or dislike very much
detour *n*	a roundabout route replacing the regular way
develop *v*	to grow or improve gradually

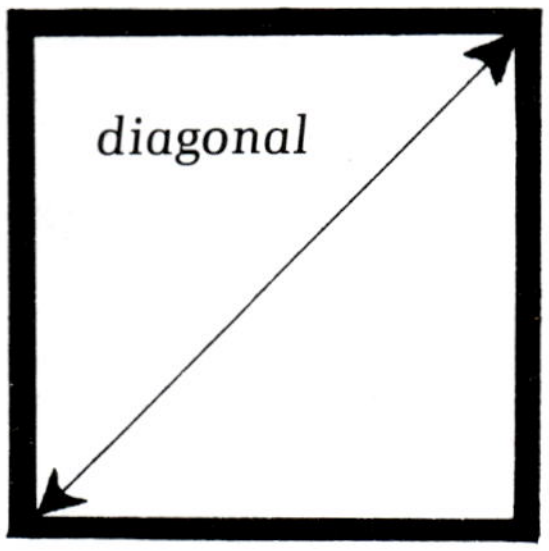

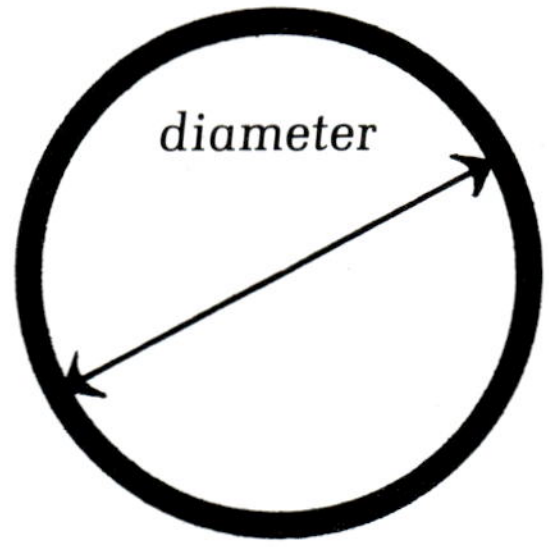

device *n* any tool, instrument, or machine that helps you

devil *n*
1 an evil spirit
2 a wicked person

devote *v* to give your full attention to

devour *v* to eat greedily

dew *n* drops of water that form on cool surfaces at night out of doors

diagnose *v* to decide what illness someone is suffering from

diagonal *n* a straight line drawn between two opposite corners

diagram *n* a drawing or plan that explains something

dial *n* the face of a clock, phone, speedometer, and other instruments

dial *v* to make a 'phone call

diameter *n* a line right across a circle passing through the centre

diamond *n* a very hard, brilliant, precious stone

diary *n* a daily record of events

dice *n (pl)* [**die** *(singular)*] small cubes marked with spots 1 to 6

dictionary *n* a book listing words in alphabetical order, telling you what each word means

die *v* to stop living, to lose your life

diesel engine *n* an engine that burns fuel oil

diet *n*
1 the food and drink normally eaten by a person or animal
2 special food eaten by a person who may be ill, or is trying to lose or gain weight

difference *n* the way in which one thing is unlike another

different *adj* unlike; not the same

difficult *adj* not easy to do; hard to understand

dig *v* to turn over the earth with a spade or machine

digest *v* to change food in the stomach, so that the body can use it

digit *n*
1 a finger or toe
2 any numeral from 0 to 9

dike *n*
1 a bank to hold back water
2 a ditch

dilute *v* to make something weaker by adding water to it

dim *adj* not bright or clear

dimension *n* the measurement of length, breadth, depth etc.

diminish *v* to make or become less

din *n* a loud and continuous noise

dinghy *n* a small, open boat

dingo *n* an Australian wild dog

dinner *n* the main meal of the day

dinosaur *n* any of the various prehistoric reptiles

dip *v*
1 to put in and out of liquid
2 to slope down

direct *adj* straight and to the point

direct *v*
1 to show the way
2 to aim
3 to order, to tell someone what to do

direction *n* the way from one place to another

directly *adv* very soon; in a direct way

director *n* a person who manages or controls

directory *n* a book in which names and addresses are printed in alphabetical order, such as a telephone directory

dirt *n* mud, dust, filth; anything unclean

disabled *adj* unable to do certain things because of being injured, crippled etc.

disagree *v* to have different ideas about something; to quarrel

disappear *v* to pass out of sight; to vanish

disappoint *v* to make someone sad by not doing what they had expected

disaster *n* a great misfortune, accident, or tragedy

disc/disk *n*
1 a flat, circular object
2 a plastic disc with a recording on it, for a record player
3 a device for storing computer information

discard *v* to throw aside

disciple *n* someone who follows and learns from a leader

discipline *n* orderly behaviour; training and self control

disc jockey *n* someone who introduces pop records

disco *n* a place where people dance to recorded music

disconnect *v* to unfasten, to unplug

discover *v* to find out, to see for the very first time

discovery *n* the finding of something new

discuss *v* to talk about something with other people

disease *n* illness, sickness

disgrace *v* to bring shame upon

disguise *v* to change what something or someone looks like

disgust *n* a strong dislike

dish *n*
1 a plate for holding food
2 a particular kind of food

dishonest *adj* not honest

dislocate *v* to put out of joint; to put out of order

dismal *adj* gloomy; sad; dreary

dismay *v* to fill with fear, despair

dismiss *v* to send away; to order someone to leave their job

disobedient *adj* not obeying, not doing what you are told

disobey *v* not to do what you are told

display *n* a show, an exhibition

dispute *n* an argument; a quarrel

dissatisfied *adj* not happy; not satisfied

dissolve *v* to mix something with a liquid until it disappears, such as sugar in a cup of tea

distance *n* the space between two places

distant *adj* a long way off

distinct *adj* heard or seen clearly

distinguish *v* to make or notice a difference between two or more things

distract *v* to take your mind away from something

distress *n* great trouble, pain, sorrow

distribute *v* to give out or share

district *n* an area or region; a part of a town, city or country

disturb *v* to trouble, unsettle, to interfere

ditch *n* a narrow channel for water

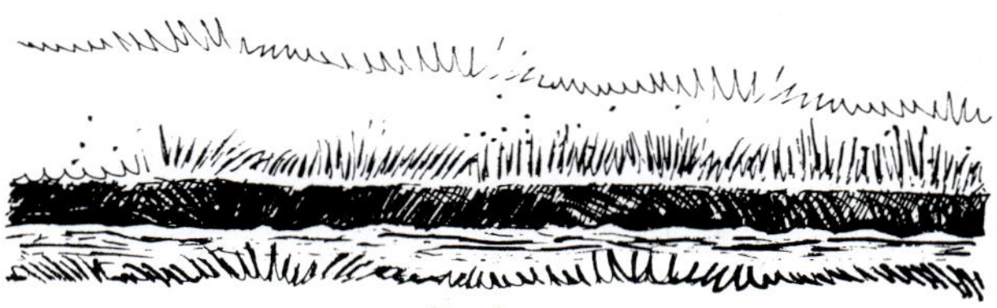

ditch

Dd

Dd

dive *n* a downward plunge, usually into water
divan *n* a low seat or bed
divide *v* 1 to separate or cut into parts
2 to find out how many times one number will go into another
divorce *n* the legal ending of a marriage
dizzy *adj* unsteady; confused
do *v* to be busy; to make, to work, to start something
dock *n* a place by water where ships are loaded and unloaded
doctor *n* a person qualified to treat the sick and injured
document *n* a paper containing written information
dodge *v* to get quickly out of the way
doe *n* a female rabbit or deer
dog *n* a common domestic animal, related to the fox and wolf
doll *n* a small model of a baby or person, usually for a child to play with
dollar *n* the unit of money used in many countries including Australia, New Zealand, Canada and USA
dolphin *n* a sea mammal that looks like a small whale
dome *n* a rounded roof like an upside down bowl
domestic *adj* 1 to do with the home
2 tame, not wild
domino *n* one of the flat, oblong pieces marked with spots used in the game of dominoes
donate *v* to make a gift
donation *n* a gift
donkey *n* an ass; an animal with long ears and looks like a small horse
door *n* the entrance to a building, house, room or cupboard
dose *n* the amount of medicine to be taken at one time
dot *n* a small spot
double *adj* twice as much
double *n* a person exactly like someone else
doubt *v* to be suspicious of; not to be sure
dough *n* a mixture of flour and other dry materials and water for baking
doughnut *n* a small, round piece of fried cake with a hole in the centre
dove *n* a bird of the pigeon family
down *n* the very soft feathers of a bird
down *prep* from a higher to a lower place
downpour *n* a very heavy rainfall
doze *v* to have a light sleep
dozen *n* a set or group of twelve things
drab *adj* of dull colour
drag *v* to pull or haul something slowly
dragon *n* an imaginary fire-breathing monster
dragonfly *n* a brightly coloured insect with long wings that lives near water

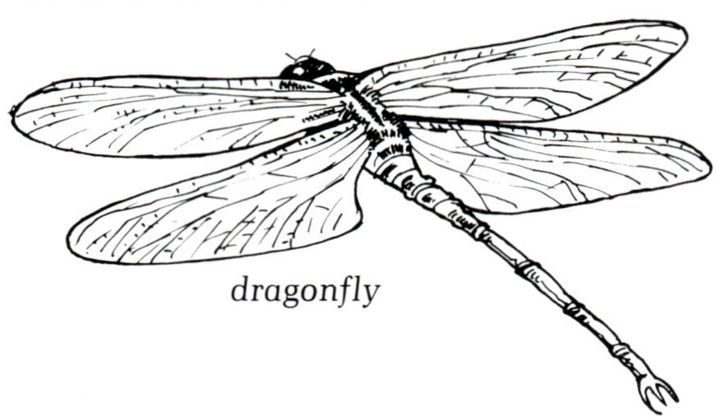

dragonfly

Dd

drain *n* a pipe or channel to carry off waste fluid
drama *n* 1 a play for the theatre, television or radio
2 an exciting real-life story
draught *n* a current of air
draughts *n (pl)* a game for two played with 24 circular pieces on a squared board
draw *v* 1 to make a picture or diagram with pencil, felt-tip, pen, crayon etc.
2 to end a game with equal scores
drawbridge *n* a bridge that can be lifted, lowered, or moved
drawer *n* a sliding box in a piece of furniture
drawing *n* a sketch, picture or design
dream *n* something you think is happening during sleep
dreary *adj* dull, uninteresting
drench *v* to wet completely
dress *n* a piece of clothing worn by women and girls
dressing *n* 1 a bandage on a cut or wound
2 a sauce, such as salad dressing
drift *n* snow or sand blown into a pile by the wind
drift *v* 1 to be carried along by the wind; to wander off course
2 to be heaped into a pile
drill *n* 1 a pointed tool that is turned to make holes
2 exercises being done over and over again
drink *v* to swallow water or other liquid
drink *n* liquid for drinking
drip *v* to fall in drops
drive *v* to steer and control a vehicle
drive *n* 1 a wide path from the street to a house
2 a journey by car
drizzle *n* a light fall of rain
drone *n* a male bee
droop *v* to hang down limply; to sag
drop *n* a tiny amount of liquid
drop *v* to fall down from a height
drought *n* a long period of dry weather
drown *v* to die by being choked by water
drug *n* 1 a medicine
2 a habit-forming substance
drum *n* 1 a round, hollow musical instrument with a skin stretched over a frame
2 a large metal container for liquids
dry *adj* not wet; without moisture
dryer/drier *n* 1 a machine for drying clothes
2 a small machine for drying hair
duck *n* a small, web-footed water bird with a flat bill
duckling *n* a young duck
duet *n* a piece of music for two performers
dull *adj* 1 not bright or clear
2 not interesting
dumb *adj* not able to talk
dummy *n* 1 a model of a person, often seen in shop windows
2 a teat for a baby to suck
dump *v* to put in a heap
dump *n* a rubbish tip
dune *n* a low hill of sand
dumpling *n* a small suet pudding
duplicate *v* to make an exact copy or copies of
duration *n* the length of time that something lasts or continues
during *prep* throughout; in the time of

dusk *n* — the time just before it gets dark in the evening

dust *n* — fine powdered dirt that floats in the air

dust *v* — to clean with a cloth

dustbin *n* — a container for household rubbish

duty *n* — something you have to do

dwarf *n* — any living thing that is much smaller than the usual size

dwell *v* — to live somewhere

dwindle *v* — to become smaller; to grow less

dye *n* — a liquid or powder used to colour materials

dynamite *n* — a powerful explosive used for breaking up rock

dynamo *n* — a machine for producing electricity

dynamite

dynamo

Ee

each *adj, pron* — every single one

eager *adj* — keen; enthusiastic

eagle *n* — a large and powerful bird that hunts small animals

ear *n* — *1* the part of the body that allows you to hear
2 the grain on a stalk of corn

early *adj, adv* — in good time; before the start

earn *v* — to get payment for working

earring *n* — a small ring or jewel worn on the ear

earth *n* — *1* the planet on which we live
2 ground, soil

earthquake *n* — a shaking movement of the surface of the earth

earwig *n* — an insect with a pincer-like tail

ease *n* — rest; comfort; freedom from pain

easel *n* — a stand on which to rest a picture

easily *adv* — without trouble

east *n* — the direction of sunrise; opposite to west

Easter *n* — the day on which Christians remember Jesus Christ's rising from the grave

easy *adj* — not difficult, not hard to do

eat *v* — to take food through the mouth

eaves *n (pl)* — the overhanging edges of a roof

ebb *v* — to flow back or drain away

ebony *n* — a black wood, very hard and heavy

echo *n* — a sound that bounces back when you shout at a hill or the wall of a cave

eclipse *n* — a darkening of the face of the sun or moon

edge *n* — *1* a rim or border
2 the sharp side of a blade

editor *n* — a person in charge of a newspaper, magazine, books of all types etc.

educate *n* — to teach or train people

eel *n* — a long, thin fish that is shaped like a snake

eel

eerie *adj* — strange, weird; causing fear

effect *n* — the result of an action

effort *n* — using strength or energy to do something

eggs *n (pl)* — roundish objects, with a thin shell, laid by birds, reptiles etc. from which young are hatched

either *adj* — one or the other

eject *v* — to throw out, to send out

elastic *adj* — stretchy; able to go back to its own shape after being squeezed or pulled

elbow *n* — the joint between your lower arm and your upper arm

elderly *adj* — becoming old; past middle age

elect *v* — to choose by voting

election *n* — a time when people choose by voting the people who will govern

electricity *n* — a power used to give us light and heat, and to drive machines

electronics *n (pl)* — the science dealing with things like television, radio, video recorders etc.

elephant *n* — the world's largest land animal which has a trunk and two curved tusks made of ivory

elevate *v* — to lift up, to raise

elevator *n*
1 a lift
2 the part of an aircraft which makes it climb or dive
3 a machine for raising grain, coal etc. to a higher level
4 a building for storing grain

Ee

elf *n* — in stories, a small fairy

elk *n* — a large deer of North America

elm *n* — a tall, broad-leaved tree

elsewhere *adv* — in some other place

embarrass *v* — to make someone feel uncomfortable or ill at ease

emblem *n* — a badge or sign or symbol

embroidery *n* — decoration on cloth made by sewing a pattern of coloured stitches.

emerald *n* — a bright green precious stone

emergency *n* — a sudden happening that must be attended to at once

emigrate *v* — to go to another country to live

emotion *n* — a strong feel of love, joy, fear, hate etc.

employ *v*
1 to pay people to work
2 to use

employment *n* — work; a job; an occupation

empty *adj* — having nothing inside

emu *n* — a large Australian flightless bird

enamel *n* — a smooth hard coating

enclose *v* — to shut in on all sides

encourage *v* — to give someone hope and courage to do something

encyclopaedia *n* — a reference book with information on many subjects

end *n* — the last part, the finish

enemy *n* — a person or country that is on the other side in a quarrel or war

Ee

energy *n* the strength or power to do work; liveliness; vigour
engagement *n* 1 a promise to marry
2 an appointment
engine *n* a machine which produces power
engineer *n* 1 a person who works with engines and machinery
2 a person who plans and builds bridges, roads, machines and big buildings
enjoy *v* to get pleasure from
enjoyment *n* pleasure, happiness
enlarge *v* to make or become bigger
enormous *n* very big, huge
enough *adj* as much or as many as are needed or wanted
enter *v* 1 to go or come into
2 to take part in a competition
entertain *v* 1 to amuse
2 to hold a party and have guests
entrance *n* a way in, a doorway
envelope *n* a folded and sealed paper cover for a letter
envious *adj* feeling full of jealousy
epidemic *n* a disease which a large number of people have at the same time
equal *adj* of the same number or value as something else
equator *n* an imaginary line around the middle of the earth that is drawn on maps
equipment *n* what is needed for a particular job, sport etc.
erect *adj* upright
ermine *n* the white winter fur of a stoat
errand *n* a short journey made to collect or deliver a message or package
error *n* a mistake
erupt *v* to burst out violently; to shoot out lava
escalator *n* a moving staircase
escape *v* to get away from or get free
Eskimos *n (pl)* a people living on the coastlands of the Arctic
especially *adv* most of all
espionage *n* spying
essential *adj* really necessary
estimate *v* to guess the size, amount, or value of something
estuary *n* the mouth of a large river
etc. *abbr* short for "et cetera" which means 'and the other things', 'and so on'
Europe *n* the smallest of the five continents
evaporate *v* to change from liquid into vapour or gas, usually when heated
even *adj* 1 smooth, level
2 able to be divided by two
evening *n* the end of the day and early part of the night
event *n* 1 some special happening
2 an item in a sports programme
eventually *adv* in the end, at last
ever *adv* always, at any time
evergreen *n* a tree that is always green and does not drop its leaves all at once
every *adj* each one
everybody *pron* each person, all the people
everything *pron* each thing, all the things
everywhere *adv* in every place
evidence *n* information that proves something
evil *adj* very bad, wicked
ewe *n* a female sheep
exactly *adv* just right; without mistake
exaggerate *v* to make something seem greater than it actually is

examine *v*	*1* to look at something very carefully *2* to test
examination *n*	*1* a careful check *2* a test of what you know
example *n*	something which shows what something else is like and how it works
excavate *v*	to dig or scoop out from the earth
excellent *adj*	very, very good
except *prep*	other than; not including
exceptional *adj*	out of the ordinary, outstanding
exchange *v*	to give one thing in return for another
excite *v*	to thrill; to make someone look forward to something
exciting *adj*	thrilling
exclaim *v*	to shout out with excitement
exclude *v*	to shut out; to keep out from
excuse *n*	to let someone off
execute *v*	to put someone to death
exercise *n*	*1* something that gives you practice *2* an activity for training your body or mind
exhaust *n*	the used gases from an engine
exhaust *v*	to use up completely; to make very tired
exhibit *v*	to show or display something
exhibition *n*	a public show or display
exist *v*	to live; to be real
exit *n*	a way out
expand *v*	to get larger
expect *v*	to think something will happen
expedition *n*	a journey for some special purpose
expel *v*	to compel to leave, to drive out
expense *n*	cost
expensive *adj*	costing a lot
experience *n*	*1* something learned from doing and seeing *2* anything that happens to you

Ee

excavate

exhibition

Ee Ff

experience *v*	to feel; to have happen to you
experiment *n*	a test to find what will happen
experiment *v*	to test or try out
expert *n*	someone who knows a lot about something
explain *v*	to show or make the meaning clear
explanation *n*	a reason
explode *v*	to blow up with a loud noise
explore *v*	to look carefully around a place where you haven't been before
exports *n (pl)*	goods sent and sold to another country
expose *v*	to uncover
express *n*	a fast train or bus that makes only a few stops
express *v*	to explain something in words
express *adj*	fast
expression *n*	a look on a person's face
extend *v*	to stretch out, to lengthen
exterior *n*	the outside of anything
extinct *adj*	dead; no longer existing
extinguisher *n*	a device for putting out fires
extra *adj*	more than usual
extreme *adj*	*1* the farthest
	2 very great indeed
eye *n*	the part of the body that allows you to see
eyebrow *n*	the small ridge of hair over each eye
eyelashes *n (pl)*	the hairs on the edge of your eyelid
eyelid *n*	the movable cover of skin over each eye
eyesight *n*	the power to see
eyewitness *n*	someone who sees an event happening
eyrie *n*	the nest of a bird of prey, especially an eagle

Ff

fable *n*	a short story that tries to teach us something
fabric *n*	cloth
fabulous *adj*	amazing, unbelievable
face *n*	*1* the front of your head
	2 the front of anything
face *v*	to look towards; to have the front towards
fact *n*	something that is true or real
factory *n*	a building where people and machines work together to make things
fade *v*	to grow dim, pale or weak
fail *v*	to be unsuccessful, not to do something you try to do
failure *n*	lack of success
faint *adj*	weak; dim; pale
faint *v*	to feel dizzy and ill; to pass out
fair *adj*	*1* light in colour
	2 honest; just
	3 not raining
	4 less than good
fair *n*	*1* a group of outdoor amusements, with sideshows and roundabouts etc.
	2 a very large show of goods, products etc.
fairy *n*	an imaginary little creature with magical powers
faith *n*	strong belief, trust
faithful *adj*	loyal, honest, to be trusted
fake *n*	something copied, not real, made to look like something better
falcon *n*	a bird of prey, of the hawk family
fall *v*	to drop from a high place
fall *n*	*1* a drop
	2 autumn, especially in Canada and U.S.A.
false *adj*	not true; not real

fame *n* being well known, or famous

familiar *adj* well known; friendly

family *n* a group of people who are all related to each other

famine *n* a great shortage of food

famous *adj* very well known

fan *n*
1 something that moves the air to make a cooling breeze
2 someone who likes very much a sportsperson, pop singer, tv and film actor etc.

fancy *adj* not plain, highly decorated

fancy *v* to have a liking for

fang *n* a long, sharp tooth

fantastic *adj* amazing, unbelievable, extraordianry

far *adj* a long way off

far *adj* not near

fare *n* the price of a journey by bus, ship, train, plane or taxi

farewell *n* a good-bye, a parting wish

farm *n* land and buildings where crops are grown and animals reared

farmer *n* a person who looks after a farm

farrier *n* a person who shoes horses

farrow *n* a litter of pigs

fascinate *v* to hold your attention, to be of great interest

fashion *n* a up-to-date style

fast *adj*
1 quick, speedy
2 firm; secure

fast *adv* quickly

fast *v* to go without food

fasten *v* to tie, join or close

fat *n* the fat, greasy part of an animal's body

fat *adj* plump

father *n* a man who is a parent

fathom *n* a measure of depth, 1.8 metres or 6 feet

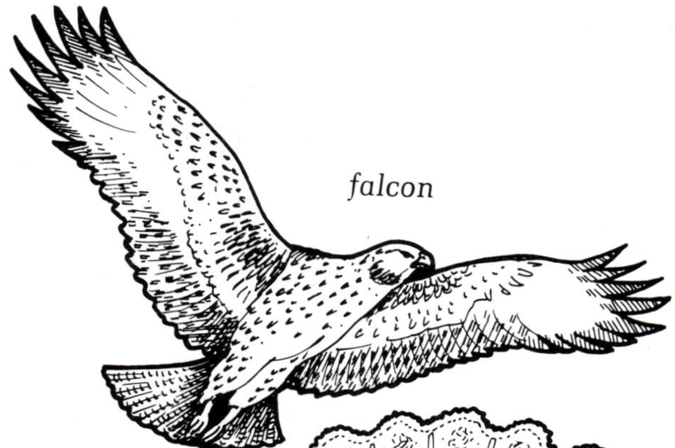
falcon

fan 1

fan 2

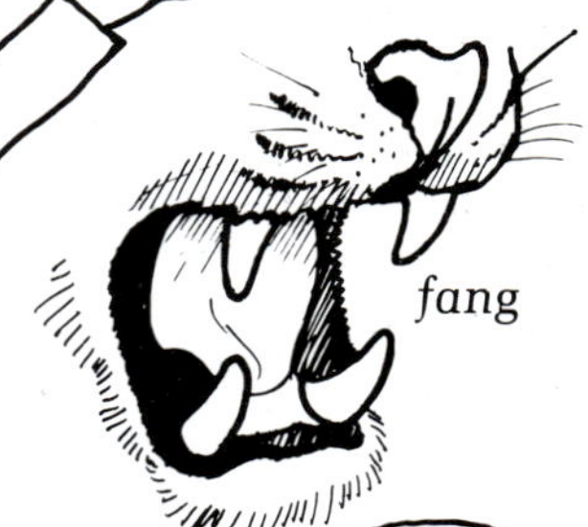
fang

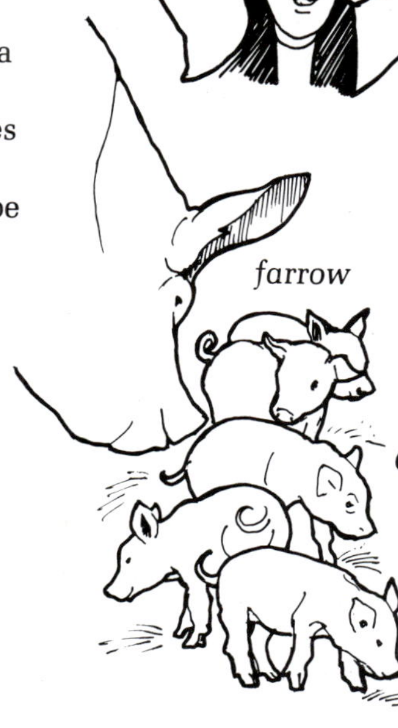
farrow

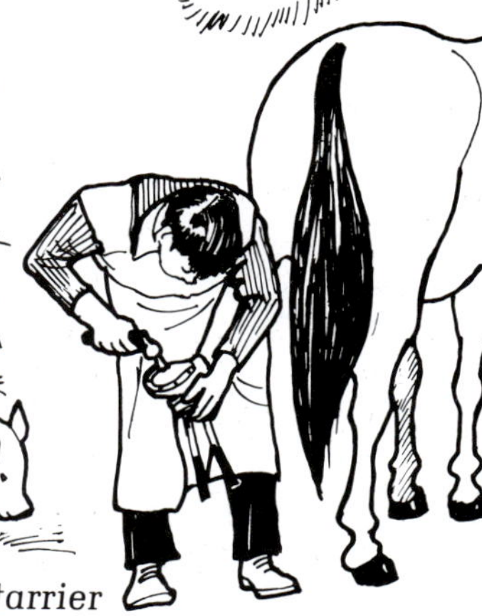
farrier

Ff

Ff

fathom *v* to get to the bottom of a problem etc.
fault *n* something that is wrong, a mistake
fauna *n* the animal life of a region
favour *n* an act of kindness or help
favour *v* to prefer
favourite *adj* the best liked person or thing
fawn *n* a young deer
fear *n* a feeling that something dangerous or bad is going to happen
fear *v* to feel frightened
fearless *adj* brave; without fear
feast *n* a very large and grand meal
feat *n* a deed of courage or strength
feather *n* one of the many light coverings that grow on a bird's body
feeble *adj* weak, not strong
feed *v* to give food to a person or animal
feel *v* to touch
felt *n* a thick kind of cloth
female *n* a girl, a woman; an animal able to give birth to young
fen *n* low-lying marshy land
fence *n* a barrier of wood, metal, wire etc., supported by posts, and enclosing a field or a garden
fence *v* to fight with swords
fern *n* a plant with feathery leaves, which does not produce flowers
ferocious *adj* fierce, savage, cruel
ferret *n* a small, fierce animal which hunts rabbits and rats
ferry *n* a boat that carries people, vehicles and goods for short distances
fertile *adj* able to produce a lot of good crops
fertilizer *n* a substance added to soil, to make it better for growing crops
festival *n* a celebration or time of happiness, often with music, drama, art etc.
fetch *v* to go and get
fever *n* an illness in which you have a high temperature
few *adj* small in number, not many
fibre *n* a thread of any kind
fiction *n* a made-up-story
fiddle *n* a violin
fidget *v* to move about restlessly
field *n* a piece of ground used for crops or pasture
fierce *adj* savage; violent; wild
fig *n* a soft, sweet fruit, with many seeds
fight *v*
1 to struggle with
2 to battle with
figure *n*
1 a sign for a number such as 1, 3, 7 etc.
2 the shape of someone's body
file *n*
1 a steel tool with a rough rubbing-surface used for smoothing wood, metal etc.
2 drawers, shelves, cases etc. in which papers, records etc. are kept
fill *v* to put into a container until there is no more room
filly *n* a young female horse
film *n*
1 a thin layer or covering
2 a roll of thin material that you put into a camera for taking photographs
3 moving pictures shown on a screen
filthy *adj* very dirty

fin *n*		a short wing-like part of a fish
final *adj*		the last, the end
finally *adv*		at last
finch *n*		a small, songbird
find *v*		to discover or locate something
fine *adj*	1	very thin, delicate
	2	bright and sunny
fine *n*		money paid as punishment
finger *n*		one of the end parts, or digits, of the hand
fingerprint *n*		the mark left on something by the tip of your finger
finish *v*		to bring to an end; to complete
finish *n*		the end, the last part
fiord *n*		a long, narrow sea inlet between steep cliffs, especially of Norway
fir *n*		a tall, evergreen tree that has needle-like leaves
fire *n*		the heat and light from something burning
fire *v*		to shoot with a gun
fire-engine *n*		a vehicle that carries firemen and their equipment to a fire
fire-escape *n*		a ladder or stairway used when a building is on fire
fireman *n*		a person trained to put out fires
firefly *n*		a winged insect with a tail that shines at night
fire station *n*		a building for firemen and their fire-fighting machines
fireworks *n (pl)*		small containers filled with chemicals that burn with loud noises and pretty colours
firm *n*		a business, a company
firm *adj*		steady; solid; fixed
first *adj*		coming before all others
first aid *n*		treatment given to a sick or injured person before a doctor is present
first-class *adj*		of the highest or best quality
fish *n*		an animal that breathes through gills and lives only in water
fisherman *n*		a person who catches fish
fist *n*		a tightly closed-hand
fit *n*		a sudden attack
fit *adj*		in good health or condition
fit *v*		to be of the right size
fix *n*	1	to mend something
	2	to fasten or make firm
flabby *adj*		hanging loosely; soft and limp
flag *n*		a piece of cloth with an emblem or decoration on it
flake		a thin, light piece of something, such as snow
flame *n*		the burning gas of a fire
flamingo *n*		a pink, tropical bird with long legs and neck
flan *n*		an open tart
flannel *n*		a soft, woollen cloth
flap *n*		a piece of material that hangs down over an opening
flap *v*		to move up and down or from side to side
flare *n*		a very bright blaze of light which may be used as a signal
flare *v*		to blaze up suddenly
flash *n*		a sudden burst of light
flash *v*		to shine out suddenly
flask *n*	1	a narrow-necked bottle
	2	a container for keeping liquids hot or cold
flat *adj*		level and smooth
flat *n*		a home having all the rooms on the same floor

Ff

flock

floppy disk

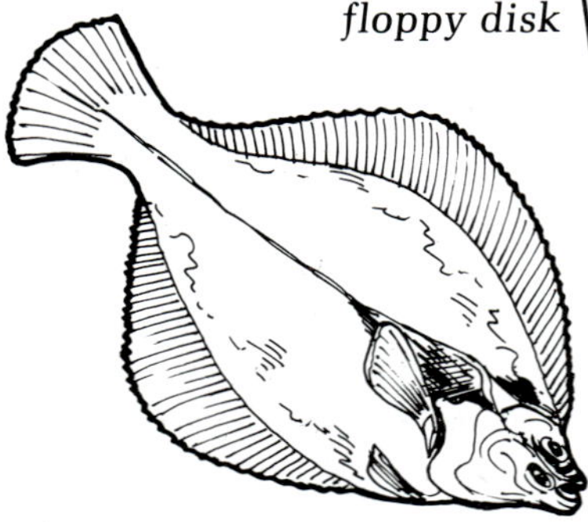

flounder

flatter	*v*	to say too many nice things to someone
flavour	*n*	the taste and smell together
flaw	*n*	a fault; a crack; a weak spot
flax	*n*	a plant from which linen is made
flea	*n*	a small, hopping insect without wings
fledgeling	*n*	a young bird that is just able to fly
flee	*v*	to run away from danger or trouble
fleece	*n*	the woolly coat of a sheep
fleet	*n*	a number of ships, vehicles, planes etc.
flesh	*n*	the soft part of your body that covers the bones
flex	*n*	insulated wire which carries electric current
flexible	*adj*	easily bent this way and that
flick	*v*	to strike lightly
flicker	*v*	to shine with a blinking light
flight	*n*	*1* the movement of birds, insects, aircraft etc. through the air *2* a trip by an aircraft *3* a set of stairs
flinch	*v*	to draw back
fling	*v*	to throw with force
flipper	*n*	the flat limb of a seal, walrus or turtle, used for swimming
float	*v*	to stay on the surface of a liquid
flock	*n*	a large group of animals or birds
flood	*n*	a great overflow of water
floor	*n*	*1* the bottom of a room on which we walk *2* one level or storey of a building
floppy disk	*n*	a disc made of soft magnetized plastic, on which computer instructions can be stored
florist	*n*	a person or shop that sells flowers
flounder	*n*	a small, flat fish
flour	*n*	the fine powder made by grinding grain
flow	*v*	to move along easily
flower	*n*	the blossom of a plant, that produces seeds or fruit
flu	*n (abbr)*	short for influenza
fluffy	*adj*	*1* covered with soft hair or fur or very fine feathers *2* soft and light
fluid	*n*	a liquid or gas that flows easily
flush	*v*	*1* to go red with excitement, to blush *2* to clear out with a sudden rush of water

flute *n* a wind instrument made of wood or metal
flutter *v* to wave back and forth in the breeze
fly *n* one of several kinds of insects with two wings
fly *v*
1 to move through the air with wings or in an aircraft
2 to leave suddenly
foal *n* a young horse
foam *n* a white mass of small bubbles or froth
fodder *n* dried food for cattle.
foe *n* an enemy
fog *n* a thick mist that is difficult to see through
foil *n* a thin, silvery sheet of metal
fold *v* to double something over on itself
foliage *n* the leaves of plants
folk *n (pl)* people
follow *v*
1 to go or come after
2 to understand
font *n* the basin for holding water for baptism
food *n* what people, animals, and plants eat to keep alive
fool *n* a silly person
foolish *adj* without much sense
foot *n*
1 the part of each leg on which you stand
2 the bottom part
3 a measure of length equal to about 30cm
football *n* a game played between two teams
footlights *n (pl)* the lights along the front of a theatre stage
footprint *n* the mark of a foot on soft ground or a clean floor
footsteps *n (pl)* the sound of someone walking
for *prep*
1 in return
2 because of
3 as far as, as long as
4 with a purpose
forbid *v* to tell someone not to do something
force *n* strength, power
force *v*
1 to make someone do something against their wishes
2 to break open
fore a prefix meaning ‘in front of’ or ‘before’
forecast *v* to say in advance what is likely to happen
forehead *n* the part of your face above your eyes
foreign *adj* belonging to another country other than your own
foreman *n* a person in charge of a group of workers
forest *n* a large area of land covered thickly with trees
forge *n* a place where metal is made very hot and then hammered into shape
forgery *n* writing or a picture that is made to look as if someone else has done it; a false copy
forget *v* to fail to remember
forgive *v* to stop being angry with someone for something they have done to you; to let off
fork *n*
1 a tool with two or more points for lifting food to your mouth
2 a garden tool with prongs for digging earth
3 a place where a road or river divides

Ff

Ff

form *n*
1 the shape something has
2 a printed paper with spaces where answers have to be filled in
3 a school class
4 a long seat or bench

fort *n* a strong building that can be defended

fortnight *n* a period of two weeks

fortunate *adj* lucky

fortune *n*
1 a lot of money
2 luck

forward *adj* in front of; at the front

forward *adv* towards the front

forward *n* a position in football and other games

fossil *n* the remains of a prehistoric animal animal or plant that have turned to stone

foster-parents *n (pl)* parents who care for a child as their own, even though they are not related to the child

foul *adj*
1 dirty, disgusting, bad
2 rough, stormy

foul *n* a breaking of the rules in a game

foundations *n (pl)* the strong base of a building, usually below ground

fountain *n* a jet of water shooting upwards and falling back into a pool

fowl *n* a bird, particularly that which is kept for their eggs or meat

fox *n* a wild animal of the dog family with red-brown fur and a bushy tail

foxglove *n* a tall plant with purple or white bell-shaped flowers

fraction *n*
1 a number that is less than a whole number such as $^{1}/_{2}$, $^{3}/_{8}$, $^{7}/_{10}$ etc.
2 a part of something

fracture *n* a break; a crack

fragile *adj* delicate; easily broken

fragrance *n* a sweet, pleasant smell

fragrant *adj* sweet-smelling

frail *adj* weak, feeble; delicate in health

frame *n* a border of wood or metal around something, such as a window frame, a picture frame

franc *n* unit of currency in France Belgium, Switzerland etc.

frank *adj* saying what you really think

frantic *adj* almost mad with excitement

fraud *n* cheating; a dishonest trick

freckles *n (pl)* light brown marks on the skin

free *adj*
1 costing no money
2 able to do what you want

free *v* to let go

freedom *n* being free

freeze *v* to change into ice

freezer *n* a special box or cupboard in which frozen food can be kept for a long time

freight *n* cargo, goods carried by a ship, plane, train, lorry etc.

frequent *adj* happening or appearing often

fresh *adj*
1 new
2 not stale

fridge *n (abbr)* short for refrigerator

friend *n* someone you know well and like

frieze *n* a decorated border along the top of a wall

frighten *v* to make someone afraid

frill *n* lace or cloth on the edges of material

fringe *n* loose threads hanging from the edge of cloth

frog *n* a small, jumping animal that lives in and out of water; it grows from a tadpole

from *prep* starting from; out of; because of; at a distance of

front *n* the part of something that faces forward

frontier *n* the boundary between two countries

frost *n* the powdery ice you see on the ground on a cold day

frown *v* to pull the eyebrows together when you are cross or thinking hard

fruit *n*
1 a juicy food from a tree, bush, or vine
2 the part of any plant that contains the seeds.

fry *v* to cook in hot fat or oil

fuel *n* anything that is burned to give heat or energy

full *adj* filled completely

fumble *v*
1 to handle something awkwardly
2 to feel about

fumes *n (pl)* strong-smelling smoke or gases

fun *n* enjoyment, amusement

fund *n* money to be used for a certain purpose

funeral *n* a burial service for a dead person

fungus *n* a plant that has no leaves, flowers or green colouring, such as a mushroom

funnel *n* a tube with a wide top and a narrow bottom

funny *adj* amusing, making you laugh

fur *n* the soft, hair coat of some animals

furious *adj* very, very angry

furniture *n* the things needed in a room, such as chairs, tables, beds etc.

fury *n* rage; violent anger

fuse *n*
1 a safety device to protect electrical goods
2 a device that sets off explosions

fuselage *n* the body of an aircraft

fuss *n* excitement, bother over small things

future *n* the time still to come

foxglove

freckles

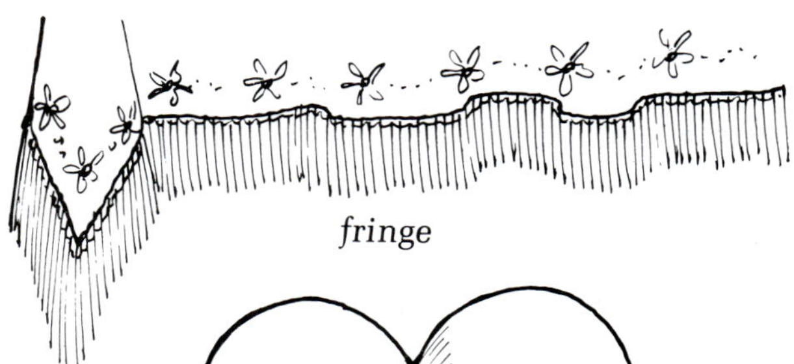
fringe

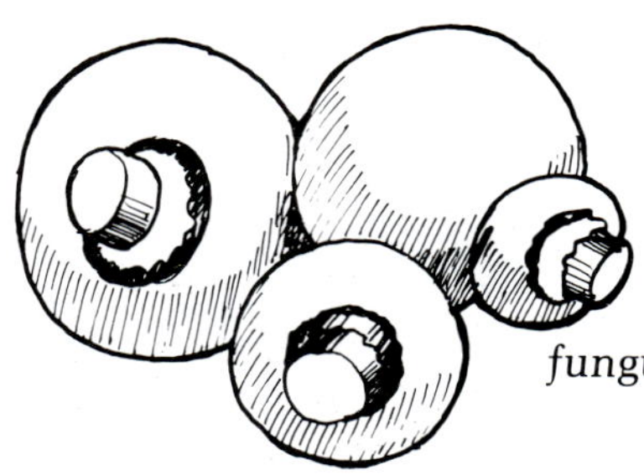
fungus

Gg

gabble	*v*		to say words so quickly that they cannot be heard clearly
gable	*n*		the triangular wall at the end of a ridged roof
gadget	*n*		a small and useful device
gag	*n*		something tied round someone's mouth to stop them speaking
gaggle	*n*		a flock of geese
gain	*v*	*1*	to get or obtain
		2	to increase
gala	*n*		a fête or festival
galaxy	*n*		a very large group of stars in outer space
gale	*n*		a very strong wind, a storm
galleon	*n*		a large Spanish sailing-ship of olden times
gallery	*n*		a building where paintings or other works of art are displayed
galley	*n*	*1*	a ship's kitchen
		2	an ancient ship using sails and oars
gallon	*n*		a liquid measure equal to about 4.5 litres
gallop	*n*		the fastest pace of a horse
gallop	*v*		to run with leaping strides
gamble	*v*		to risk money in the hope of gaining more; to bet
game	*n*	*1*	a form of indoor or outdoor play in which the players follow certain rules
		2	wild birds or animals that are hunted
gander	*n*		a male goose

gander

gang	*n*		a group of people working together, sometimes for a bad purpose
gannet	*n*		a large, fish-eating seabird
gap	*n*		an opening or space
garage	*n*	*1*	a building where motor vehicles are kept
		2	a place where petrol can be bought and cars repaired
garbage	*n*		rubbish; unwanted waste
garden	*n*		a piece of ground used for growing flowers, fruit, or vegetables
garlic	*n*		a strong-smelling plant bulb, used for flavouring in cooking
garment	*n*		any piece of clothing
gas	*n*		a substance like air, that is not solid or liquid
gash	*n*		a deep cut
gasp	*v*		to breathe with difficulty
gate	*n*		a hinged door in a fence or wall
gather	*v*		to bring or come together
gauge	*n*		an instrument for measuring
gauze	*n*		a very thin cloth
gay	*adj*		lively, cheerful, full of fun
gaze	*v*		to look at something for a long time
gear	*n*		a set of toothed wheels working together in a machine
gelignite	*n*		an explosive used for blasting
gem	*n*		a jewel or precious stone
general	*adj*		to do with most people or things
general	*n*		a senior officer in the army
generous	*adj*		ready to give freely and happily
genius	*n*		someone who is very clever
gentle	*adj*		mild, quiet, kind

genuine *adj* real, true; not a copy
geography *n* the study of the world and what happens on it
gerbil *n* a small pet that looks like a mouse
germ *n* a very tiny living thing that can cause illness and disease
get *v*
1 to obtain
2 to arrive
3 to become
geyser *n* a natural hot spring from which hot water and steam rise into the air
ghost *n* the spirit of a dead person, which some people think walks about at night
giant *n* an animal or plant of enormous size
giddy *adj* dizzy and unsteady
gift *n* something that is given to someone; a present
gig *n* a public pop, rock or jazz performance
gigantic *adj* very large indeed
giggle *v* to laugh in a silly way
gills *n (pl)* two openings in the head of a fish, used for breathing
gin *n* a colourless alcoholic drink
ginger *n* the hot-tasting root of a plant used for flavouring
ginger *adj* reddish-brown
giraffe *n* a tall African mammal with very long legs and neck
girl *n* a female child
give *v*
1 to hand over as a present
2 to begin to crack or break
glacier *n* a huge body of ice that moves very slowly down a mountain side or along a valley
glad *adj* pleased, happy
glance *n* a quick look

gerbil

glare *n* a strong light
glare *v* to stare at someone in an angry way
glass *n*
1 a hard substance you can see through, used in making windows
2 a drinking vessel
glasses *n (pl)* lenses in a frame to help you see better; spectacles
glaze *n* a mixture coated onto pottery to give it a shiny surface
glaze *v* to fit glass into window frames
gleam *n* a brief flash of light
gleam *v* to shine; to flash;
glide *v* to move very smoothly
glider *n* a light aircraft that flies without an engine
glimmer *n* a faint, unsteady light
glisten *v* to shine, to sparkle
glitter *v* to throw out rays of light
globe *n*
1 a ball, or anything in the shape of a ball
2 the earth
gloomy *adj*
1 dark, dim
2 sad, miserable
glory *n* beauty, fame, praise
gloss *n* a smooth, shiny surface
glove *n* a covering for your hand
glow *v* to give out light and warmth, without flames
glue *n* a sticky liquid or paste used to hold things together
gnaw *v* to chew at, as a dog does with a bone

gnome

Gg

gnome *n* a little dwarf in fairy tales

go *v*
1 to move away; to leave
2 to be moving

goal *n*
1 the posts between which a ball must be sent in some games such as football and hockey
2 an aim

goat *n* an animal with horns and long hair

gobble *v*
1 to eat something quickly and greedily
2 to make the noise of a turkey

goblin *n* an ugly and mischievous elf in fairy tales

God *n* in some religions, the creator of everything

goggles *n (pl)* large, strong glasses worn to protect the eyes

gold *n* a very valuable, shiny, yellow metal

goldfish *n* a small fish often kept as a pet in glass bowls and in garden ponds

golf *n* an outdoor game played with clubs and a small, hard ball

gong *n* a large metal disc that gives a booming sound when hit

good *adj* of high quality; kind; well-behaved

goodbye *n* farewell

goods *n (pl)*
1 things that are bought and sold
2 property; belongings

goose *n* a large bird with webbed-feet

gooseberry *n* a hairy berry that grows on a small bush

gorge *n* a deep, narrow valley

gorgeous *adj* magnificent, beautiful

gorilla *n* the largest and strongest ape

gorse *n* a prickly, yellow shrub

gosling *n* a young goose

gospel *n* an account of the life and teachings of Jesus Christ

gossip *n* talk about other people that is not always true, and is sometimes unkind

govern *v* to rule; to control people or a country

government *n* the people chosen to rule a country

gown *n* a woman's dress

grab *v* to snatch or grasp something suddenly

graceful *adj* charming; beautiful in movement

gradient *n* the slope of a road, railway etc.

gradual *adj* happening slowly

graduate *n* someone who has gained a university degree

grain *n*
1 the seed of wheat, oats, corn and other cereal plants
2 the natural pattern in wood

gram *n* [g = gram] a measure of weight; 1000g = 1 kilogram

grammar *n* the rules for the correct use of words

grand *adj*
1 great in size
2 splendid, magnificent

grandchild *n* a child of a son or daughter; a granddaughter or grandson

grandfather, grandad, grandpa *n* the father of a person's father or mother

grandmother, grandma *n* the mother of a person's father or mother

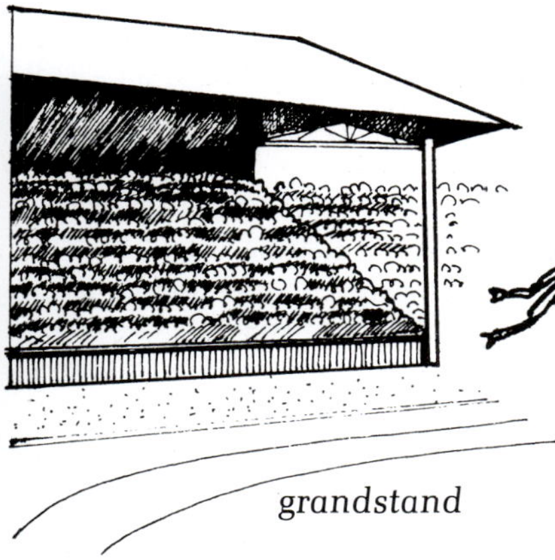
grandstand

grasshopper

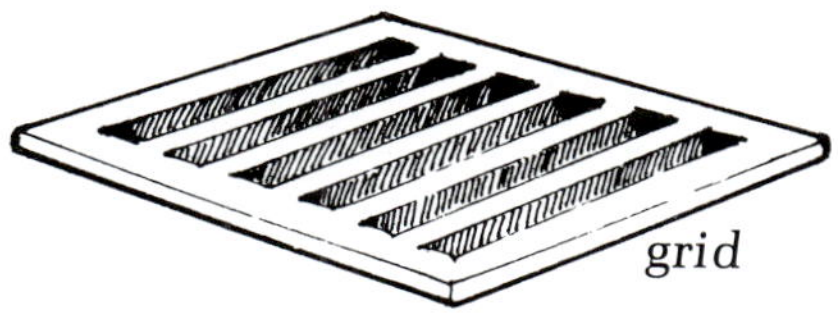
grid

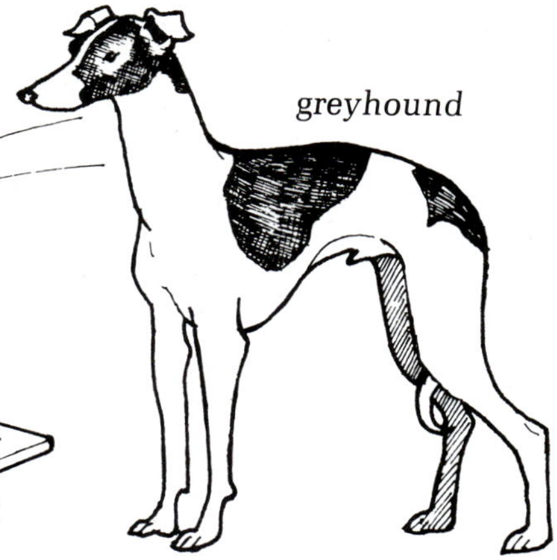
greyhound

Gg

grandstand *n* rows of seats at a sports ground, usually covered

granite *n* a very hard rock

grant *v* to give, to allow

grape *n* the juicy fruit that grows in clusters on a vine

grapefruit *n* a fruit that looks like a large orange and has a yellowish skin

graph *n* a diagram that shows facts and figures by means of a line on squared paper

grasp *v* to seize hold of

grass *n* a plant with thin green leaves grown on lawns and fields

grasshopper *n* a jumping insect which chirps

grateful *adj* feeling of thanks for something

grave *n* a hole in the ground in which someone is buried

gravel *n* small pebbles and stones

gravity *n* the force that pulls things towards the earth

gravy *n* hot sauce made with meat juices

graze *v* to eat growing grass

grease *n* any soft, oily substance

great *adj* *1* of large amount, size, weight etc. *2* important *3* famous, well-known

greedy *adj* wanting more than your share

green *n* the colour of grass

greenbelt *n* the area of countryside around a town where building is not allowed

greengrocer *n* a person who sells fruit and vegetables

greenhouse *n* a glasshouse where plants are grown

greet *v* to welcome

grenade *n* a small, explosive shell thrown by hand

grey *n* a colour between black and white; ash-coloured

greyhound *n* a powerful, fast racing or hunting dog

grid *n* a frame made of bars; a grating

grief *n* sadness, sorrow

grim *adj* fierce-looking; stern; without joy

grimy *adj* dirty, soiled

grin *n* a wide smile

grin *v* to smile broadly

Gg

grind *v* 1 to crush to powder
2 to rub together
grip *v* to hold tightly
grit *n* 1 tiny pieces of stone or stand
2 courage; staying power
grizzly bear *n* a large, fierce brownish-grey bear from the Rocky Mountains, North America
groan *n* a deep sound of pain, sadness or disappointment
grocer *n* a trader who sells food and household goods
groom *n* 1 a man on his wedding day
2 a person who looks after horses
groom *v* to make neat and tidy
groove *n* a long, narrow cut or channel
ground *n* 1 the earth we walk on
2 a sports field
group *n* a number of people doing something together
grow *v* 1 to get bigger, to increase
2 to plant
growl *v* to make a deep, angry noise, as made by a dog
grown-up *n* any person who is an adult; a full-grown person
grub *n* a newly-hatched insect
grudge *n* a bad feeling
grumble *v* to complain, to find fault
grunt *n* the kind of sound that a pig makes
guarantee *n* a promise; an agreement that if something goes wrong, it will be repaired or replaced
guard *n* someone who keeps watch and protects
guard *v* to protect; to keep safe
guess *v* to say what you think is true, without knowing for certain
guest *n* a visitor, someone you invite to your home
guide *v* to show someone the way; to lead
guide *n* someone who shows the way; a leader
guilty *adj* having done wrong or taken part in a crime
guinea-pig *n* a small, furry, tail-less rat-like animal often kept as a pet
guitar *n* a stringed musical instrument played by plucking
gulf *n* a large inlet of sea
gull *n* a largish, flying sea-bird
gulp *v* to swallow quickly
gum *n* 1 the flesh around your teeth
2 a kind of glue
3 chewing gum
gun *n* a firearm; a weapon firing bullets, shells etc.
gunpowder *n* a black explosive powder
guru *n* a religious teacher, especially Sikh
gush *v* to flow out suddenly
gust *n* a sudden blast of wind
gutter *n* a small channel for carrying away rain-water
guy *n* 1 a rope support for a tent
2 a dummy figure of Guy Fawkes which is burnt on November 5th
guzzle *v* to eat greedily
gym/gymnasium *n* a large room for exercises, training and sports
gymkhana *n* a competition for horses and ponies and their riders
gymnast *n* someone who trains to do special physical exercises and acrobatics
gypsy *n* a person belonging to a group of wandering people

Hh

habit *n* — something you do the same way all the time

haddock *n* — a seafish of the cod family and important as food

hag *n* — an ugly old woman

hail *n* — frozen rain

hair *n* — 1 one of the fine threads that grow on the skin
2 the covering of your head, or of an animal's body

haircut *n* — the cutting and trimming of your hair

hairdresser *n* — a person who cuts and looks after people's hair

half *n* — one of two equal parts that make up a whole

halibut *n* — a large flatfish that can be eaten

hake *n* — a seafish, related to the cod, and eaten as food

hall *n* — 1 the entrance space behind the door of a building
2 a large room for meetings, concerts, parties etc.

Hallowe'en *n* — the night of October 31 when it was once believed that witches and ghosts roamed about

halo *n* — a circle of light

halt *v* — to stop

halve *v* — to divide into two equal parts

ham *n* — salted or smoked meat from a pig's thigh

hamburger *n* — a round cake of minced beef inside a bun, eaten hot

hamlet *n* — a small village

hammer *n* — a tool used for driving in nails, shaping metal, or breaking up stones

hamper *n* — a large basket with a lid

hand *n* — the end part of your arm

handbag *n* — a small bag or purse, usually carried by women

handcuffs *n (pl)* — steel bracelets used to hold a prisoner's hands together

handful *n* — as much as your hand will hold

handicap *n* — something that puts a person at a disadvantage

handkerchief *n* — a cloth for wiping your nose

handle *n* — the part of a cup, pan, or tool by which it is held

handle *v* — to feel something with the hands

handlebar *n* — the part of a bicycle or motor cycle that the rider holds and uses for steering

handsome *adj* — good-looking

handwriting *n* — a person's style of writing

handy *adj* — 1 clever with your hands
2 useful to have by you, such as a handy tool

hang *v* — to hold from above so that the lower part can move

hangar *n* — a large building where aircraft are kept

hanger *n* — a wooden or wire frame on which to hang clothes

hang-gliding *n* — the sport of gliding using a type of large kite

happen *v* — to take place

happy *adj* — pleased, cheerful, glad

harbour *n* — a sheltered place for ships

hard *adj* — 1 firm or solid; not soft
2 difficult

hardly *adj* — only just

hardware *n* — 1 metal items such as locks, tools, pans etc.
2 electronic parts of a computer

hare *n* — an animal like a large rabbit with long ears and long back legs

harm *v* — to damage, to hurt

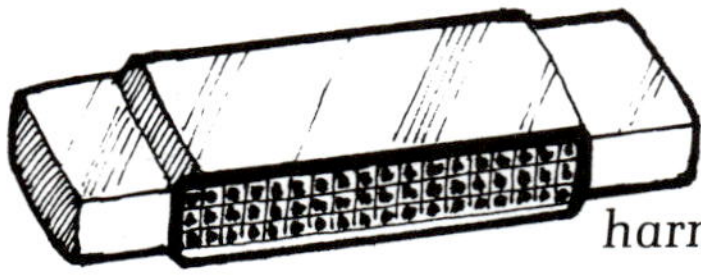

Hh

harmful *adj* causing harm, dangerous
harmless *adj* safe; not dangerous
harmonica *n* a small, musical instrument, also called a mouth organ
harmony *n* a pleasing musical sound
harp *n* a large musical instrument played by plucking strings with the fingers of both hands
harsh *adj* rough, unkind
harvest *n* the gathering of grain, fruit, and other crops at the end of the growing season
haste *n* great hurry
hat *n* a covering for the head, usually with a brim
hatch *v* to be born from an egg
hatch *n* a movable covering over an opening
hatchet *n* a small axe
hate *v* to dislike very much, to detest
hatred *n* a very strong dislike of someone or something
haul *v* to pull or drag with effort
haunted *adj* believed to be visited by ghosts
have *v* to own; to possess
hawk *n* a bird of prey with a strong, hooked beak and long, curved claws
hawthorn *n* a thorny bush whose fruits are red
hay *n* grass, cut and dried as food for animals
haze *n* a slight mist or smoke
hazel *n*
1 a small tree with nuts that can be eaten
2 a greenish-brown colour
hazy *adj* misty
he *pron* a man or boy
head *n*
1 the top part of the body above the neck
2 the chief person, such as a Head teacher
headache *n* a pain in the head
headlights *n (pl)* the main front lights of a car, bus, lorry etc.
headquarters *n* the main office of an organisation
heal *v* to make well again
health *n* the condition of your mind and body, whether you are well or ill
heap *n* a pile of things
hear *v* to receive sounds through the ears
hearse *n* a car used in a funeral, in which the coffin is carried
heart *n* the organ or part of the body that pumps blood around the body
heartless *adj* without feeling or pity
heart-break *n* great sorrow; terrible disappointment
hearth *n* the floor or base of a fireplace
heat *n* warmth, hotness
heat *v* to warm up
heater *n* something which provides warmth
heath *n* wasteland covered with rough grass, heather etc.
heather *n* a heath plant with small, purple, pink or white flowers
heave *v* to raise up with effort
heaven *n* the place where God or the gods are supposed to live
heavy *adj* hard to lift; of great weight
hectare *n* a unit of measurement for area

hedge *n* bushes that grow close together and form a kind of fence
hedgehog *n* a small animal covered in prickly spines
hedgerow *n* a hedge of bushes, brambles, or small trees
heel *n* the back of your foot, under the ankle
heifer *n* a young cow that has not had a calf
height *n* how high anything is
helicopter *n* an aircraft able to take off and land vertically, to fly and to hover
hell *n* according to some religions where the souls of the wicked are punished after death
hello *n* a greeting
helmet *n* a hard hat protecting the head
help *v* to aid someone; to assist
helpless *adj* not able to look after yourself
hem *n* the edge of a piece of cloth that is turned over and sewn
hemisphere *n* half a sphere; half the earth
hemlock *n* a poisonous plant
hen *n* a female bird, but especially a farmyard chicken
her *pron* a female person or animal already named
her *adj* of, or belonging to, a female
herb *n* a plant used to provide flavour in cooking, or as a medicine
herd *n* a group of cattle or other animals
here *adv* in or at this place
hermit *n* a person who chooses to live alone and stays away from other people
hero *n* a man or boy who has done something very brave
heroin *n* a powerful, pain-killing but dangerous drug which one can become addicted to
heroine *n* a girl or woman who has done something very brave
heroism *n* great bravery
heron *n* a large wading bird with a long beak, a long neck, and long legs
herring *n* a small sea fish used for food
hesitate *v* to pause because you are not sure whether to do or say something
hexagon *n* a figure with six equal sides
hibernate *v* to spend the winter asleep, as many animals do
hidden *adj* *1* concealed *2* kept secret
hide *v* *1* to keep out of sight *2* to put out of sight
hide *n* the skin of an animal
hi-fi *n* high fidelity apparatus to give good quality recorded sound
high *adj* tall, a long way up from the ground
high-rise *n* a tall building with many floors
highway *n* a main road
hijack to take over control unlawfully of an aircraft, ship, train or vehicle by force
hike *n* a long walk in the country
hill *n* a raised part of the land, lower than a mountain
him *pron* a male person or animal already named
hind *n* a female deer
hinder *v* to prevent or make difficult

Hh

Hh

Hindu *n* a person who follows Hinduism, a religion of India and other Asian lands

hinge *n* a joint on which a door or lid can move

hint *n* a clue; a helpful piece of advice

hip *n* the joint where the leg joins the trunk of the body

hippopotamus *n* a very large, thick-skinned animal living in and near lakes and rivers in Africa

hire *v*
1 to rent; to pay for the use of something
2 to arrange for someone to do work for pay

his *pron* belonging to him

history *n* the study of what happened in days gone by

hit *v* to strike or knock something

hit *n* something popular, such as a record or a show

hitch *v* to fasten with a loop

hitch *n* a setback; a hold-up

hive *n* a place for bees to live in

hoard *v* to store or to collect

hoard *n* a hidden store of foods, treasure etc.

hoarse *adj* sounding deep, rough or husky

hoax *n* a practical joke

hobble *v* to limp, to stumble along

hobby *n* a favourite pastime

hockey *n*
1 a game played with curved, wooden sticks and a ball, between two teams of eleven players
2 a game played on a skating rink where the players hit a puck with curved sticks

hoe *n* a long-handled tool for loosening soil and digging out weeds

hippopotamus

hog *n*
1 a pig
2 a greedy person

hoist *v* to lift up something by ropes

hold *v*
1 to keep firmly in the hand
2 to contain
3 to have

hold *n* a part of a ship where cargo is stored

hole *n* an opening or hollow in something

holiday *n* a time free from work or school

hollow *adj* not solid; empty

holly *n* a prickly evergreen shrub with red berries

hollyhock *n* a tall flowering plant

holster *n* a leather case for a handgun, attached to a person's belt

holy *adj* to do with God or religion

home *n* the place where you live

homesick *adj* sad because you are away from home

homework *n* schoolwork that is done at home

honest *adj* always truthful and fair, never cheating or stealing

honey *n* a sweet, thick liquid made by bees

honeymoon *n* the holiday taken by a newly married couple

honeysuckle *n* a climbing plant with sweet-smelling flowers

honour *n*
1 great respect
2 fame and glory

hood *n* a covering for the head and neck

hoof *n* the horny foot of a horse, cow, sheep etc.

hook *n* a bent piece of metal made to hold something, such as a fish hook
hoot *n* 1 the cry of an owl
2 the sound of a horn or siren
hop *v* to jump on one leg, or with two feet together
hop *n* a climbing plant belonging to the nettle family, the flowers of which are used in making beer
hope *v* to wish that something would happen
horizon *n* the line where sea and sky, or earth and sky, seem to meet
horizontal *adj* lying flat or level with the ground
horn *n* 1 the hard, usually pointed growth on the head of some animals
2 a musical instrument that you blow
3 a warning signal
hornet *n* a large insect of the wasp family
horrible *adj* unpleasant, frightening, awful
horrify *v* to upset or shock someone
horror *n* great fear, terror, fright
horse *n* a hoofed animal used for riding and pulling loads
horsepower *n* a measure of the power of an engine
horseshoe *n* a U-shaped piece of iron used to protect a horse's hoof
horticulture *n* the art of gardening
hose *n* a long, flexible tube through which liquids can pass
hospital *n* a building where sick or injured people are cared for by doctors and nurses
host *n* a person who entertains guests
hostage *n* a person held prisoner until certain demands are met
hostess *n* a woman who entertains guests
hostile *adj* unfriendly
hot *adj* full of heat
hot dog *n* a hot sausage in a bread roll
hotel *n* a building where travellers pay to stay and have meals
hound *n* a dog used for hunting
hour *n* a length of time equal to 60 minutes
house *n* a building in which people live
household *n* all the people who live together in a house
hover *v* to stay in the air in one place
how *adv* in what way
however *adv* by whatever means
howl *n* a long wailing cry
huddle *v* to press close together
hue *n* a colour; a shade of colour
huff *n* a fit of anger
hug *v* to clasp close in your arms
huge *adj* enormous in size
hull *n* the frame or body of a ship
hum *v* 1 to make a noise like a bee
2 to make a singing sound with your lips
human *adj* having to do with people, not animals
humble *adj* feeling not important or less important; modest
humid *adj* moist, damp
humidity *n* dampness in the air
humorous *adj* funny, laughable
humour *n* the ability to see the funny side of things
hump *n* a large bulge or lump, usually on the back
hundred *n* the number 100

hunger *n*	the feeling that you need food
hunt *v*	*1* to chase after something in order to catch or kill it *2* to search for
hurdle *n*	a movable fence for runners or horses to jump over in a race
hurl *v*	to throw something with all your strength
hurricane *n*	a violent storm with a very powerful wind and heavy rain
hurry *v*	to move quickly
hurt *v*	to cause pain or harm to someone
husband *n*	a married man
hush *v*	to keep quiet
husky *n*	a strong dog, used in very cold places for pulling sledges
husky *adv*	rough-voiced
hut *n*	a small building, generally of wood
hutch *n*	a cage or box for rabbits or other small animals
hyacinth *n*	a spring flower that grows from a bulb, often with pink, blue, or white flowers
hydrant *n*	a water pipe in a street, to which hoses can be attached
hydrofoil *n*	a large type of motor-boat that raises itself out of the water on wing-like struts as it gathers speed
hydrogen *n*	a colourless, odourless, tasteless gas that is lighter than air
hyena *n*	a wild, wolf-like animal found in India and parts of Africa
hygiene *n*	the rules of good health and cleanliness
hymn *n*	a song of praise to God
hyphen *n*	a short dash (-) used to join words or divide a word into parts
hypnotist *n*	a person who can put you into a sleep-like state
hypocrite *n*	a person who pretends to be good

I *pron*		myself, me, the person is who is talking or writing
ice *n*		frozen water
iceberg *n*		a mountain of ice floating in the sea
ice cream *n*		a kind of soft, sweet, frozen mixture
ice hockey *n*		a team game of six players and a goalkeeper on each side played on ice
ice skate *n*		a boot with a blade underneath for skating on ice
icicle *n*		a pointed stick of hanging ice
icing *n*		a sweet covering for cakes
idea *n*		a thought, a plan in the mind
identical *adj*		exactly the same
idiot *n*		a stupid or foolish person
idle *adj*		lazy; not working
idol *n*	*1*	a statue that is worshipped as a god
	2	someone or something admired or loved greatly
if *conj*	*1*	on the condition that, supposing that
	2	whether
igloo *n*		an Eskimo hut made of blocks of snow
ignite *v*		to set fire to
ignition *n*	*1*	the part of the car that starts the engine
	2	a setting on fire
ignorant *adj*	*1*	knowing little
	2	rude, impolite
ignore *v*		to take no notice of someone or something
iguana *n*		a large, climbing lizard
ill *n*		unwell; sick
illegal *adj*		against the law
illiterate *adj*		unable to read or write
illuminate *v*		to give light to something

illustrate *v*		to draw pictures to show something more clearly
illustration *n*		a drawing or picture in a book, magazine etc.
imaginary *adj*		not real, only thought of
imagination *n*		being able to picture things in your mind; having ideas
imagine *v*		to picture a thing in your mind
imitate *v*		to copy someone or something
immediately *adv*		at once
immense *adj*		very large, enormous
immigrant *n*		a person who comes into a new country to live
immunize *v*		to protect against disease
impatient *adj*		restless, finding it hard to wait
import *v*		to bring goods into the country from other countries
important *adj*		mattering very much
impossible *adj*		not able to be done
imprison *v*		to put into prison
improve *v*		to make better, or become better
impudent *adj*		not polite; insolent
in *prep*	*1*	inside — in the house
	2	at — we live in a town
	3	during — it can be done in a few minutes
in		a prefix meaning 'not': 'incomplete' means not complete
inch *n*		a measure of length, equal to about 2.5cm
include *v*		to count in; to put in
income *n*		money that you receive for your work, etc.
increase *v*		to become bigger in size or power
incubate *v*		to hatch eggs by keeping them warm

Ii

indeed *adv*	really; certainly
independent *adj*	free; not controlled by another person, thing or country
index *n*	a list of names, subjects etc. in alphabetical order and the pages on which they appear, at the end of a book
indicate *v*	to point out; to show
indigestion *n*	a feeling of illness when your body doesn't digest food properly
individual *n*	one person, animal or thing
indoors *adv*	inside a building
industry *n*	work done in factories, on farms etc.
inexpensive *adj*	cheap, not expensive
infant *n*	a very young child
infantry *n*	soldiers who fight on foot
infection *n*	an illness that can be spread by harmful germs
inform *v*	to tell, to pass on information
information *n*	news, facts, knowledge
ingredient *n*	one of the things you put in a mixture
inhabit *v*	to live in a place
inhabitant *n*	someone who lives in a place
inhale *v*	to breathe in
inherit *v*	to receive money or property from someone who has died
initial *n*	the first letter of a name
injection *n*	the putting of medicine etc. into the body with a special needle
injure *v*	to harm, to damage
injury *n*	damage or harm, particularly to the body
ink *n*	coloured liquid used for writing, drawing or printing
inland *adj*	away from the coast
inlet *n*	a narrow strip of water or small bay
inn *n*	a public house where food and drink are served, and sometimes where people can stay
inner *adj*	inside
innings *n*	the time when a cricket player or team is batting
innocent *adj*	not guilty; not having done wrong
inquire *v*	to ask about someone or something; to find out
inquisitive *adj*	wanting to find out about things; curious
insane *adj*	mad; very foolish
insect *n*	a small creature with six legs and three parts to its body
inside *adj*	within
insist *v*	to say firmly and strongly
inspect *v*	to examine very closely
inspector *n*	1 someone who visits schools, factories, hospitals, etc., to see that all is well 2 a police officer
instalment *n*	a part of something, especially a story or payment
install *v*	to put in place
instant *n*	a brief moment of time
instantly *adv*	at once
instead *adv*	in place of
instinct *n*	a natural feeling or ability that makes living creatures do things without being taught
instruct *v*	to teach, to show someone how to do something
instructions *n (pl)*	directions, an explanation of how to do things
instructor *n*	a teacher

instrument *n* 1 a tool, implement, or piece of apparatus
2 something used for making musical sounds

instrument 1  *instrument 2*

insult *v* to be rude to someone

intelligence *n* being able to learn and understand well

intelligent *adj* clever and able to understand easily

intend *v* to mean to do something

interest *n* 1 something you enjoy doing or want to learn more about
2 money that a bank or building society pays you when you have savings with them: money you pay if you have a loan

interesting *adj* holding your attention

interface *n* a device for linking computers

interfere *v* to meddle in other people's affairs

interior *n* the inside of anything

international *adj* having to do with two or more nations

interrupt *v* to disturb someone who is doing or saying something

interval *n* the space between two things

interview *n* a meeting when you can talk to someone to find out more about him or her

into *prep* to the inside of

introduce *v* to make people known to each other

invade *v* to enter another country to attack it

invalid *n* someone who is ill or weak

invent *v* to plan or make something for the first time

invention *n* a new thing that has been invented

investigate *v* to examine carefully

invisible *adj* not able to be seen

invitation *n* spoken or written words that ask you, or invite you to come to some place or to do something

invite *v* to ask someone to come somewhere or to do something

iris *n* 1 the coloured part of your eye
2 a tall flowering plant with pointed leaves

iron *n* 1 a strong metal with many uses
2 an appliance for pressing clothes

iron *v* to make clothes smooth after washing them

irrigate *v* to supply water to dry land in order to help crops to grow

irritate *v* to annoy, to make angry

Islam *n* the religion of the followers of Mohammed. Members of this religion are called Moslems

island *n* a piece of land with water all round it

isle *n* a small island

isolate *v* to put something away from other things

itch *n* a tickling irritation of the skin

item *n* one thing on a list

ivory *n* the white, bone-like material from which elephants' tusks are made

ivy *n* an evergreen climbing plant, often having shiny green leaves

jab *v*		to stab, to poke
jack *n*		a tool for raising heavy weights off the ground
jacket *n*		a short coat
jagged *adj*		rough with sharp edges
jaguar *n*		a wild animal like a leopard, but much heavier
jail *n*		a prison
jam *n*	1	fruit boiled with sugar until it is thick
	2	a tight crowd of people or traffic, unable to move
jam *v*		to push things together tightly
jamboree *n*		a large rally of Boy Scouts
jangle *v*		to make a loud, clashing noise
jar *n*		a pot or glass container
jar *v*		to make a harsh, grating noise
javelin *n*		a spear made to be thrown
jaw *n*		the bones of the mouth
jazz *n*		a lively kind of music
jay *n*		a noisy, bright-feathered bird
jealous *adj*		being unhappy because you want what others have
jeans *n (pl)*		trousers made of strong, cotton cloth
jeep *n*		a kind of vehicle able to travel over rough ground
jelly *n*		a soft, wobbly kind of food usually brightly coloured and flavoured with fruit
jellyfish *n*		a sea creature with a body like jelly
jerk *n*		a quick tug
jersey *n*		a close-fitting, knitted upper garment
Jesus *n*		Jesus Christ, the founder of the Christian religion
jet *n*	1	a steam of liquid or gas, sent with force
	2	a type of aircraft pushed forward by jets of hot gas
Jew *n*		a person whose religion is Judaism
jewel *n*		a precious stone
jeweller *n*		a person who deals in jewels
jewellery *n*		precious stones, necklaces, rings, watches and other personal ornaments
jig *n*		a lively dance
jigsaw puzzle *n*		a picture cut into pieces that have to be put together again
jingle *n*		a tinkling noise; a clinking sound; a catchy tune or rhyme
jittery *adj*		nervous
job *n*	1	work that is done for money
	2	a piece of work
jockey *n*		a person who rides horses in races
jog *v*		to run along at a slow pace
join *v*	1	to fasten; to put together
	2	to become part of a group of people
joiner *n*		a person who works with wood
joint *n*		a place where two parts meet
joke *n*		something said or done to make you laugh
jolly *adj*		merry, full of fun
jolt *v*		to move with a sudden jerk
jostle *v*		to knock or push against
jot *v*		to make a note; to write down briefly
jotter *n*		a notebook
journal *n*		a magazine or newspaper
journalist *n*		a person who writes for a newspaper, magazine or journal

journey *n* travel from one place to another
joy *n* happiness, pleasure
joyful *adj* full of joy
Judaism *n* the religion of the Jews based on the belief in one God
judge *n* 1 a person in charge of a court of law
2 someone who decides the result of a sports event, a dog show, a beauty contest etc.
judo *n* a Japanese form of self-defence
jug *n* a container for liquids, with a handle and a lip for pouring
juggernaut *n* a very large, long-distance lorry
juggler *n* an entertainer who tosses things in the air, catches and throws them up again
juice *n* the liquid in fruits or vegetables, and in meat
jumble *v* to mix things up; to muddle
jumble *n* a mixed-up mess
jump *v* to leap up, or over something
jump *n* a leap from the ground
jumper *n* a knitted garment worn on the upper body, pulled on over the head; a sweater
junction *n* a place where roads or railway lines join
jungle *n* a thick forest in hot, wet countries
junior *adj* younger or less experienced
junk *n* 1 rubbish
2 a Chinese sailing-boat
jury *n* a group of people who sit in a court of law to decide if someone is innocent or guilty
just *adj* fair; honest
just *adv* 1 exactly
2 a moment ago
justice *n* 1 fairness; being just
2 the power of the law
jut *v* to stick out; to project
juvenile *n* a young person
juvenile *adj* to do with young people

Jj

judge 1

judge 2

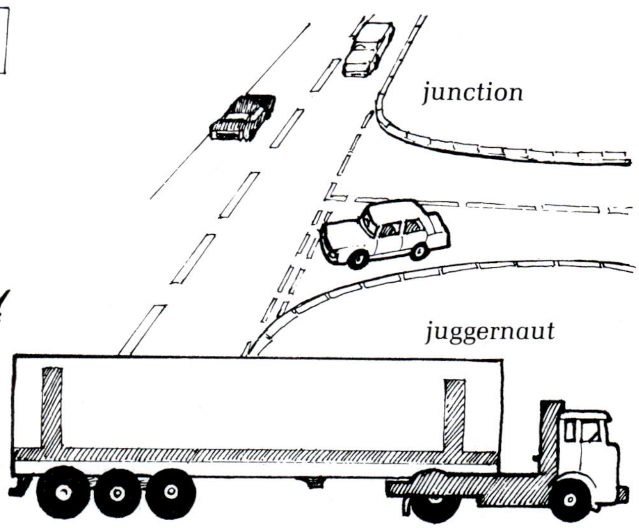

Kk

kale *n*		a green vegetable similar to cabbage
kangaroo *n*		an Australian animal that jumps along on its large, strong legs: a female has a pouch in which she carries her baby
karate *n*		a style of unarmed combat, using kicks and punches
kayak *n*		an Eskimo canoe made of animal skin
keel *n*		the bottom ridge of a boat or ship's framework
keen *adj*	*1*	eager; enthusiastic
	2	sharp, as a knife's blade
keep *v*	*1*	to have something and not give it to anyone else
	2	to stay in good condition
	3	to look after something for somebody
keeper *n*		someone who looks after people or things, particularly animals in a zoo
keg *n*		a small barrel
kelp *n*		a kind of seaweed
kennel *n*		a shelter for a dog
kerb *n*		the edge of a pavement or path
kernel *n*		the inside part of a nut, the part you eat
kestrel *n*		a small bird of prey
ketchup *n*		a sauce made from tomatoes and other things
kettle *n*		a metal container used for boiling water in
key *n*	*1*	a piece of metal shaped so that it will open a lock
	2	one of the parts pressed down with the fingers on a piano, typewriter or computer
	3	an explanation or list of answers
kibbutz *n*		a settlement in Israel where many people live and work
kick *v*		to hit with your foot
kick-off *n*		the start of a football game
kid *n*		a young goat
kidnap *v*		to carry off a person by force
kidney *n*		an organ in your body that removes waste matter from the blood
kill *v*		to put to death; to cause the death of
kiln *n*		a type of oven or furnace for baking bricks or pottery to make them hard
kilo *prefix*		a Greek word for one thousand
kilogram *n*		a measure of mass (weight); kg is the symbol: 1kg = 1000g
kilometre *n*		a measure of distance; km is the symbol: 1km = 1000m
kilt *n*		a short, pleated skirt worn by Scotsmen
kind *n*		a sort
kind *adj*		helpful, friendly, pleasant
kindergarten *n*		a school for very young children
king *n*	*1*	the male ruler of a country
	2	a piece in the game of chess
kingdom *n*		a country ruled by a king or queen
kingfisher *n*		a small bird with bright feathers that feeds on fish
kink *n*		a twist in a rope, etc.
kiosk *n*		a telephone box, or a small, covered stall often selling newspapers
kipper *n*		a smoked, salted herring
kiss *n*		touch with the lips as a sign of love or friendship
kit *n*		a set of tools or other equipment

kitchen *n* a room where food is prepared

kite *n* a frame of wood covered with a light material which can be made to fly

kitten *n* a young cat

kiwi *n* a New Zealand bird that cannot fly

knack *n* a skill or ability

kingfisher

kiwi

knight

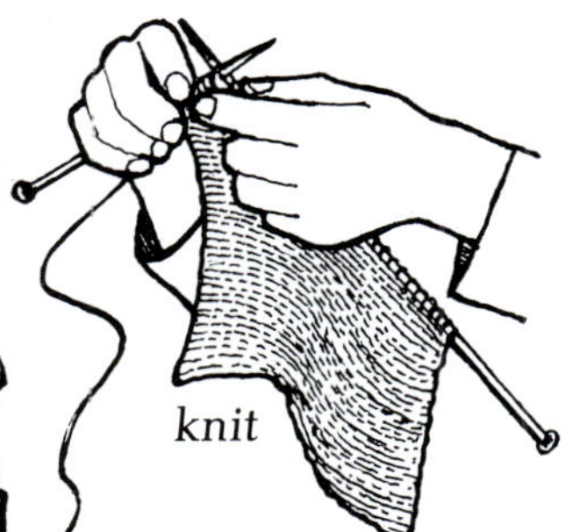
knit

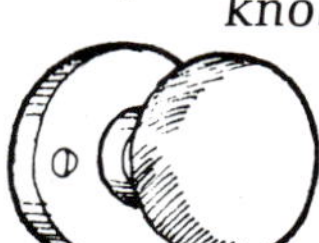
knob

koala

knead *v* to work a flower mixture into dough by pressing and twisting with the fingers

knee *n* the joint between the upper and lower part of your leg

kneecap *n* the flat, movable bone over your knee

kneel *v* to go down on your knees

knife *n* a sharp bladed cutting tool with a handle

knight *n*
1 a man with the title 'Sir'
2 a piece in a game of chess
3 a noble soldier on horseback, in olden times

knit *v* to make wool or other yarn into cloth, using long needles

knob *n* a round handle of a door or drawer

knock *v* to hit; to strike

knot *n*
1 a fastening made by tying together pieces of rope, string, cord etc.
2 a unit of speed (nautical miles per hour) used for ships
3 the hard section of wood on a tree where a branch grows out

know *v*
1 to understand
2 to have some information
3 to tell apart from others

knowledge *n* understanding; having information

knuckle *n* a joint in a finger

koala *n* a small, furry Australian that lives in trees

kookaburra *n* an Australian bird with a cry like laughter

Koran *n* the holy book of the Muslims

kosher *n* food that is lawful for Jews to eat

Ll

label *n* a piece of card or paper fixed to something on which is written what it is, where it is go etc.

laboratory *n* a place used for scientific experiments

labour *n* hard work; effort

Labrador *n* a sporting dog with a black or golden coat originally from Newfoundland

laburnum *n* a tree bearing long stems of yellow flowers whose seeds are poisonous

lace *n*
1 material made of thin threads that form a pattern
2 a string or cord, such as a shoe lace

lack *v* to be without something

lad *n* a boy

ladder *n* a set of steps or rungs fastened between two poles

ladle *n* a serving spoon with a long handle

lady *n*
1 a grown-up female person
2 a woman who is kind, polite and honest

ladybird *n* a small flying beetle; often red with black spots

lag *v* to fall behind; to dawdle

lager *n* a light-coloured beer

lagoon *n* an enclosed lake of sea-water

lair *n* a wild animal's den

lake *n* a large body of water with land all around

lamb *n* a young sheep

lame *adj* not able to walk properly

lamp *n* a device that provides light

land *n*
1 the solid part of the earth's surface
2 ground, soil

land *v*
1 to come on to the ground from the air or from water
2 to put an aircraft onto the land

landing *n*
1 a level space at the top of a flight of stairs
2 an aircraft's coming down to earth

landmark *n* something that stands out clearly and can be used as a guide

landscape *n* a view of the countryside

lane *n*
1 a narrow road, usually in the country
2 one part of a wide road

language *n* words, spoken or written by the people of a country

lantern *n* a container that protects a light

lap *n*
1 the part from waist to knees when you are sitting
2 once around a race track

lap *v* to lick up liquid with the tongue, as a cat does

lapwing *n* a type of bird, with raised feathers on its head

larch *n* a cone-bearing tree that is not an evergreen

lard *n* pig's fat used in cooking

larder *n* a small room or cupboard where food is kept

large *adj* big, great in size

lark *n* a high-flying, singing bird

larva *n* the early form of an insect

laser *n* a device for sending out extremely narrow and strong light waves

lash *n*
1 a hair on the eyelid
2 a stroke from a whip

lass *n* a girl

lasso *n* a rope with a loop at the end, used for catching cattle

last *adj*		following all the others; at the end
last *v*		to stay or continue
latch *n*		a fastening on a gate or door
late *adj*		coming after the usual time
lately *adv*		not long ago
lathe *n*		a machine for turning wood, metal etc. into circular and rounded shapes
lather *n*		a foam made from soap, shampoo, shaving cream etc.
laugh *n*		the sound you make when you think something is funny
launch *n*		a small motor-boat
launch *v*	*1*	to put a boat into water
	2	to send a spacecraft or rocket into the air
launderette *n*		a room with coin-operated washing machines and driers
laundry *n*	*1*	a place where clothes are sent to be washed
	2	clothes to be washed
lava *n*		the hot melted rock flowing from a volcano
lavatory *n*		a toilet and washroom
lavender *n*		a plant with sweet-smelling pale purple flowers
law *n*	*1*	a rule made by a government
	2	any rule that is to be obeyed
lawn *n*		an area of short grass in a garden or park
lawn mower *n*		a machine used for cutting the grass on a lawn
lawyer *n*		a person with expert knowledge of the law, such as a solicitor or barrister
lay *v*	*1*	to place something down
	2	to produce eggs
lay-by *n*		a place at the side of a road where vehicles can pull off and stop
layer *n*		a thickness, a coating
lazy *adj*		not willing to work; idle
lead *n*		a soft, heavy metal
lead *n*		a strap with which to hold a dog
lead *v*		to go in front, to show the way
leader *n*		someone who goes in front and shows the way or takes charge
leaf *n*		a part of a plant growing from a stem or branch
leaflet *n*		a printed piece of paper that tells people about something
league *n*		a group of sports clubs that play matches against each other
leak *n*		a hole through which liquid or gas can escape
lean *adj*	*1*	thin
	2	having little fat
lean *v*	*1*	to rest against
	2	to be in a sloping position
leap *v*		to jump high or far
leap year *n*		a year, every fourth year, when February has 29 days instead of 28
learn *v*		to find out; to get knowledge or skill
least *adj*		smallest
leather *n*		a material made from the skin or hide of animals
leave *v*	*1*	to go away from
	2	to let something stay where it is
ledge *n*		a narrow shelf on a wall or cliff
leek *n*		a vegetable in the onion family

Ll

Ll

left *adj* in the direction opposite of right
leg *n* one of the limbs on which people or animals stand or walk
legal *adj* to do with the law
legend *n* a story from the past that is probably not completely true
leisure *n* rest, time free from work
lemon *n* a pale yellow fruit with a sour taste
lemonade *n* a lemon-flavoured drink
lend *v* to let someone use something of yours for a time
length *n* how long a thing is
lengthen *v* to make or become longer
lens *n* a curved piece of glass used in spectacles, cameras, telescopes etc.
leopard *n* a large animal belonging to the cat family with black spots on a yellowish coat
leotard *n* a tight, one-piece garment worn by gymnasts, dancers etc.
less *adj* smaller; fewer; not as much
lesson *n* *1* a period of time when pupils learn
2 something to be learned or taught
let *v* to permit, to allow
letter *n* *1* one of the symbols of an alphabet
2 a written message put in an envelope and sent to someone
lettuce *n* a green vegetable with large leaves, eaten raw in salads
level *adj* smooth and flat, not sloping
lever *n* a bar used for raising and lowering something
leveret *n* a young hare
liar *n* someone who does not tell the truth
liberty *n* freedom
librarian *n* a person who is in charge or helps to run a library
library *n* a room or building where books are kept and borrowed from
licence *n* a piece of paper showing that the law allows you to do or have something
lichen *n* a moss-like plant that grows on rocks and trees
lick *v* to wet with your tongue
lid *n* a cover for a box, pan etc.
lie *n* something that is not true
lie *v* *1* to tell an untruth
2 to rest, stretched flat
lieutenant *n* an officer in the armed forces
life *n* *1* being alive, as animals and plants
2 the time between birth and death
lifeboat *n* a special boat for rescuing people at sea
lift *v* to raise up; to take up
lift *n* a machine that takes people or goods from one floor to another in a high building
light *n* brightness which makes it possible to see things
light *adj* *1* not heavy
2 not dark in colour
light *v* to set fire to something
lighter *n* something that lights or sets on fire
lighthouse *n* a tower with a powerful, flashing light to guide ships or warn them of rocks
lightning *n* a flash of electricity in a thunderstorm

like *v*	*1* to be fond of *2* to enjoy doing something
like *adj*	similar to
likely *adj*	expected to happen
likeness *n*	a copy
lilac *n*	a shrub with fragrant white or purple flowers
lily *n*	a flowering plant that grows from a bulb
limb *n*	*1* an arm or a leg *2* a tree branch
lime *n*	*1* a greenish fruit that looks like a small lemon *2* a white powder obtained from heating limestone and used in making cement
limit *n*	a point you cannot or should not pass; the edge
limp *adj*	not stiff or firm; hanging loosely
limp *v*	to walk lamely
line *n*	*1* a long, thin mark *2* a row of people or things *3* a piece of string, cord, rope etc.
linen *n*	cloth made from the fibres of the flax plant
liner *n*	a large passenger ship
linger *v*	to wait about; to be slow in leaving
lining *n*	the covering of an inner surface
link *n*	one of the rings or loops in a chain
link *v*	to join things together
lion *n*	a large and powerful wild animal of the cat family
lip *n*	one of the two pink, fleshy edges of your mouth
lipstick *n*	a stick of make-up used to colour the lips
liquid *n*	a substance that flows like water or oil
liquorice *n*	a black sweet made from the root of the liquorice plant
list *n*	a column or columns of names, numbers, words etc.
listen *v*	to hear, to pay attention to
literature *n*	stories, poetry and plays
litre *n*	a liquid measure; l is the symbol
litter *n*	*1* a number of animals all born together *2* waste papter and other rubbish left lying around
little *adj*	small; not much
live *adj*	living, not dead
live *v*	*1* to be alive, to have life *2* to have your home; to dwell
lively *adj*	full of life and energy
liver *n*	a very important organ in the body
livestock *n*	farm animals
living-room *n*	a sitting room; a main room in the house
lizard *n*	a four-legged reptile with a tail
llama *n*	a large South American animal with long hair
load *n*	something that is carried
load *v*	to place goods on a ship, or in a car, train, lorry etc.
loaf *n*	bread shaped and baked in one large piece
loan *n*	something that has been lent to you
lobe *n*	the fleshy lowest part of your ear
lobster *n*	a large shellfish with eight legs and two strong claws
local *adj*	nearby; belonging to a fairly small area
locate *v*	to find the exact position of someone or something
loch *n*	a Scottish lake

Ll

lock	*n*	*1*	a fastening for a door, box, suitcase etc., often needing a key to open it
		2	a curl of hair
		3	a section of canal where boats are raised or lowered to different levels
lock	*v*		to fasten something with a lock
locker	*n*		a small cupboard that can be locked
locomotive	*n*		a railway engine
locust	*n*		an insect, similar to a grasshopper, that destroys crops
lodge	*v*		to pay to live in rooms in another person's house
lodge	*n*		a beaver's home
loft	*n*		a room where you store things at the top of a house, under the roof
log	*n*	*1*	a sawn-off part of a tree trunk or thick branch
		2	a diary of a ship's voyage
loiter	*v*		to move along very slowly, often stopping
lollipop	*n*		a big sweet on a stick
lonely	*adj*	*1*	sad because you are alone, with no friends
		2	far away from other places
long	*adj*	*1*	a big distance from end to end
		2	taking much time
long	*v*		to wish for very much
look	*n*		a glance
look	*v*		to use your eyes to see something
look after	*v*		to take care of
look forward to	*v*		to wait for something with pleasure
look into	*v*		to study something carefully
look up	*v*		to find a word or some information in a dictionary, enclyclopaedia or other reference book
look up to	*v*		to admire someone
loom	*n*		a machine for weaving threads into cloth
loop	*n*		a round shape of a piece of string, ribbon etc., when it crosses itself
loose	*adj*		slack; not fastened or tight
loot	*n*		property taken by thieves
Lord	*n*		God
lord	*n*		a nobleman
lorry	*n*		a large motor vehicle for carrying goods
lose	*v*	*1*	to be without something because you have dropped it or left it somewhere
		2	to be beaten in a game
lot	*n*		a large number
lotion	*n*		a liquid or cream for healing, soothing or cleaning the skin
loud	*adj*		making a lot of noise
loudspeaker	*n*		the part of a stereo, radio or TV from which the sound comes
lounge	*n*		a sitting room with easy chairs
lounge	*v*		to sit or stand in a lazy way
love	*n*		a great liking or fondness
love	*v*		to like very much, to care a lot about
lovely	*adj*		attractive; pretty; beautiful
low	*adj*		not high; near the ground
lower	*adj*		not as high as
lower	*v*		to let or bring something down
loyal	*adj*		faithful and true
luck	*n*		chance; good or bad fortune
lucky	*adj*		fortunate

luggage *n*		the suitcases and a bags that a traveller carries
lukewarm *adj*		neither hot nor cold; slightly warm
lullaby *n*		a song that is sung to send a baby to sleep
lumber *n*		roughly-cut timber
lumberjack *n*		a person who cuts down trees, especially in N. America
lump *n*	*1*	a swelling or bump on the skin
	2	a hard piece of something
lunar *adj*		having to do with the moon
lunch *n*		a meal you eat in the middle of the day
lung *n*		one of the two organs inside the chest that you fill with air when you breathe in
lupin *n*		a tall plant with flowers on a long spike
lurch *v*		to stagger or roll to one side
lurk *v*		to hide and wait
luxury *n*		something that is enjoyable, often expensive, but not really needed
lynx *n*		a wild cat with pointed ears, a short tail and large paws
lyrics *n (pl)*		the words of a modern, popular song

luggage

lynx

macaroni *n*		long tubes of flour paste often eaten with cheese or tomato sauce
machine *n*		an arrangement of moving parts working together to do work; such as a washing machine etc.
mackerel *n*		a silvery fish that lives in the oceans
mackintosh *n*		a waterproof coat
mad *adj*	*1*	crazy; not in one's right mind
	2	very angry
magazine *n*		a thin book with pictures and stories or articles
maggot *n*		a grub that changes into a fly
magic *n*		the use of clever tricks to make impossible things seem to happen
magician *n*		someone who does magic tricks
magistrate *n*		a person appointed to judge cases in a law court that deals with small crimes; a Justice of the Peace
magnet *n*		a piece of iron or steel that attracts pieces of iron or steel towards it
magnificent *adj*		marvellous; wonderful; splendid
magnify *v*		to make something look larger
magpie *n*		a black and white bird related to the crow
maid *n*	*1*	a young unmarried girl
	2	a female servant
mail *n*	*1*	letters, cards, parcels etc. sent by post
	2	armour made of metal plates or rings
mail *v*		to send by post
main *adj*		the most important; chief

Mm

maintain *v* 1 to keep in good order
2 to carry on

maize *n* a cereal crop, also called sweetcorn and Indian corn

majesty *n* a title for a king or queen

major *n* an army officer, next in rank above captain

major *adj* larger, more important

majority *n* the greater number or part

make *n* kind, brand

make *v* 1 to build or shape something
2 to force
3 to bring about
4 to add up to

make believe *v* to pretend

make for *v* to go towards

make off *v* to run away

make up *v* 1 to become friends again after a quarrel
2 to invent, such as a story, poem etc.

make-up *n* powder, lipstick, rouge etc.

male *n* 1 a boy, a man
2 an animal that cannot have baby animals
3 a plant that does not have fruit

mallet *n* a wooden hammer

malt *n* barley or other grain used to make beer

mammal *n* an animal that produces milk on which it feeds its young

mammoth *n* a large animal like an elephant, but now extinct

mammoth *adj* very big

man *n* a grown-up male human being

manage *v* 1 to take charge and look after
2 to be able to do something

manager *n* a person in charge of a business, hotel, shop etc.

mane *n* the long hair on the neck of a horse, lion and some other animals

mango *n* a tropical fruit with sweet yellow-coloured flesh

manhole *n* an opening with a cover through which a worker can go down to examine and repair sewers, telephone cables etc.

mankind *n* all people — men, women and children — everywhere

man-made *adj* artificial; made by humans

manner *n* the way a thing is done or happens

manners *n (pl)* how you behave towards others

manor *n* a large country house

mansion *n* a large, grand house

manslaughter *n* the killing of a person unlawfully, but not on purpose

manual *n* a book of instructions or information; a hand-book

manual *adj* done with the hands

manufacture *v* to make things, usually in a factory

manure *n* animal droppings and straw put in the ground to make plants grow better

many *adj* a large number

map *n* a drawing of the earth's surface or part of it, showing towns, roads, rivers, high land etc.

maple *n* a broad-leaved tree, one kind of which is tapped for its sweet syrup

marathon *n* a very hard, long-distance race of 42.19km (26 miles 385 yards)

marble *n* 1 a hard stone that can be carved and polished
2 a small stone or glass marble used in games

march *v* to walk with a regular step

mare *n* a female horse

margarine *n* a spread made from oils and fats, often used in place of butter

margin *n* space left at the top, bottom, and sides of written or printed pages

marigold *n* a garden plant with bright yellow or orange flowers

marina *n* an area near the sea where small boats can come into harbour

marionette *n* a puppet moved by strings

mark *n* 1 a scratch, stain, line, pattern etc. on something
2 a score on a test

mark *v* to make a mark on something

market *n* a place, often in the open, where people go to buy and see goods

marmalade *n* a jam made of oranges, lemons, lime etc., usually eaten at breakfast

maroon *n* a brownish-red colour

maroon *v* to leave a person in a deserted place

marquee *n* a large tent

marriage *n* 1 living together as husband and wife
2 a wedding

marrow *n* 1 the soft material in the centre of bones
2 a dark green vegetable which can grow very big

marry *v* to become husband and wife

marsh *n* low-lying, wet, swampy ground

marsupials

marsupial *n* one of a group of mammals in which the females carry their young in a pouch e.g. a kangaroo

martin *n* a small bird related to the swallow

martyr *n* a person who suffers or dies for his or her beliefs

marvellous *adj* wonderful; excellent

marzipan *n* a sweet paste made from almonds

mascara *n* colouring used on eye-lashes

mascot *n* an animal, person or thing supposed to bring good luck

mash *v* to crush or squash food to make it soft

mask *n* a covering over the face, worn as a disguise or a protection

mason *n* a stone-worker

mass *n* a large lump or quantity

massacre *n* a killing of a large number of people without mercy

massage *v* to treat some muscles and joints by rubbing and pressing with the hands

massive *adj* large and heavy

mast *n* 1 a tall pole supporting a ship's sails
2 a high frame to hold a radio or television aerial

Mm

master	*n*	*1*	a male teacher
		2	an expert
		3	the captain of a merchant ship
		4	a man in control of people, animals or things
masterpiece	*n*		a work of art done with great skill
mastiff	*n*		a large, powerful dog
mat	*n*	*1*	a small rug to wipe your feet on
		2	a thin pad to protect a surface, such as a table mat
matador	*n*		a bullfighter
match	*n*	*1*	a game or contest between two people or teams
		2	a small piece of wood or cardboard with a head that lights when rubbed
		3	something that is the same shape, colour, size etc.
match	*v*		to be equal or similar to
mate	*n*		a friend, companion
mate	*v*		to produce young
material	*n*		any substance from which something is or can be made
mathematics	*n (pl)*		the study of numbers, measurements, shapes etc. usually called 'maths' for short
matinée			an afternoon performance of a play, film, concert etc.
matter	*n*	*1*	what things are made of
		2	something you are concerned about
matter	*v*		to be of importance
mattress	*n*		the thick, soft part of a bed
mauve	*n*		a pale purple colour
maximum	*n*		the greatest number or quantity
maybe	*adv*		perhaps; possibly
mayonnaise	*n*		a kind of salad cream
mayor	*n*		the chief person of a city or town
mayoress	*n*	*1*	the wife of a mayor
		2	a female mayor
maze	*n*		a network of winding paths from which it is difficult to find a way out
meadow	*n*		a field of grass
meal	*n*	*1*	food eaten each day at a certain time
		2	grain ground into a powder
mean	*adj*	*1*	wanting to keep everything for yourself
		2	unkind; unfriendly
mean	*v*	*1*	to stand for; to show
		2	to plan to do something
mean	*n*		a mid-point or average
meaning	*n*		what is meant
means	*n*		a method or way of doing something
measles	*n*		a catching disease that causes red spots on the body
measure	*n*		the size or amount of something
measure	*v*		to find the size or amount of a thing
meat	*n*		animal flesh used as food
mechanic	*n*		a person who is skilled in using and repairing machinery
mechanical	*adj*		having to do with a machine
medal	*n*		a piece of metal, usually like a coin, that is given as a prize or reward
meddle	*v*		to interfere in other people's affairs
medical	*adj*		having to do with doctors and medicine
medicine	*n*	*1*	the science of healing
		2	a liquid, pill, or other substance taken for an illness

medium *adj* middle; not big and not small
meet *v* to join, to come together
meeting *n* a coming together of people to talk or listen to someone
melody *n* a pleasant piece of a music; a tune
melon *n* a large, sweet, juicy fruit
melt *v* to change from solid to liquid
member *n* someone who belongs to a club, group, team etc.
memorize *v* to learn by heart
memory *n* 1 the power of remembering things
2 something you remember
mend *v* to repair something
mental *adj* having to do with your mind
mention *v* to make a remark about
menu *n* a list of the foods that are served in a restaurant
merchant *n* someone who makes a living by buying and selling things
mercury *n* a heavy, silvery liquid metal
mere *n* a lake or pond
merely *adv* simply, only
merit *n* what is good in someone or something
mermaid *n* an imaginary creature with a woman's body and a fish's tail
merry *adj* laughing; happy; full of fun
mess *n* many things all in the wrong place; untidy and dirty
message *n* information sent from one person to another
messenger *n* someone who carries a message
metal *n* a substance such as gold, iron, tin, silver, lead etc.
meteor *n* a small piece of rock or metal that rushes through space and burns up when it nears the earth
meteorite *n* a meteor that has fallen through space and landed on earth
meter *n* a machine that measures how much of something has been used e.g. a gas meter
method *n* a way of doing something
metre *n* a measure of length; m is the symbol: 1m = 100cm
microbe *n* a very tiny living thing so small it can only be seen through a microscope
micro-light *n* a small aircraft like a hang-glider with an engine
microphone *n* an electrical instrument that enables sounds to be broadcast, recorded or made louder
microscope *n* an instrument for making tiny things big enough to see
microwave-oven *n* a type of oven which heats food very quickly

Mm

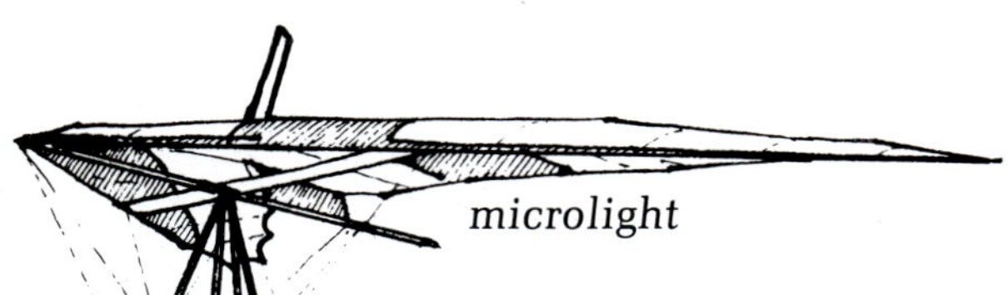
microlight

microwave

Mm

mid- a prefix meaning 'middle': 'midday' means the middle of the day: 'midnight' means halfway through the night

middle *n* the point halfway between two things

midget *n* a very small person

midnight *n* 12 o'clock at night

midweek *n* the middle days of the week

might *n* power, strength

mighty *adj* powerful, strong

migrate *v* to move from one place to another place or country

mild *adj* gentle; not strong

mile *n* a measure of distance on land equal to about 1610m

milk *n* the white liquid female mammals produce to feed their young

milkshake *n* a drink made of milk and flavouring of fruit, chocolate etc. mixed with ice cream

mill *n*
1 a building where machines grind grain into flour
2 a factory where things are made e.g. a cotton-mill, a steel-mill

million *n* a thousand thousands; the number 1 000 000

millionaire *n* a very rich person who has more than a million pounds, dollars etc.

mime *v* to act out a story using actions but no words

mimic *v* to copy the way someone does or says something

mince *v* to cut or chop into small pieces

mincemeat *n* a sweet mixture of chopped fruit and other things that is cooked in tarts and pies

mind *n* the part of a person that feels, thinks and remembers

mind *v*
1 to look after, to care
2 to watch out for
3 to object to something

mine *pron* belonging to me

mine *n*
1 a place where coal or other minerals are dug from the ground
2 a bomb hidden in the ground or sea that explodes when something comes near or touches it

miner *n* a person who works in a mine

mineral *n* anything dug out from the earth, such as coal, gold, diamonds etc.

mingle *v* to mix together

miniature *adj* very small in size

minimum *adj* the least possible amount

minister *n*
1 a clergyman
2 the head of a government department

mink *n* an animal like a weasel which has valuable fur

minnow *n* a very small freshwater fish

minor *adj* smaller; less important

mint *n*
1 a plant whose leaves are used in cooking to give food flavour
2 a place where coins are made

minus *prep* less; when you take away

minute *n* a very short period of time; 60 seconds

minute *adj* very tiny

miracle *n* a wonderful happening, which didn't seem possible

mirror *n* a piece of glass in which you can see yourself

misbehave *v* to behave badly

mischief *n* silly or bad behaviour that can cause trouble or harm

miser *n* a greedy person who keeps money and will not spend it

miserable *adj* very unhappy, very sad

misery *n* great unhappiness

misfortune *n* bad luck

misplace *v* to put in the wrong place

Miss *n* a title put in front of an unmarried woman or girl

miss *v*
1 to fail to catch, find, reach, hit or hear something
2 to be sad for someone who is away from you

missile *n* an object or weapon that is thrown or sent through the air, often by a rocket

mission *n*
1 a special job or task
2 a group of people sent to do religious work, usually in another country

missionary *n* someone who goes to another place to tell people about his or her religion

mist *n* a thin fog or haziness in the air

mistake *n* something that is wrong

mistletoe *n* an evergreen plant with white berries which grows as a parasite on trees, especially apple trees, used as a Christmas decoration

misunderstand *v* to get the wrong idea about something

mittens *n (pl)* gloves that cover four fingers together and the thumb separately

mix *v*
1 to stir or shake different things together
2 to meet and mingle with other people

mixture *n* two or more things mixed together

moan *v* to make a long, sad sound to show you are hurt, unhappy etc.

moat *n* a deep ditch dug round a castle

mob *n* a disorderly, noisy crowd of people

moccasin *n* a shoe made of soft leather

mock *v* to make fun of

model *n*
1 a small copy of something
2 someone who poses for an artist or a photographer
3 someone who wears new clothes to show people what they are like

modern *adj* up-to-date; to do with present times

module *n* a part which can be either used on its own or fitted to other parts; a part of a spacecraft

moist *adj* slightly wet; damp

molar *n* a back tooth

mole *n*
1 a small, furry animal that makes tunnels under the ground, leaving molehills on the top
2 a small, dark spot on the skin

moment *n* a very small amount of time

monarch *n* a royal ruler such as a king, queen, or emperor

monastery *n* a building where monks live and work

money *n* coins and paper notes used in buying and selling things

mongrel *n* a dog of mixed breed

monk *n* a man who lives with a group of other men to serve God

monkey *n* a furry animal that belongs to the same group as apes and people

Mm

monorail *n* a railway using only one rail
monster *n* a strange and frightening creature in stories
month *n* one of the twelve parts in which the year is divided
monthly *adv* once a month; every month
monument *n* a statue or building put up in memory of someone or some happening
moo *v* to make a long, low sound a cow makes
mood *n* the way that you feel at a certain time
moon *n* the small planet that circles round the earth
moor *n* an area of rough land often covered with heather
moor *v* to tie up a boat so that it will not float away
moose *n* a large North American deer
mop *n* a bundle of strings or other material fastened to a handle and used for cleaning floors
moped *n* a bicycle with a small engine
more *adj* bigger in number, amount, size etc.
more *adv* again
morning *n* the early part of the day, between night and afternoon
mortar *n*
1 a mixture of sand, cement and water, used in building to stick bricks together
2 a type of gun that fires shells
mortgage *n* an agreement to borrow money to buy a house
mosaic *n* a picture made with coloured pieces of glass, stone etc.
mosque *n* a building where Muslims go to worship
mosquito *n* a small, two-winged, insect that sucks blood
moss *n* a small, smooth green plant that grows on damp trees and stones, and has no flower
most *adj* the greatest number or amount
most *adv*
1 very
2 more than all the others
motel *n* a hotel that is built near a main road especially for motorists
moth *n* a winged insect usually seen at night
mother *n* a female parent
motor *n* a machine or engine that makes something move
motor *v* to travel in a motor car
motor bike *n* a kind of bicycle with a petrol engine
motorboat *n* a small boat powered by an engine
motorist *n* a person who drives a car
motorway *n* a wide, modern road where cars, lorries, coaches etc., can travel a long way fast
mould *n* a container for making things like jelly, blancmange set in the shape that is wanted
mound *n* a pile of earth or stones; a small hill
mount *v* to get on a bicycle or horse so that you can ride it
mountain *n* a very high hill
mountaineer *n* someone who climbs mountains
mourn *v* to feel very sorry because someone or something has died

mouse *n*	a small, gnawing animal with a pointed nose and a long tail
moustache *n*	hair that grows above a man's top lip
mouth *n*	the part of the face that opens for eating and speaking
movable *adj*	able to be moved
move *v*	to go, or to take something, from one place to another
movie *n*	a film shown in a cinema or on TV
mow *v*	to cut grass short
mower *n*	a machine that cuts grass
Mr *(abbr)*	short for Mister, a title put in front of a man's name
Mrs *(abbr)*	a title put in front of a married woman's name
Ms *(abbr)*	a title put in front of a woman's name. It does not show whether or not she is married
much *adj*	large in number, size, amount etc.
mud *n*	a soft mixture of soil and water
muddle *v*	to mix things up and make a mess of something
muesli *n*	a mixture of cereal, nuts, dried fruit etc.
mug *n*	a kind of drinking cup
mug *v*	to attack and rob someone, usually in the street
Muhammadan *n*	a Muslim
mule *n*	an animal that is part horse and part donkey
multiply *v*	to make something a number of times bigger
mum *n*	mother
mumble *v*	to speak low and unclearly
mummy *n*	1 the body of a person preserved after death, as was the custom of ancient Egypt 2 mother
mumps *n*	a catching illness that makes your face and neck swell up

Mm

Mr Mrs Miss Ms

munch *v*		to chew in a noisy way
mural *n*		a picture painted on a wall
murder *v*		to kill someone on purpose
murmur *v*		to speak in a very soft, low voice
muscle *n*		one of the parts of your body that can be tightened or loosened making the body move
museum *n*		a building where a lot of interesting things are displayed for people to go and see
mushroom *n*		a kind of fungus which can be eaten
music *n*		a series of pleasant sounds made by singing or by playing an instrument
Muslim *n*		someone who believes in Muhammed and what he taught
mussel *n*		a small sea creature that lives in a pair of black shells
must *v*		to have to
mustard *n*		a yellow mixture which gives a hot flavour to food
mutiny *n*		the time when soldiers or sailors attack their own officers
mutter *v*		to speak or grumble in a low voice
mutton *n*		the meat from a sheep
muzzle *n*	1	an animal's nose and mouth
	2	a cover put over an animal's mouth and nose to keep it from biting
my *adj*		belonging to me
mysterious *adj*		strange and puzzling
mystery *n*		something very strange and hard to understand
myth *n*		an old story that deals with strange and magical people and things

Mm

Nn

Nn

nag *v*		to keep on finding fault
nail *n*	1	the thin, hard part that covers the end of each finger and toe
	2	a small piece of metal with a sharp point, used for fastening pieces of wood together
naked *adj*		bare; without any clothes on
name *n*		what a person or thing is called
nanny goat *n*		a female goat
nappy *n*		a piece of soft cloth put round a baby's bottom
narcissus *n*		a flowering plant that grows from a bulb
narrate *v*		to tell a story
narrow *adj*		not wide, small in width
nasty *adj*		unpleasant; not nice
nation *n*		a country and the people who live in it
national *adj*		belonging to one country
native *n*		a person born in a certain place or country
Nativity *n*		the birth of Jesus
natural *adj*		found in nature; not made by people
nature *n*	1	the world of plants, trees, animals, land, sea, stars etc.
	2	the way someone or something is
naughty *adj*		badly behaved
navel *n*		the little round hollow in the centre of the front part of your stomach
navigate *v*		to guide or plan the route of a ship or aircraft
navy *n*		all the warships of a country, with officers and men
near *prep*		not far away
nearby *adv*		very close
nearly *adv*		almost, not quite

neat *adj*		smart and tidy
necessary *adj*		needed; required
neck *n*		the part of the body that joins the head to the shoulders
necklace *n*		a string of beads or jewels worn round the neck
need *v*		to require or want something
needle *n*	1	a very thin, pointed piece of metal with a hole at one end, used in sewing
	2	one of a pair of metal, wood or plastic rods used for knitting
neglect *v*		to give little care to
Negro *n*		someone with black skin
neigh *v*		to make the noise a horse makes
neighbour *n*		someone who lives near you
neighbourhood *n*		the area or district in which you live
neither *adj*		not one or the other
nephew *n*		the son of a brother or sister
nerve *n*	1	one of the fibres in the body that carries feelings and messages to the brain
	2	brave or calm behaviour in face of danger
nervous *adj*	1	timid, easily frightened
	2	tense, easily excited or upset
nest *n*		a home of twigs, straw, grass etc., made by birds and other animals
net *n*		a woven material, of string, plastic or metal, with large or small spaces between the threads
netball *n*		a team game in which a ball has to be thrown into a net on a tall post
nettle *n*		a stinging plant
neutral *adj*		not taking either side in a quarrel or war
never *adv*		not at any time
new *adj*	1	not old
	2	not seen or known before
news *n*		information about what is going on
newspaper *n*		a daily or weekly paper with news, stories, pictures, advertisements etc.
newt *n*		a small animal like a lizard that lives near water
next *adj*	1	nearest, closest
	2	the one after
nib *n*		the pointed part of a pen that needs ink
nibble *v*		to eat something in small bites
nice *adj*		pretty, pleasant, friendly
nickel *n*		a hard, silver-white metal
nickname *n*		a name given to someone in fun, instead of the real name
niece *n*		the daughter of a brother or sister
night *n*		the time when it is dark between sunset and sunrise
nightingale *n*		a small, brown bird that sings at night
nightmare *n*		a frightening dream
nimble *adj*		able to move quickly and easily
nip *v*		to pinch or bite sharply
no *adj*		not any; not one
no *adv*		opposite of yes
nobody *pron*		no person; no one
nocturnal *adj*		active at night
nod *v*		to bow the head slightly
noise *n*		a sound that is loud and often unpleasant
noisy *adj*		making a lot of noise
nomad *n*		a member of a wandering group or tribe
none *pron*		not one, not any

nonsense *n* foolish and silly talk
noodles *n (pl)* a food made of flour, water and eggs, shaped into long strips
nook *n* a quiet little corner
noon *n* twelve o'clock in the daytime; the middle of the day
no one *pron* nobody; no person
noose *n* a loop of rope
nor *conj* and not; and no more
normal *adj* ordinary; usual
north *n* one of the points of the compass
nose *n* the part of your face that is used for breathing and smelling
nosy *adj* curious, always wanting to know what others are doing
nostril *n* one of the two openings in your nose

Nn

not *adv* a word that gives an opposite meaning to another word or sentence
notch *n* a mark like a 'v' cut into something
note *n* 1 a short message
2 a musical sound, or a sign that stands for it in music
notebook *n* a book with pages on which to write
nothing *n* not anything
notice *n* something written down or shown to people to tell them something, such as a poster, sign etc.
notice *v* to see something or someone
nought *n* nothing; the number 0; zero
noun *n* the word naming a person, thing, idea etc.
novel *n* a long story which fills up a whole book
novelty *n* something new or unusual
now *adv* at the present time
nowhere *adv* in no place; not anywhere
nozzle *n* the nose or spout fitted to the end of a hose-pipe
nuclear *adj* to do with atomic energy
nude *adj* without any clothes; naked
nudge *v* to push someone with your elbow to make him or her notice something
nugget *n* a rough lump of metal, usually gold
nuisance *n* something or somebody that causes trouble
numb *adj* without any feeling
number *n* 1 a word or sign that tells you how many such as '2', 'two', '30', 'thirty' etc.
2 several
number *v* to count; to put a number to something
numerous *adj* very many
nun *n* a woman who has taken vows to lead a religious life
nurse *n* a person who looks after the sick, the old, and the very young
nurse *v* 1 to look after a baby
2 to look after sick, injured, and elderly people etc.
nursery *n* 1 a place where very young children go to play and be looked after
2 a place where young plants and trees are grown
nut *n* 1 the fruit of certain plants, with a hard shell
2 a piece of metal with a hole in the centre that is screwed on to a bolt to fasten it
nylon *n* a man-made material used in making clothes, brushes and many other things

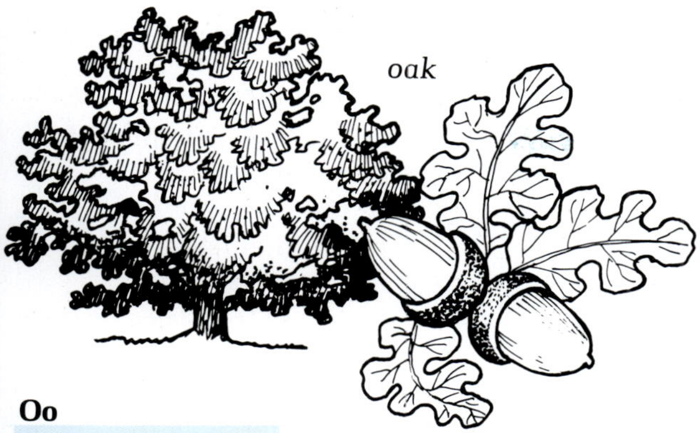

Oo

oak *n* — a large tree on which acorns grow; its wood is hard

oar *n* — a long pole with a flate blade at one end, used for rowing a boat

oasis *n* — a place in a desert with water and trees

oath *n* — a serious promise to tell the truth or to do something

oats *n (pl)* — a grain used for cereal and as feed for animals

obedient *adj* — willing to do what you are told to do

obey *v* — to do what you are told

object *n* — a thing you can see and touch

object *v* — to say that you do not like or agree with something

oblong *n* — a rectangle; a shape like the page of this book

observatory *n* — a building from which stars, planets etc. are watched through telescopes

observe *v* — to watch or notice

obstacle *n* — something that is in the way

obstruct *v* — to be in the way so that something cannot pass

obtain *v* — to get

obvious *adj* — easy to see or understand

occasion *n* — the time when something happens

occasional *adj* — happening now and then

occupation *n* — *1* a person's job *2* a pastime

occupy *v* — *1* to live in or be in *2* to fill in time

occur *v* — to take place, to happen

ocean *n* — a great area of sea such as the Pacific, Atlantic etc.

o'clock *adv* — by the clock

octopus *n* — a sea creature with eight arms

odd *adj* — *1* strange, unusual *2* not even *3* not making a pair

odour *n* — a smell

of *prep* — *1* made from *2* belonging to *3* about

off *prep* — away from

off *adv* — *1* away *2* not on

offence *n* — the breaking of a law or rule

offend *v* — *1* to hurt someone's feelings *2* to do wrong

offensive *adj* — rude, insulting, unpleasant

offer *n* — a price suggested by a person who wants to buy something

offer *v* — *1* to hold a thing out for someone to take *2* to say what you are willing to do

office *n* — a room with desks, typewriters, telephones etc. where people work

officer *n* — *1* someone who holds an important position *2* someone in command, such as an officer in the armed forces

offspring *n* — the child or children of a family; young animals

often *adj* — many times

Oo

ogre	*n*		in fairy tales, a monster who eats people
oil	*n*		a greasy liquid used for fuel, cooking, etc.
oil	*v*		to put oil on something to make it move more smoothly
oil-rig	*n*		a special structure and machinery for getting oil from beneath the sea-bed
ointment	*n*		a medicine made in a paste or cream
okay, OK	*adj, adv*		all right, yes, correct
old	*adj*	*1*	born or made a long time ago
		2	not new
old-fashioned	*adj*		out-of-date, not modern
olive	*n*		a small, oily fruit grown on an evergreen tree in warm places
Olympics	*n (pl)*		international athletic contests held every four years in a different country
omelette	*n*		a kink of pancake made of fried, beaten eggs often with a meat or vegetable filling
omit	*v*		to leave out
on	*prep*	*1*	on top of
		2	during
		3	about
on	*adv*	*1*	not off
		2	further
once	*adv*	*1*	one time
		2	in the past
one	*n*		the number 1
one	*adj*		single
one-way street	*n*		a street with traffic going in one direction only
onion	*n*		a round, strong-smelling bulb that is used as a vegetable
only	*adj*		alone; by itself
only	*adv*		not more than; singly
ooze	*v*		to leak; to flow slowly through
opal	*n*		a precious stone
open	*adj*	*1*	not closed; not covered
		2	wide and clear
open	*v*	*1*	to make a thing open
		2	to begin; to start
opening	*n*		a gap; a space
opera	*n*		a play set to music, with the performers singing their parts
operation	*n*	*1*	something done by surgeons to a sick person's body to make it healthy again
		2	the working of a machine
opinion	*n*		what you think or believe
opponent	*n*		someone on the opposite side, such as in a game or contest
opportunity	*n*		a good chance to do something
oppose	*v*		to fight or argue against
opposite	*n*		a person or thing that is completely different
opposite	*prep*		across from
optician	*n*		someone who makes or sells spectacles
orange	*n*	*1*	a round, reddish-yellow, juicy fruit with thick peel
		2	a reddish-yellow colour
orbit	*n*		the path that a satellite, planet, or other heavenly body takes around another body in space
orchard	*n*		a large number of fruit trees
orchestra	*n*		a group of musicians who play together
orchid	*n*		a plant that has beautiful flowers
order	*v*		to tell someone to do something

order *n*	*1*	a list of things that you want
	2	tidiness, good arrangement
ordinary *adj*		not special in any way
ore *n*		rock or earth containing metal
organ *n*		a large musical instrument with black and white keys like a piano
organize *v*		to plan and arrange something
original *adj*		earliest; first; not copied
ornament *n*		something which is used as a decoration
orphan *n*		a child whose parents are dead
ostrich *n*		a very large bird that has a long neck and long legs but cannot fly
other *adj*	*1*	not the same
	2	opposite
otter *n*		a long-tailed furry animal that lives in or near rivers or streams
ought *v*		should; must
ounce *n*		a measure of mass or weight equal to about 28g
our *adj, pron*		belonging to us
out *adv*	*1*	away from a place or not in it
	2	in the open air
outback *n*		the interior of Australia; the bush
outboard *n*		a small engine fitted to the stern of a small boat
outdoor *adj*		in the open air
outer *adj*		on the outside
outer space *n*		space beyond the earth's atmosphere
outfit *n*		all the clothes or equipment needed for a special purpose
outing *n*		a day or afternoon out somewhere
outlet *n*		a way out, an opening
outline *n*		a line showing the shape of an object
outnumber *v*		to be more than
out-patient *n*		someone who visits hospital for treatment but does not sleep there
outside *n*	*1*	the outer part of something
	2	the opposite of inside
	3	the outdoors
outskirts *n*		the edges of a town
outstanding *adj*		very good; much better than the others
oval *adj*		having the shape of an egg
oven *n*		a space in a cooking stove where food can be baked or roasted
over *adv*	*1*	across
	2	more than needed
	3	ended; finished
over *prep*	*1*	on top of
	2	above; higher than
	3	across; to the other side of
over *n*		a number of balls, usually six, bowled from one end in the game of cricket
overalls *n (pl)*		clothing worn over others to keep them clean
overboard *adv*		over the side of a boat and into the water
overcoat *n*		a long coat worn over other clothes in cold weather
overdue *adj*		behind time; late
overflow *v*		to spill over; to flood
overhead *adv*		high above; over you
overhear *v*		to hear someone speaking, who does not know you are listening
overjoyed *adj*		delighted, very pleased
overlap *v*		to cover part of something
overseas *adv*		across the sea; abroad
overtake *v*		to pass another moving thing, especially a vehicle

overture *n*	a piece of music performed at the beginning of a concert or opera
overturn *v*	to turn something over
overweight *adj*	too heavy
owe *v*	to have to pay money to someone
owl *n*	a night-flying bird with large eyes that hunts smaller animals at night
own *v*	to have something that belongs to you
own *adj*	belonging to a certain person
owner *n*	the person who owns something
ox *n*	an animal like a cow, kept for its meat or for pulling carts
oxygen *n*	a gas in the air without colour or smell that everyone needs to breathe in order to stay alive
oyster *n*	a kind of shellfish

ox

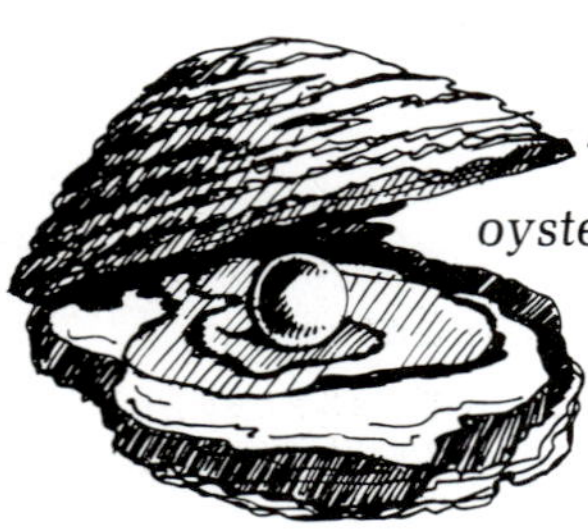
oyster

Pp

pace *n*	*1* one step in walking *2* the speed of moving
pack *n*	*1* a bundle or bag of things wrapped together for carrying *2* a group of animals that run and hunt together *3* a set of cards used in games *4* a group of Brownies or Cubs
package *n*	a parcel or bundle
packet *n*	a small parcel
pad *n*	*1* sheets of writing paper joined together at one edge *2* the launching area for space rockets *3* a soft material used as a protection against damage or injury
paddle *n*	a short oar used to move a canoe
paddle *v*	to walk about in shallow water
paddock *n*	a small field
padlock *n*	a lock joined to something by a metal loop
page *n*	one side of a sheet of paper
pageant *n*	a parade or play, usually in the open air
pail *n*	a bucket
pain *n*	the feeling you have when part of your body is injured or sick
paint *n*	coloured liquid put on a surface, often by a brush
paint *v*	*1* to cover something with a coloured liquid *2* to make a picture or design with paint
pair *n*	two things of a kind that go together; a couple
palace *n*	the home of a ruler of a country, a bishop etc.

pale *adj*		not having much colour
palm *n*	*1*	the inside of your hand
	2	a tropical tree without branches but many large leaves near the top
pamper *v*		to spoil with too much kindness
pamphlet *n*		a thin paper-covered booklet
pan *n*		a flat dish for cooking
pancake *n*		a thin, flat, round cake of eggs, flour, and milk, mixed together and fried
panda *n*		a large black and white animal found in China
pane *n*		a piece of glass in a window frame
panel *n*	*1*	a flat piece of wood, glass, metal etc. often part of a door or wall
	2	a group of people taking part in a quiz etc.
panic *n*		a sudden fear that cannot be controlled
pansy *n*		a small, garden flower with brightly coloured petals
pant *v*		to gasp for breath
panther *n*		a leopard, especially a black one
pantomime *n*		a Christmas entertainment usually based on a fairy story
pantry *n*		a room or cupboard where food is kept
pants *n*	*1*	underclothes for the lower part of the body
	2	trousers
paper *n*	*1*	material used for writing or printing on, and for wrapping things etc.
	2	a newspaper
paper *v*		to paste wallpaper on a wall or ceiling
paperback *n*		a book with a soft cover
parable *n*		a story told by Jesus which teaches a lesson
parachute *n*		an umbrella-shaped apparatus used for dropping safely from an aircraft
parade *n*		a procession or display moving past spectators
paradise *n*		a place where you are totally happy
paraffin *n*		an oil used for burning in jet engines, heaters etc.
paragraph *n*		several sentences grouped together dealing with one idea
parallel *adj*		lines that are the same distance from each other along their full length
paralysed *adj*		unable to move or feel
paratroops *n (pl)*		highly trained soldiers carried in an aircraft and dropped by parachute
parcel *n*		something wrapped up ready to be posted or carried
pardon *v*		to forgive; to excuse
parent *n*		a father or mother
park *n*	*1*	a public garden or place where you can walk, sit, and play games
	2	a place where cars and other vehicles may be left for a time
parka *n*		a kind of outdoor jacket with a hood
parliament *n*		a gathering of people chosen to make the laws of a country
parrot *n*		a brightly coloured bird that can learn to repeat things that are said to it
parsley *n*		a green plant used in cooking to flavour foods

parsnip *n* a pale yellow vegetable with a sweet taste

part *n*
1 a piece of something
2 a person or character in a play

part *v*
1 to leave someone
2 to divide into parts

particle *n* a very tiny piece

particular *adj*
1 very special; important
2 having to do with one person or thing

partly *adv* in part; not all

partner *n* a person who shares or does something with someone else

partridge *n* a wild bird that has grey, white, and brown feathers

party *n* a group of people enjoying themselves together

pass *n*
1 a way or opening between mountains
2 kicking, throwing, or hitting the ball to someone in the same team in football, netball, hockey, etc.
3 a special paper letting you in or out

pass *v*
1 to go past
2 to be successful in a test or exam
3 to hand something to someone

passage *n*
1 a way through; a corridor
2 a part of a book, story etc.

passenger *n* someone who is travelling on a bus, train, ship, aircraft etc.

Passover *n* a Jewish religious festival, lasting eight days in March or April, celebrating the Jewish people's freedom from slavery

passport *n* an important little book with your name, photograph etc. that you must have to travel in a foreign country

past *n* the time gone by

pasta *n* an Italian food made from cooked flour paste in varieous shapes, such as macaroni, spaghetti etc.

paste *n* a thick, damp mixture used for sticking things together

pastel *n* a coloured, chalk crayon

pasteurize *v* to heat milk enough to kill germs

pastime *n* something you do or play in your spare time

pastry *n* a mixture of flour, fat, and water baked in an oven

pasture *n* a field or piece of land for cattle or sheep to graze on

patch *n*
1 a small piece of material put over something to mend it or protect it
2 a small piece of ground

path *n* a narrow way for people to walk on

patience *n* the ability to wait a long time or work on a hard job without complaining

patient *n* someone who is being treated by a doctor, dentist etc.

patient *adj* able to wait a long time or work steadily without getting cross

patio *n* a paved area beside a house

patriot *n* a person who loves his or her country and all it stands for

patrol *n* a group of men, ships, aircraft etc. who keep watch and keep guard

pattern *n* — *1* shapes and colours on something; a design
2 anything that is copied to make something else

pause *v* — to stop what you are doing for a short time

pavement *n* — a path for people to walk on at the side of a street or road

pavilion *n* — a building at a sports ground for the use of players and spectators

paw *n* — the foot of animal with claws

pawn *n* — in chess, one of the 16 pieces of the lowest value

pay *n* — the money received for work done

pay *v* — to give money in return for something

payment *n* — money that is paid

pea *n* — a round, green seed that grows in a pod and is used for food

peace *n* — *1* a time when there is no war
2 a time of quiet and rest

peaceful *adj* — quiet and calm

peach *n* — a round, soft juicy fruit that has a thin fuzzy, yellow-red skin and a large stone

peacock *n* — a large male bird with brightly coloured tail feathers that it can spread out like a fan

peak *n* — *1* the top of a mountain
2 the front part of a cap

peal *n* — a ringing of bells

peanut *n* — a nut that grows in a pod under the ground

pear *n* — a sweet, juicy fruit, round at the bottom and smaller near the stem end

pearl *n* — a silver-white, precious gem found in some oyster shells

peat *n* — a kind of turf cut from bogs and used in gardening or, sometimes, as a fuel

pebble *n* — a small, round stone

peck *v* — to jab at food and pick it up with the beak

peculiar *adj* — strange

pedal *n* — a part that is pressed by the foot to make something work

pedestrian *n* — someone who travels on foot

peel *n* — the skin or rind of some fruit and vegetables

peep *v* — to look at something quickly

peer *v* — to look closely at, as if unable to see properly

peg *n* — *1* a small piece of wood or other material for hanging things on
2 a fastener for fixing clothes to a washing line

pelican *n* — a large bird that has a big pouch under its long beak

pelt *n* — the skin of an animal, usually with its fur

pen *n* — *1* an instrument used for writing
2 an enclosed space in which animals are kept

penalty *n* — a kind of punishment

pencil *n* — a tool used for writing and drawing

pendant *n* — an ornament hung round the neck on a long chain

pendulum *n* — a swinging wire or rod with a weight on the end

penetrate *v* — to find or make a way through something

penguin *n* — a black and white sea bird that cannot fly, found near the South Pole

peninsula *n* — a piece of land that sticks far out into the water

penknife *n* a small knife that folds up so that you can carry it safely

penknife

pennant *n* a long, tapering flag

penny *n* a bronze coin

pension *n* money that is paid to someone who has retired from work

pentagon *n* a shape with five sides

people *n (pl)* persons; men, women, boys and girls

pepper *n* 1 a hot-tasting powder that adds flavour to food
2 a green or red vegetable, to be cooked or eaten raw in salads

peppermint *n* a plant with a strong scent: its leaves are used to flavour some sweets, toothpastes etc.

per cent *n* parts of a hundred: 5 per cent (5%) means 5 out of every hundred

perch *n* 1 a fish that lives in rivers and lakes
2 a stick or twig that a bird can rest on

perch *v* to sit on the edge of something, like a bird on a branch

percussion instrument *n* a musical instrument that is played by striking or shaking

perfect *adj* so good that it cannot be made better

perform *v* to do something in front of an audience

performance *n* something that is done so that people can see or hear it

perfume *n* a liquid with a sweet smell

perhaps *adv* possibly; maybe

peril *n* danger

perimeter *n* the distance round the edge of something

period *n* a length of time

perish *v* to die

permanent *adj* always there; not changing

permission *n* words that allow someone to do something

permit *v* to allow

permit *n* written permission to do something

perpendicular *adj* exactly upright; at right angles to the base

person *n* a human being

persuade *v* to get someone to agree to something

pest *n* a person or thing that bothers you or causes trouble

pester *v* to annoy and worry someone continually

pet *n* an animal friend that you keep and take care of

petal *n* one of the separate, coloured parts of a flower

petrol *n* a liquid fuel made from oil and used to power motor vehicles

pew *n* a long, wooden bench in a church

pharmacist *n* a person qualified to prepare medicines

pheasant *n* a game bird with long, brightly coloured tail feathers

phone *n* short for telephone

photograph *n* **photo** (abbr) a picture taken with a camera and printed on special paper

photocopier *n* a machine for copying written or printed papers

Pp

physical *adj* 1 able to be touched and seen
2 having to do with the body

piano *n* a large musical instrument with a keyboard and strings which are struck by hammers

pick *n* a pointed tool used for breaking up hard ground

pick *v* 1 to choose
2 to take flowers or fruit from plants and trees

picket *n* a group of people who, during a strike, try to prevent others from working

pickles *n (pl)* vegetables stored in vinegar

pickpocket *n* a thief who steals things from people's pockets

picnic *n* a meal eaten of doors

picture *n* a drawing, painting, or photograph

pie *n* fruit or meat baked in pastry

piece *n* a part of something

pier *n* a long structure built out over water

pierce *v* to make a hole through something

pig *n* a farm animal raised for its bacon and pork

pigeon *n* a bird in the dove family

pike *n* a fierce freshwater fish

pile *n* a number of things lying on top of each other

pilgrim *n* someone who makes a journey to a holy place

pill *n* a little tablet or ball of medicine to be swallowed

pillar *n* a strong post that helps to hold up a building

pillow *n* the cushion that you rest your head on in bed

pilot *n* 1 the person who flies an aeroplane
2 the person who guides a ship the safe way up a river into harbour

pimple *n* a small, sore place on the skin

pin *n* a small, straight piece of wire with a head at one end and a point at the other

pinch *v* to squeeze between the thumb and a finger

pinch *n* a small amount

pine *n* a tall evergreen tree with cones, and leaves that look like green needles

pineapple *n* a large, sweet, juicy tropical fruit with a prickly covering

pineapple

pink *n* a very light red colour

pint *n* a measure of capacity, equal to about 0.5 litre

pioneer *n* 1 one of the first people who go to live in a new place
2 someone who is the first to do something

pipe *n* 1 a tube along which water, gas etc. can flow
2 a tube with a small bowl at one end in which tobacco is burned

pipeline *n* a line of pipes, sometimes very long, for carrying gas, oil, and other substances

Pp

pirate *n* someone who attacks and robs ships while they are on the sea

pistol *n* a small gun that is held in one hand

pit *n*
1 a deep hole with steep sides
2 a coal mine

pitch *n*
1 a ground marked out for football, cricket, or other games
2 a black, sticky liquid made from tar

pitch *v*
1 to throw
2 to put up a tent

pitchfork *n* a long-handled fork for lifting hay

pity *n* the feeling you have when you are sorry for someone who is ill or in trouble

pivot *n* a pin or point on which a wheel or other object turns

pixie, pixy *n* a small fairy

pizza *n* a flat dough covered with tomato sauce, cheese and other foods; it is baked until crusty

place *n* where something or someone is

place *v* to put something in a certain spot

plague *n* a very dangerous disease that spreads quickly

plaice *n* a kind of flatfish, eaten as food

plain *n* a large area of flat or almost flat land

plain *adj*
1 clear, easy to see or understand
2 simple, not fancy

plan *n*
1 an outline or idea of something to be done
2 a drawing for a new building, machine etc.

plan *v* to decide what is going to be done

plane *n*
1 a tool used for smoothing wood
2 a tall tree with large leaves and bark that peels
3 short for aeroplane

planet *n* one of the heavenly bodies that move round the sun

planetarium *n* a building with a domed ceiling on which there are displays of the stars and planets

plank *n* a long, flat piece of wood

plant *n* any living thing that is not an animal

plaster *n*
1 a soft mixture spread on walls and ceilings to form a smooth surface
2 a dressing for a wound

plastic *n* a light, strong material made from chemicals

plasticine *n* a soft, clay-like substance used for modelling

plate *n* a flat dish for eating from

plateau *n* a raised area of flat land

platform *n*
1 a small, raised stage
2 the raised place beside the railway lines where passengers wait at a station

platinum *n* a heavy and very valuable greyish-white metal

platypus *n* an Australian mammal that has brown fur, webbed feet, a wide bill, and lays eggs

play *n*
1 a story that is acted
2 games; what children do for fun

play *v*
1 to be in a game
2 to perform on a musical instrument

playground *n* an area or ground where children play

Pp

play-group *n* a class for children too young to go to school

playing-card *n* one of a set of cards used in some games

playtime *n* a period when children can stop working and enjoy themselves

pleasant *adj* nice; pleasing; enjoyable

please *v* to make someone happy

please *interj* a word that you say when you ask for something politely

pleasure *n* the feeling of being happy

pleat *n* a fold made in cloth

pledge *v* to make a serious promise; to give your word

plenty *n* a large number; as much as you need

pliers *n (pl)* a tool for gripping things, bending wire etc.

plimsoll *n* a light, rubber-soled shoe

plod *v* to walk slowly and heavily

plot *v* to plan secretly

plot *n*
1 a small piece of ground
2 a secret plan
3 the main points of a story

plough *n* a machine used on farms for turning over the soil

pluck *v*
1 to pull feathers off a bird
2 to pick flowers or fruit
3 to sound a string on a musical instrument, such as a guitar

plucky *adj* brave

plug *n*
1 a piece of solid material that fills a hole
2 a device that joins a lamp, television, drill etc., to a place in the wall where there is electricity

plum *n* a soft, juicy fruit with a stone in it

plumber *n* someone who fits and repairs water pipes, taps etc. in a building

plume *n* a bird's long and beautiful feather

plump *adj* round and fat

plunge *v*
1 to jump suddenly into water
2 to put something suddenly into water

plural *adj* a word which shows that there are more than one

plus *prep* added to

plywood *n* a strong wood made of thin layers of wood glued together

p.m. *abbr* the time from noon to midnight

pneumonia *n* a serious illness of the lungs

poach *v*
1 to cook an egg, without the shell, in boiling water
2 to hunt or fish on someone's land without permission

pocket a bag sewn into some clothes, for keeping things in

pod *n* a long seed holder on some plants

poem *n* a piece of writing; its lines have a rhythm and often rhyme

poet *n* a person who writes poems

point *n*
1 a dot, mark, or place
2 the sharp end or tip of something
3 a mark scored in a game

point *v*
1 to show where something is by holding your finger towards it
2 to aim a weapon

pointed *adj* sharp; with a point at the end

poison *n* a substance that could kill or harm a living creature

poke *v* to push hard with the end of your finger or a stick

poker *n*
1 a metal rod for stirring a fire
2 a card game

polar *adj* having to do with the North or South Pole, or both

polar bear *n* a very large, white bear that lives in the Arctic

pole *n*
1 a long, thin rounded piece of wood or metal
2 either of the two ends of a magnet
3 the North or South Pole, the earth's most northern or southern points

police *n (pl)* the men and women whose job is to keep law and order

policeman *n* **policewoman** a member of the police force

polish *v* to make something smooth and shiny by rubbing it

polite *adj* showing good manners

pollen *n* a yellowish powder in the centre of flowers, which helps to make seeds

Pp

pollute *v* to the make the air, land, or water dirty or impure

polo *n* a game like hockey, played on horseback

polyethene *n* a plastic material used for making wrappings and bags

pond *n* a small area of water; a tiny lake

pony *n* a small horse

poodle *n* a dog with very curly hair

pool *n*
1 a very small area of water
2 a swimming pool
3 a game somewhat like snooker

poor *adj*
1 having very little or no money
2 not good

poorly *adv* not well

pop *n*
1 a small bang
2 a fizzy soft drink
3 short for popular, as in 'pop' music

Pope *n* the head of the Roman Catholic Church

poplar *n* a tall, quick-growing tree

poppy *n* a wild or garden flower; usually red or scarlet in colour

popular *adj* liked by a lot of people

population *n* the total number of people living in one place

porch *n* a covered entrance to a building

porcupine *n* a small, rat-like animal covered with pointed spines

pore *n* a tiny opening in the skin

pork *n* meat from a pig

porpoise *n* a small sea animal of the whale family

porridge *n* a breakfast food made by boiling oatmeal in water

port *n*
1 a town or city with a harbour
2 the left side of the ship as you face the front or bow
3 a wine from Portugal

portable *adj* able to be carried about

porter *n* someone at a station, airport or hotel who carries people's luggage

portion *n* a part or share of something

portrait *n* a picture of a person

position *n* the place where someone or something is

positive *adj* completely sure

possess *v* to have, to own

possible *adj* able to happen or to be done

possibly *adv* perhaps

post *n*
1 a pole or pillar
2 the mail

post *v*		to send a letter, card or parcel
postage *n*		the charge for sending a letter or package by mail
postcard *n*		a card, often with a picture on one side, which you can write a message on and send through the post
postcode *n*		numbers and letters of the alphabet that are written at the end of your address to help the sorting of mail at the post office
poster *n*		a large notice for everyone to read
postman *n*		a person who collects and delivers mail
post office *n*		a place that sells stamps and deals with pensions, parcels, licences etc.
postpone *v*		to put off until later
potato *n*		a vegetable that grows under the ground and can be boiled, baked, fried etc.
pottery *n*		cups, plates, bowls etc., made of baked clay
pouch *n*		a small bag in which to hold things
poultry *n*		chickens, turkeys, ducks etc., raised for their meat and often for eggs
pounce *v*		to swoop down on, to leap on
pound *n*	*1*	a measure of weight equal to about 0.5kg
	2	a unit of money, also written £
pound *v*		to thump hard and often
pour *v*	*1*	to let liquid flow from a jug or other container
	2	to rain heavily
powder *n*		very fine particles; anything crushed or ground into dust

power *n*	*1*	the ability to do something
	2	strength, energy
powerful *adj*		very strong or important
practical *adj*	*1*	able to do useful things
	2	useful
practically *adv*		almost, nearly
practice *n*		something done many times so you improve
practise *v*		to do something many times in order to do better
prairie *n*		a huge area of flat land with few or no trees, in parts of Canada and USA
praise *v*		to say good things about someone or something
pram *n*		a small, four-wheeled vehicle to carry a baby
prance *v*		to jump about in a lively way
prank *n*		a trick played on someone
prawn *n*		a small sea creature with a thin shell and five pairs of legs
pray *v*		to speak to God
prayer *n*		what is said when talking to God
preach *v*		to talk about God to a group of people
precious *adj*		very valuable
precipice *n*		the very steep side of a mountain or high cliff

prefer *v* to like one thing more than another

pregnant *adj* having an unborn baby growing inside the body

prehistoric *adj* living or existing a very long time ago, before history was written down

preparation *n* getting ready

prepare *v* to get ready

prescription *n* a doctor's order for medicine

present *n*
1 a gift to someone
2 the time now, not the past

present *v* to give a prize or gift to someone

presently *adv* soon

preserve *v*
1 to keep safe from harm
2 to keep food etc., in good condition

president *n* head of a country or organisation

press *n*
1 a machine used for printing
2 a machine used to flatten clothes
3 newspapers

press *v*
1 to push hard on something
2 to make something flat or smooth

pretend *v* to make it seem that something is true when it is not

pretty *adj* pleasant to look at

prevent *v* to stop something from happening

previous *adj* earlier in time

prey *n* any animal hunted by another for food

price *n* the cost of something

priceless *adj* too valuable to have a price

prick *v* to make a tiny hole in something

prickle *n* a sharp point that grows on a plant or an animal

pride *n*
1 feeling pleased about something that you or others have done, own etc.
2 a high opinion of yourself

priest *n* a religious person who looks after a church and its people

primary *adj* first; earliest

primary school *n* the school you attend when you are about five years old

Prime Minister *n* the leader of the government in some countries

primrose *n* a spring flower with yellow petals

prince *n* the son of a king or queen

princess *n* the daughter of a king or queen; the wife of a prince

principal *adj* the most important

principal *n* the head of a college or school

principle *n* an important rule, law or belief

print *n*
1 letters that you do not join together
2 a mark made by pressure, such as a footprint
3 a printed picture or photograph

print *v*
1 to write with letters that are not joined together
2 to use a machine to put letters or pictures on to paper

prison *n* a place where criminals are kept as a punishment

prisoner *n*
1 someone who has been captured
2 someone in prison

private *adj*
1 not open to everyone
2 not known to other people

prize *n*		a reward for doing well or winning a contest
probable *adj*		likely to happen or to be true
probably *adv*		very likely
problem *n*		something that is not easy to do or understand
proceed *v*		to continue, to go on
process *n*		a way of making something
procession *n*		a line of people and vehicles moving along together
produce *n*		things that are made or grown
produce *v*	*1*	to make
	2	to bring something out so that it can be seen
producer *n*		a person who organizes a play, film etc.
product *n*		something that is made or grown
professor *n*		a senior teacher at a university
profit *n*		the money you make by selling something for more than you paid
programme *n*	*1*	a list of events or things that are going to take place
	2	a broadcast on television or radio
	3	a printed pamphlet giving details of a play, sporting event etc.
progress *n*		a forward movement
progress *v*		to move forward; to show improvement
prohibit *v*		to say that people must not do something
project *n*		a plan or activity to be done
project *v*	*1*	to throw forward
	2	to stick out
projector *n*		a machine used to show moving or still pictures on a screen
promenade *n*		a kind of road by the sea where people can walk
promise *v*		to say that you will certainly do or not do something
promote *v*		to give someone a higher job, etc.
promotion *n*		a better job; a higher position
prompt *adj*		done at once; quick
prong *n*		one of the pointed ends of a fork
pronounce *v*		to say a sound or a word in a certain way
proof *n*		something that shows beyond doubt that a thing is true
prop *n*		a support such as wood, metal etc.
propel *v*		to drive forward
propeller *n*		a set of blades that spin round to drive a ship or a plane forward
proper *adj*		right; correct
property *n*		anything a person owns
prophet *n*		a person who tells what is going to happen in the future
propose *v*		to suggest something
prosecute *v*		to bring someone to trial before a court of law
prosper *v*		to do well; to succeed
protect *v*		to keep safe from danger
protest *v*		to object to something; to complain
proud *adj*	*1*	pleased at having done something well
	2	thinking that you are better than others
prove *v*		to show for certain that something is true
provide *v*		to supply what is needed

prowl *v* to move around silently, often looking for something to eat or steal

prune *n* a dried plum

prune *v* to cut short the unwanted branches of a tree or bush

pry *v* to be too curious about other people's affairs

psalm *n* a sacred song; a hymn

pub *n* a building where you can go to drink beer etc. and talk to friends

public *adj* belonging to or open to everyone

publish *v* to prepare a book, newspaper, or magazine for sale

pudding *n* a sweet food that you eat at the end of a meal

puddle *n* a small pool, usually rain-water

puff *n* a small amount of breath, smoke, or wind

puffin *n* a sea bird with a large bill

Pp

pull *v* to haul towards to you

pulley *n* a wheel with rope round it, used for lifting heavy things

pullover *n* a knitted garment which covers the top part of the body

pulp *n*
1 the soft part of fruits
2 ground-up wood mixed with chemicals, that is used to make paper

pulpit *n* a place where the preacher stands in church to talk to the people

pulse *n* the beat of the heart that you can feel in different parts of the body

pump *n* a machine that forces liquids or gases into or out of things

punch *n* a tool for making holes

punch *v* to hit with the fist

punctual *adj* on time

punctuation *n* the use of full stops, commas, and other marks in a piece of writing to make it easier to read

puncture *n* a small hole in something, such as a tyre, which lets the air out

punish *v* to make someone suffer for a wrong he or she has done

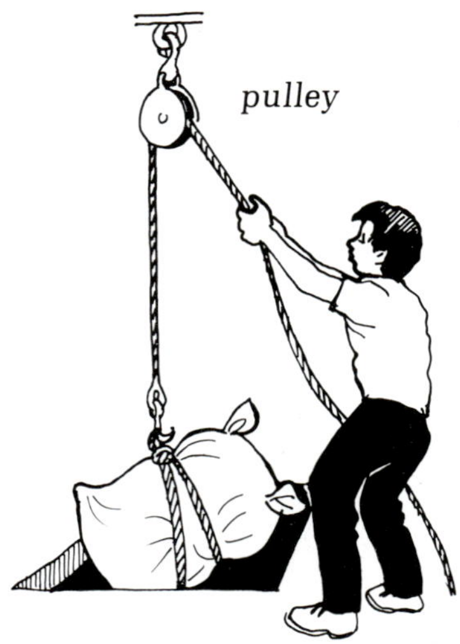

pulley

puffin

puppet

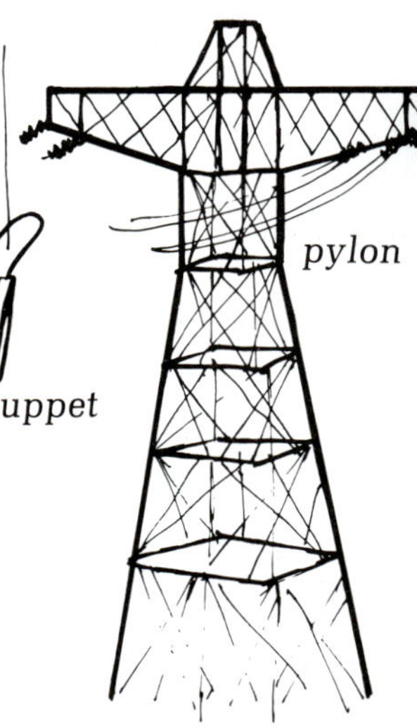

pylon

pupil *n*
1 someone who is learning from a teacher
2 the circular opening in the centre of your eye.

puppet *n* a doll that can be moved and made to perform

puppy *n* a very young dog

purchase *v* to buy something

pure *adj* clean, not mixed with other things

purple *n* a colour made by mixing red and blue

purpose *n* the reason for doing something

purr *n* the sound that a happy cat makes

purse *n* a small bag for holding money, keys etc.

pursue *v* to chase after

push *v* to press on something in order to move it

push-chair *n* a chair on wheels to carry a young child

put *v* to place something somewhere

putty *n* a greyish paste which hardens when dry and is used for fixing glass into window frames

puzzle *n*
1 a problem or question that is hard to work out
2 a kind of pastime or game which requires skill

pyjamas *n (pl)* a thin coat and trousers for sleeping in

pylon *n* a tall, steel tower used for supporting electric cables

pyramid *n* a structure that has a square base and four sides shaped like triangles

python *n* a large snake that crushes its prey

Qq

quack *n* the noise made by a duck

quadruped *n* an animal with four feet

quadruplet *n* one of four babies born at the same time to the same mother

quail *n* a small bird of the partridge family

quaint *adj* unusual or odd in a pleasant or interesting way

quake *v* to shake; to tremble with fear

quality *n* how good or bad a thing is

quantity *n* an amount

quarrel *v* to disagree and argue, often using angry words

quarry *n*
1 a place where stone for building and other purposes is taken out of the ground
2 an animal that is being hunted

quarter *n* one of four equal parts

quay *n* a place where ships load and unload

quarry

quay

queen *n* 1 a woman who is ruler of a country or the wife of a king
2 the most powerful piece in chess
3 a female bee or ant that lays eggs

queer *adj* strange, unusual

quench *v* 1 to put an end to someone's thirst
2 to put out a fire

question *n* something that you ask when you want to find out or get something

question mark *n* a punctuation mark, like this ? which is put at the end of a sentence that asks a question

quick *adj* fast, speedy

quicksand *n* loose, wet sand into which you can sink

quiet *adj* without any noise, peaceful, calm

quilt *n* a thick, padded bed covering

quit *v* to leave; to give up

quite *adv* 1 completely
2 more or less

quiver *v* to shake because you are very cold or frightened

quiver *n* a case for carrying arrows

quiz *n* a kind of game in which people try to answer questions in order to show how much they know

quoits *n* a game in which rings are thrown onto pegs

quoits

Qq
Rr

Rr

rabbi *n* a Jewish religious leader

rabbit *n* a small brownish-grey mammal with long ears and a very short tail, which lives in a burrow

race *n* 1 a contest to see who can go the fastest
2 a group of people of the same sort with the same colour of skin etc.

race *v* to move or go very fast

rack *n* a framework or stand for holding objects

racket *n* 1 a loud noise
2 a light bat with strings used to hit balls in tennis, squash, and badminton

radar *n* an instrument in a ship or aircraft that tells you where things are when you cannot see them

radiator *n* 1 a heating device used for warming a room
2 the part of the car that keeps the engine cool

radio *n* an apparatus that receives sounds from the air by means of electrical waves and lets people hear them

radish *n* a small, red-skinned vegetable used in salads

radius *n* a straight line going from the centre to the outside of a circle

raffia *n* fibre from an African palm tree used for weaving baskets, mats etc.

raffle *n* a way of raising money by selling numbered tickets which may win a prize

raft *n* a floating wooden platform

rafter *n* one of the sloping beams that holds up a roof

rag *n*		any small piece of cloth
rage *n*		great anger
ragged *adj*		torn, with rough edges
raid *n*		a sudden attack
rail *n*	1	a long, narrow bar made of metal or wood
	2	a long, metal bar that is part of a railway line
railings *n (pl)*		a fence of posts and rails
railway *n*		a track of steel rails on which trains run
rain *n*		water falling in drops from the clouds
rainbow *n*		a coloured arch formed in the sky by the sun shining through raindrops
raincoat *n*		a waterproof coat
raise *v*	1	to lift up; to make higher
	2	to bring up young children or animals
	3	to collect money for a cause
raisin *n*		a small dried grape
rake *n*		a garden tool that has a long handle and a row of short spikes
rally *n*		a large number of people who have come together for a big meeting
ram *n*		a male sheep
ram *v*		to push or hit something very hard
Ramadan *n*		the month when Muslims fast during the day
ramble *n*		a walk for pleasure in the country
ramp *n*		a sloping floor, path etc., leading from one level to another
ranch *n*		a large farm in North America on which cattle, horses, or sheep are raised
range *n*		a row of mountains
ransom *n*		money paid for the return of someone who has been taken prisoner or kidnapped
rap *v*		to hit something quickly and lightly
rapid *adj*		very fast
rapids *n (pl)*		a part of a river where the water moves very fast, often over rocks
rare *adj*		not often found; not happening often
rascal *n*	1	a naughty child
	2	a dishonest person
rash *n*		a number of tiny red spots on the skin
rash *adj*		hasty and reckless
rasher *n*		a thin slice of bacon
raspberry *n*		a small, red juicy fruit
rat *n*		an animal like a large mouse
rate *n*		the speed something happens or is done
rather *adv*		fairly; quite; not very
ration *n*		an amount or share of something allowed to a person in a time of shortage
rattle *n*		a baby's toy which makes a rattling noise when shaken
rattle *v*		to make a series of sharp sounds
rattlesnake *n*		a poisonous snake that makes a rattling sound with its tail
rave *v*		to talk excitedly; to be very pleased about
raven *n*		a large bird that is similar to a crow
ravenous *adj*		very hungry
ravine *n*		a deep narrow valley
raw *adj*		not cooked
ray *n*		a line or beam of light
razor *n*		a cutting instrument used for shaving off hair

reach *v*
1 to stretch out and touch or get
2 to arrive at

read *v* to look at words and understand their meaning

ready *adj*
1 able and willing to do something without delay
2 fit to be used

real *adj* not a copy

realize *v* to understand clearly

really *adv* truly

reap *v* to cut and gather grain

rear *n* the back part

rear *v*
1 to bring up young children or animals
2 to rise up on the hind legs, as a horse, dog etc.

reason *n* anything that explains why something has happened

rebel *v* to refuse to obey

recall *v*
1 to remember
2 to call someone or something back

receipt *n* a note saying that you have paid for something

receive *v* to get something that has been given or sent to you

Rr

recent *adj* made, done, or happened a short while ago

recipe *n* directions for cooking food

reckless *adj* being careless and risking danger

recognize *v* to know that you have seen somebody or something before

record *n*
1 a flat disc which makes sounds when it turns round on a record-player
2 facts that are written down and kept
3 the best performance known

record *v*
1 to write something down so that it will be remembered
2 to put sounds on a record or tape

recorder *n* a musical instrument made of wood or plastic, played by blowing into one end

record-player *n* a machine for playing records

recover *v*
1 to get better after being ill
2 to get something back that you have lost

recreation *n* games, hobbies etc., done for enjoyment

rectangle *n* a shape with four straight sides and four right angles, such as a postcard

red *n* the colour of blood

reduce *v* to make something smaller or less

reed *n* a tall grass that grows in or near water

reef *n* a line of rock or coral just above or below the surface of the sea

reel *n*
1 a Scottish dance
2 a device on which film, fishing-line, thread etc. can be wound

re-entry *n* the return of a spacecraft to the earth's atmosphere

referee *n* someone who takes charge of a game or contest and sees the rules are obeyed

reference book *n* a book that provides information, such as an encyclopaedia, dictionary etc.

reflect *v*
1 to send back rays of light etc.
2 to show a picture of something, as a mirror does

refresh *v* to give new strength; to make fresh

refreshments *n(pl)*		something to eat or drink
refrigerator *n*		a kind of metal cupboard that keeps stored food cold
refugee *n*		a person who is escaping from danger to find safety or protection
refund *n*		money paid back
refuse *v*		to say 'no'
refuse *n*		rubbish
regatta *n*		a race meeting for boats and yachts
reggae *n*		a West Indian style of popular music
regiment *n*		a large army unit
region *n*		a part of a country or the world
register *n*		a written list of names and other information
registery office *n*		a place where births, marriages and deaths are recorded
regret *v*		to be sorry for something that has been done
regular *adj*	*1*	happening again and again at the same time
	2	usual, normal
regulation *n*		a rule
rehearsal *n*		a practice to get ready for a concert, play etc.
rehearse *v*		to practise something before it is done in front of an audience
reign *v*		to be king or queen; to rule
reign *n*		the period of time that a king or queen rules
reindeer *n*		a large deer that has antlers and lives in the cold, northern lands
reins *n (pl)*		the two long straps used for guiding a horse
rejoice *v*		to show how pleased or happy you are
relative *n*		someone who belongs to the same family as you
relax *v*	*1*	to rest the body by allowing it to become less tense
	2	to rest from work
relay race *n*		a race between teams in which each person covers part of the distance
release *v*		to let someone or something go free
reliable *adj*		able to be trusted and depended upon
relief *n*	*1*	the feeling you have when you are no longer in trouble, pain or danger
	2	help given to refugees etc.
relieve *v*		to take away pain, worry, danger etc.
religion *n*		what people believe about God or gods, and the way they worship
rely *v*		to depend upon, to trust
remain *v*	*1*	to stay behind
	2	to be left over
remainder *n*		what is left over
remark *v*		to say something
remark *n*		something said
remarkable *adj*		worth noticing; special
remedy *n*		something that makes you feel better; a cure
remember *v*		to be able to bring something into your mind when you want to
remind *v*		to help someone remember
remote *adj*		far off
remote control *n*		the control of a TV, video recorder, model plane, etc., from a distance, usually by a radio signal
remove *v*		to take away
rent *n*		money paid for the use of a flat, TV etc., that is owned by someone else

Rr

Rr

repair *v* to mend something

repeat *v* to say or do something again

replace *v* 1 to put something back 2 to take the place of

reply *v* to answer

report *n* a piece of news; telling about something that has happened

reporter *n* someone who obtains and writes about news for a newspaper, TV etc.

represent *v* 1 to act or speak for other people 2 to be a picture or model of something

reptile *n* a cold-blooded animal that creeps or crawls such as a snake, turtle, crocodile etc.

reputation *n* what people think or say about you

request *v* to ask for something

require *v* to need

rescue *v* to save from danger or harm

resemble *v* to look similar to

reserve *v* to arrange for something to be kept for you

reservoir *n* a place where a large amount of water is stored, often in an artificial lake

resident *n* someone who lives in a particular place

resign *v* to give up your job or position

resist *v* to fight or struggle against

resolve *v* to make a decision about something

resort *n* a holiday centre

respect *n* the feeling you have for someone you admire and like

respond *v* to answer, to reply

responsible *adj* 1 in charge of something 2 trustworthy and reliable

rest *n* 1 sleep; being still and quiet 2 the part that is left 3 the other people or things

rest *v* to stop working, to relax or to have a sleep

restaurant *n* a place where you buy and eat a meal

restless *adj* not able to be still and quiet

restore *v* 1 to put something back 2 to make something as good as it was before

result *n* 1 something that happens because of something else 2 the final score in a game

resume *v* to begin doing something again after a break

retire *v* to stop working, usually because of old age

retreat *v* to go back from

retrieve *v* to get back or to find again

return *v* to come or go back 2 to give back

reveal *v* 1 to allow something to be seen 2 to make something known

revenge *n* something done to get even with someone who has hurt you

Rev. or **Reverend** *n* a title given to a member of the clergy

reverse *n* the opposite side or way

reverse *v* to go backwards in a car

revive *v* to bring back to life or health

revolt *n* a refusal to obey orders

revolution *n* 1 a time when a government is changed by force, not by an election 2 a full turn of a wheel or other object

revolver *n* a small gun that can be fired several times without having to be loaded again

reward *n*		a prize or money given for something done
rhinoceros *n*		a very large, thick-skinned animal with one or two horns, found in Africa and Asia
rhubarb *n*		a plant with reddish, sour-tasting stalks that can be cooked and eaten
rhyme *n*		a word having the same last sound as another
rhythm *n*		the regular beat or flow of sounds or movements
rib *n*		one of the bones that curve around your chest protecting your lungs
ribbon *n*		a narrow strip of cloth such as silk, satin, velvet etc.
rice *n*		a white grain that is used as food
rich *adj*		having much money or property
riddle *n*		a puzzling question
ride *v*	*1*	to travel on something, such as a horse or bicycle
	2	to travel in a car, bus, train etc.
ridge *n*		the top of something long and narrow
ridiculous *adj*		very silly or foolish
rifle *n*		a long gun that is held against the shoulder when it is fired
rift *n*		a split, a crack
rig *n*		equipment for drilling oil wells
right *adj*	*1*	opposite of left
	2	true, correct
	3	fair
rim *n*		the outer edge of a cup, bowl, wheel etc.
rind *n*		the skin on bacon, cheese, and some fruits
ring *n*	*1*	a circle
	2	a metal band to wear on your finger
	3	the sound of a bell
ring *v*		to telephone someone
rink *n*		a place made for ice-skating and ice hockey
rinse *v*		to use clean water to wash away soap or dirt
riot *n*		a violent and noisy disturbance caused by a group of people
rip *v*		to tear something
ripe *adj*		ready to be picked and eaten
ripple *n*		a small movement on the surface of water
rise *v*	*1*	to go upwards
	2	to get up
risk *n*		the chance of danger or loss
rival *n*		someone trying to win the same prize as you are
river *n*		a large stream of water that flows into an ocean, lake, or into another river
rivet *n*		a bolt for joining metal plates together
road *n*		a hard, level way made for the use of traffic
roam *v*		to wander about
roar *v*		to make a loud, deep sound
roast *v*		to cook meat or vegetables in an oven or over an open fire
rob *v*		to take or steal things
robber *n*		someone who steals and is prepared to injure people who try to stop him
robbery *n*		stealing by force
robin *n*		a small, brown bird with orange-red feathers on its breast
robot *n*		a machine that can be made to do things that people do

Rr

rock *n* 1 a large stone
2 a kind of popular music with a strong beat

rock *v* to move gently from side to side

rocket *n* 1 a firework at the end of a stick, that goes high in the air when lit
2 a device for sending spacecraft and missiles into space

rocky *adj* full of rocks; bumpy

rod *n* a long, thin round piece of wood, metal, fibre-glass etc.

rodent *n* any of a group of animals that have sharp front teeth used in gnawing

rodeo *n* a contest of skill in riding horses, roping cattle etc.

roe *n* a mass of eggs from fish

rogue *n* a bad person whom you cannot trust

role *n* a part played by an actor or actress

roll *n* 1 a piece of material, curled into a tube shape
2 a small bun-shaped loaf of bread
3 a list of names, a register

roll *v* 1 to turn over and over
2 to sway from side to side
3 to flatten with a roller

roller *n* 1 a small cylinder put in hair to curl it
2 a heavy cylinder rolled over things to make them smooth or flat

roller-skates *n (pl)* a set of wheels attached to a boot for skating

rolling-pin *n* a long cylinder for rolling out pastry to flatten it

Roman Catholic a Christian who accepts the Pope as head of the church

romance *n* a love story

roof *n* the outside top covering of a building

rook *n* a bird belonging to the crow family

room *n* 1 one of the inside spaces of a building such as bedrooms, kitchens, lounges etc.
2 space

root *n* the part of a plant that grows in the ground

rope *n* thick, strong cord

rose *n* a beautiful flower with a thorny stem

rosemary *n* an evergreen shrub whose sweet-smelling leaves are used as a herb in cooking and making perfume

rot *v* to go bad, to decay

rotate *v* to go around and around as a wheel does

rotten *adj* 1 going or gone bad
2 not pleasant; not good

rough *adj* 1 not smooth
2 stormy
3 not gentle

round *n* a period of time in a boxing match

round *adj* in the shape of a circle, ball etc.

roundabout *n* 1 a place where a number of roads meet and traffic has to go round in the same direction
2 an amusement at a fun-fair

rounders *n* an outdoor game played between two teams using a small ball and a bat like a heavy stick

rouse *v* to wake someone up

route *n* a way of getting to a place

routine *n* a set way of doing things

rove *v* to roam, to wander

row *n*		people or things in a straight line
row *v*		to make a boat move by using oars
row *n*	*1*	a quarrel
	2	a lot of noise
royal *adj*		having to do with kings or queens or their families
rub *v*		to move something backwards and forwards on something else
rubber *n*	*1*	a springy, elastic material used for making tyres, elastic bands, balls etc.
	2	a piece of rubber, or plastic, used for wiping out pencil marks
rubbish *n*		waste matter that is thrown away
ruby *n*		a deep red precious stone
rucksack *n*		a bag worn strapped on the back by walkers and climbers
rudder *n*		a flat part fixed to the end of a ship or aircraft used for steering
rude *adj*		bad-mannered, not polite
rug *n*	*1*	a floor covering
	2	a thick blanket
rugby *n*		a kind of football played by two teams with an oval-shaped ball which can be kicked, carried or passed from hand to hand
rugged *adj*		rough and rocky
ruin *n*		the remains of an old building
ruin *v*		to spoil something completely
rule *n*		something that ought to be obeyed by everyone
rule *v*	*1*	to be in charge of a country, to govern
	2	to draw a straight line with a ruler
ruler *n*	*1*	someone who controls, governs or rules a country
	2	a strip of wood, plastic or metal, with straight edges used for measuring and drawing straight lines
rumble *v*		to make a deep, rolling sound as thunder makes
rumour *n*		a story that is passed around, but may not be true
run *n*	*1*	a quick movement on foot
	2	a score in cricket made by running between the wickets
run *v*		to use the legs to move quickly
rung *n*		one step of a ladder
runner-up *n*		the person or team that finishes second in a race or contest
runway *n*		a wide and long concrete surface for aircraft to take off and land
rural *adj*		having to do with the country
rush *v*		to hurry about; to move fast
rust *n*		a reddish-brown, rough surface that forms on iron and some other metals when they become damp
rustle *n*		a crisp sound of dry leaves
rustle *v*		to steal cattle or other animals
rut *n*		a deep track made by a wheel or a vehicle
ruthless *adj*		cruel; having no pity
rye *n*		a cereal plant grown for animal feed and making some kinds of bread

Ss

sabbath *n* a weekly day of rest and worship: Saturday for Jews, Sunday for Christians

sabotage *n* damage done on purpose to machines, buildings etc.

sack *n* a large bag made of strong material

sack *v* to dismiss someone from their job

sacred *adj* holy, having to do with religion and worship

sacrifice *n*
1 an offering made to God
2 something you value that you give up

sad *adj* not happy; sorrowful

saddle *n* a seat for the rider of a horse

safari *n* a trip through wild country, especially in Africa

safe *n* a strong metal box in which valuable things are locked

safe *adj*
1 free from danger or harm
2 careful

safety *n* freedom from danger or harm

sag *v* to bend low in the middle

sail *n*
1 a sheet of canvas or cloth that is attached to a boat
2 a short voyage

sail *v* to travel on water

sailor *n* a member of a ship's crew

saint *n* a man or woman who has lived a very holy life

salad *n* a mixture of vegetables or fruit served cold

salami *n* a spicy kind of sausage

salary *n* regular payment of money for work done

sale *n*
1 the exchange of goods for money
2 the selling of goods at prices lower than usual

saliva *n* liquid formed in your mouth

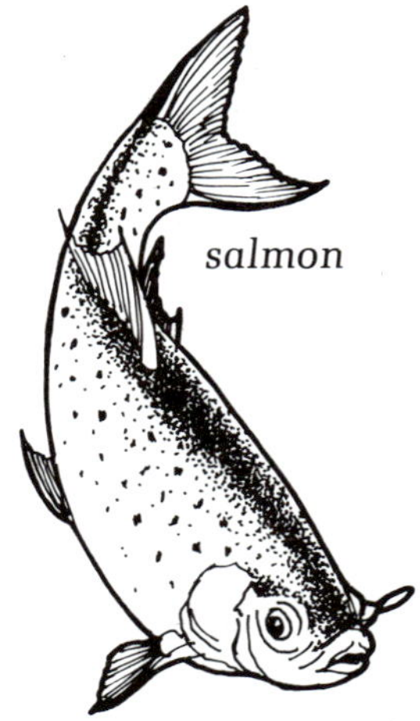

salmon

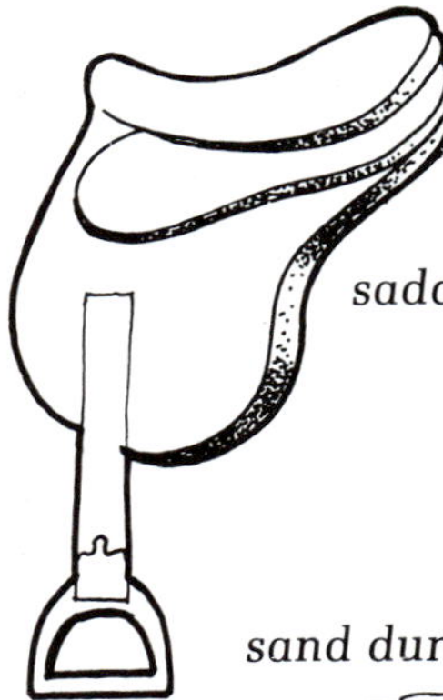

saddle

sand dune

salmon *n* a large fish with pink flesh, used for food

salt *n* a white substance used to flavour food

salute *v* to raise your hand in respect to someone

salvage *n* goods saved from a fire, a flood, a damaged ship etc.

same *adj* exactly alike, not different

sample *n* a small piece of something that shows you what the rest is like

sand *n* tiny grains of rock

sand dune *n* a mound of sand in the desert or near the sea

sandal *n* a kind of open shoe, attached to the foot by straps

sandpaper *n* a heavy paper with a coating of sand for smoothing wood

sandwich *n* two slices of bread with a filling between them

sanitary *adj* healthy, free from dirt

sap *n* the liquid inside plants and trees

sapling *n* a young tree

sapphire *n* a bright blue precious stone

sardine *n* a small, silvery fish sold for food, usually in cans

sari *n* a piece of clothing worn by women and girls in India

sash *n*
1 a wide ribbon, usually worn around the waist
2 a window frame that slides up and down

satellite *n*
1 a heavenly body moving around a planet
2 a spaceship or other man-made object sent travelling in orbit around the earth, moon etc.

satin *n* a smooth, very shiny cloth

satisfaction *n* a feeling of pleasure, enjoyment

satisfactory *adj* good enough to be pleasing

satisfy *v* to please

sauce *n* a liquid mixture served with some foods for added flavour

saucer *n* a shallow dish for a cup to stand on

sauna *n* a Finnish type of hot steam bath

sausage *n* a chopped meat mixture mixed with spices enclosed in a skin

savage *adj* wild and fierce

save *v*
1 to free someone from danger
2 to keep something to use it later on
3 to avoid waste

savings *n* money that has been saved

saw *n* a tool with sharp metal points along one edge, used for cutting wood, metal etc.

sawmill *n* a place where logs are cut into planks

saxophone *n* a musical instrument played by blowing into the mouthpiece and pushing down the keys

say *v* to speak, to tell

scab *n* a crust that forms over a wound

scaffold *n* a structure of metal tubes and planks used when a building is being put up or repaired

scald *n* a burn from a very hot liquid

scale *n*
1 a set of musical notes
2 a thin flake of skin
3 a series of measuring marks on a ruler, a thermometer etc.

scalp *n* the skin and hair on top of your head

scalpel *n* a small, very sharp knife used by surgeons

scan *v* to read over quickly

scar *n* a mark left on your skin after a cut or burn has healed

scarce *adj* in short supply; rare

scare *v* to frighten

scarecrow *n* an object in the shape of a man, put up in a field to keep birds away from crops

scarf *n* a piece of cloth worn around the neck or head

scarlet *n* a very bright red colour

scatter *v* to throw things in different directions

scene *n*
1 a view
2 a part of a play
3 a place where something happened

scenery *n*
1 what you see outside
2 a painted cloth or board at the back of a stage

scent *n* a smell; a perfume

Ss

schedule *n*
1 a list of events, usually shown with times
2 a list of details

scheme *n* a plan

scholar *n*
1 a pupil or student
2 a person who has a lot of knowledge

school *n* a place where children are educated

schooner *n* a fast sailing ship with two or more masts

science *n* knowledge got by studying, watching and testing

scientist *n* someone who studies a science such as chemistry, physics etc.

scissors *n* a cutting instrument with two blades

scone *n* a small, soft, round, flat cake

scoop *n*
1 a little shovel for sugar or flour
2 an important news story found only in one newspaper

scorch *v* to burn slightly

score *n* points made in a game

scorn *n* a feeling that someone or something is worth very little

scorpion *n* an animal that looks like a spider with a long tail

scour *v* to clean by rubbing hard with a rough material

scout *n*
1 someone sent ahead to get information
2 a member of the Scout Association

scowl *v* to frown

scramble *v*
1 to mix together
2 to climb or crawl using hands and feet

scrap *n* a small piece

scrape *v* to rub with a sharp edge

scratch *n* a mark left by something sharp

scratch *v*
1 to rub the part of your skin that itches
2 to mark with a point or edge

scream *v* to make a loud sharp cry of pain or fear

scream *n* a loud, shrill cry

screech *n* a harsh, shrill cry or sound

screen *n*
1 the surface on which films and slides are shown, and on which TV pictures are seen
2 a partition which protects from draughts, light, heat and being seen

screw *n*
1 a kind of nail with spiral grooves for gripping wood or metal
2 a ship's propeller

screwdriver *n* a tool used for turning screws

scribble *v* to write or draw in a quick and careless way

script *n*
1 writing in which the letters are joined together
2 the written words of a play, film, or TV or radio programme

scripture *n* holy writings, especially the Bible

scrub *v* to clean by rubbing hard with a stiff brush

sculptor *n* someone who carves statues or shapes

scythe *n* a tool with a curved blade for cutting grass

sea *n* the great expanse of salt water that covers almost 75% of the earth's surface

seal *n* a furry animal that lives in and by the sea

seal *v*		to join two things tightly together, often by using something sticky
sea lion *n*		a large seal that lives in the Pacific Ocean
seam *n*		a line where two pieces of cloth are sewn together
seaman *n*		a sailor
search *v*		to look everywhere for someone or something
seaside *n*		the sea-shore; the beach
season *n*		one of the four parts of the year; spring, summer, autumn, winter
season *v*		to add salt, pepper, or other flavours to food
seat *n*		something to sit on, as a chair, stool etc.
seat belt *n*		a strong belt that holds a person in the seat of a car or an aeroplane in case of a bump or crash
seaweed *n*		a green or brown plant that grows in the sea
second *n*	*1*	a very small measure of time; a sixtieth part of a minute
	2	the next after the first in order, time, position etc.
second-hand *adj*		already used; not new
secret *n*		a piece of information that is kept hidden
secret *adj*		known only to a few
secretary *n*		an office worker who types letters and makes arrangements for other people
section *n*		one of the parts into which something can be divided
secure *adj*	*1*	safe
	2	firmly fastened
see *v*	*1*	to receive a picture of something through your eyes
	2	to understand
seed *n*		the grain or nut from which a new plant grows
seek *v*		to look for; to search
seem *v*		to look as if something is true
seesaw *n*		a long plank balanced on a central support, used by children for play
seize *v*		to grasp, to catch hold of
seldom *adv*		rarely, not often
select *v*		to choose carefully
selection *n*		a collection, a choice
selfish *adj*		thinking and caring only for yourself
sell *v*		to hand over something in return for money
semi		a 'prefix' meaning 'half'
send *v*		to make something or someone go somewhere
senile *adj*		sick and feeble due to old age
senior *adj*		older or more experienced
sensation *n*	*1*	a feeling
	2	great excitement
sense *n*	*1*	the ability to smell, taste, hear, see and touch
	2	quickness of mind
	3	the meaning of something
sensible *adj*		full of good sense
sensitive *adj*	*1*	easily upset
	2	having deep feelings
sentence *n*	*1*	a number of words which together form a complete statement or thought
	2	a punishment given in a court of law
sentry *n*		a guard
separate *v*		to divide, to set apart

Ss

sequence *n*		a number of things happening one after the other
sergeant *n*	1	a police officer below the rank of inspector
	2	a non-commissioned officer in the army and airforce
serial *n*		a story that is told in parts, instead of all at one time
series *n*		a number of similar things coming one after the other; a sequence
serious *adj*	1	important and needing attention
	2	very bad
serpent *n*		a large snake
servant *n*		a person who works for someone else
serve *n*		in tennis and other games, the putting into play of the ball
serve *v*	1	to work for someone or something
	2	to give out food to others
	3	to put a ball into play
service *n*	1	a helpful act
	2	a form of worship
	3	an organisation that serves people
set *n*	1	a group of things that go together
	2	a radio or TV receiver
set *v*	1	to put things in place
	2	to become stiff
	3	to sink below the horizon, as the sun
settee *n*		a long seat with a back
settle *v*	1	to get comfortable and stay in a place
	2	to decide something
	3	to come to rest
	4	to sink to the bottom
sever *v*		to cut through
several *adj*		not many, but more than two or three
severe *adj*		strict, harsh
sew *v*		to stitch with a needle and thread
sewage *n*		waste material and water that is carried away by sewers and drains
sewer *n*		an underground drain pipe that carries away sewage
sex *n*		being female or male
sextant *n*		a scientific instrument used in navigation
shabby *adj*		old and ragged
shade *n*	1	a place hidden from the sun
	2	a slight difference in colour
shade *v*		to shield from strong light
shadow *n*		a patch of darkness caused by something standing in the way of a light
shaft *n*	1	a long handle; a pole
	2	a long passage leading down into a mine
	3	a ray of light
shaggy *adj*		having long, thick, rough hair
shake *v*	1	to move from side to side or up and down
	2	to tremble
shale *n*		a soft rock of hardened clay which divides into thin layers or flakes
shallow *adj*		not deep
shame *n*		a feeling of being unhappy or foolish because you have done wrong
shampoo *n*		a liquid soap for washing hair
shamrock *n*		a small, bright green three-leaved plant: the national emblem of Ireland

shape *n* the outline or form of anything

shape *v* to form or make something into a particular shape

share *n* the part of something that is given to one person

share *v* 1 to divide out
2 to use together

shark *n* a large, grey, ocean fish that has many sharp teeth

sharp *adj* 1 with an edge or point that can make a cut
2 quick to understand or notice

shatter *v* to break suddenly into small pieces

shave *v* 1 to remove hair with a razor
2 to scrape or graze slightly

shave *n* 1 the cutting of hair with a razor
2 a narrow miss or escape

shear *v* to cut off wool, especially off sheep

shears *n* large clipping scissors

sheath *n* a cover for a knife or sword

shed *n* a hut for storing tools or materials

shed *v* to let things fall off or drop away

sheep *n* an animal that is raised for its wool and meat

sheer *adj* 1 very steep
2 very thin, allowing you to see partly through

sheet *n* 1 a large piece of thin cloth used on a bed
2 a thin, flat piece of metal, glass, paper etc.

sheikh *n* an Arab chief or prince

shelf *n* a board on a wall or in a cupboard for putting things on

shell *n* 1 a thin hard outer covering such as an egg, nut, pod etc.
2 a large bullet that explodes when it hits something

shellfish *n* a water animal with a hard, outer shell

shelter *n* a place that gives protection and cover

shelter *v* to protect; to cover

shepherd *n* someone who looks after sheep

sheriff *n* a law officer, particularly in the USA

sherry *n* a strong wine, often drunk before a meal

shield *n* a piece of armour carried to protect the body

shield *v* to protect

shift *v* to move something; to change your position

shimmer *v* to shine with a soft, trembling light

shin *n* the front of your leg between the knee and the ankle

shine *v* 1 to give out light
2 to polish

shingle *n* pebbles, particularly on a beach

shiny *adj* bright, glittering

ship *n* a large boat or sea-going vessel

shipwreck *n* a ship that is damaged and sinks at sea

shirt *n* a thin garment worn on the upper part of the body

shiver *v* to shake with fear or cold

shoal *n* a large group of fish swimming together

shock *n* 1 a sudden fright; an unpleasant surprise
2 a very sharp feeling caused by electricity

shock *v* 1 to cause a feeling of surprise or fear
2 to give an electric shock

shoe *n* 1 an outer covering worn on the foot
2 a metal rim nailed to a horse's hoof

shoot *n* a new or young plant

shoot *v* 1 to fire a bullet, arrow, shell etc.
2 to kick the ball at the goal in football
3 to come up from the ground, to grow

shooting star *n* a small meteor from space

shop *n* a building where goods are sold

shop *v* to buy from shops, stalls, stores etc.

shopping centre *n* a group of shops of different kinds, planned and built as a whole

shore *n* land at the edge of the sea, lake, or large river

short *adj* 1 not far from one end to other
2 lasting only a little time; brief
3 less than it should be

shorten *v* to make shorter

shorthand *n* a way of writing quickly by means of symbols

shortly *adv* soon, in a little while

shorts *n* short trousers that come to just above your knee

shot *n* 1 the firing of a gun
2 lead pellets

shoulder *n* the part of your body between the neck and the upper arm

shout *n* a loud call or cry

shout *v* to raise your voice and call loudly

shove *v* to push hard

shovel *n* a large spade with a curved blade for scooping up loose materials

show *n* an entertainment

show *v* to let someone see something; to point out

shower *n* 1 a gentle fall of rain
2 a wash while standing under a spray of water

shred *n* a tiny scrap of something

shred *v* to cut or tear into strips

shrew *n* a small animal like a mouse

shriek *n* a high-pitched scream

shrill *adj* sounding very high and loud

shrimp *n* a small, grey shellfish that turns pink when cooked

shrink *v* to become smaller

shrivel *v* to become very dry and curl up, like a dead leaf

shrub *n* a low bush with several woody stems

shrug *v* to raise or lift your shoulders

shudder *v* to shake suddenly with fear or cold

shuffle *v* 1 to walk without lifting your feet
2 to mix up cards or other things

shut *v* to move a door or lid to close an opening

shuttle *n* a regular going to and fro by air, railway, bus etc.

shutter *n* 1 a strong window-cover
2 the part of the camera that opens and closes in front of the lens

shy *adj* not liking to meet or speak to other people

sick *adj* ill, not well

sickle *n* a cutting tool with a curved blade

Ss

sickness *n* illness, poor health

side *n*
1 a flat surface of an object
2 a team of players in a game
3 the part of your body between the hip and the shoulder

siege *n* the surrounding of a town by troops in an attempt to make them surrender

sieve *n* a fine metal or plastic net that lets only liquid and tiny pieces pass through

sigh *n* a heavy breathing out to show that you are tired, bored, or unhappy

sight *n*
1 the ability to see
2 something that is seen by someone

sign *n*
1 a board or other notice giving information, warning, directions etc.
2 a mark or action that has a meaning

sign *v* to write your name

signal *n* a message sent by movement, sound, or light

signal *v* to send a message by signs

signature *n* your name written by yourself in your own way

Sikh *n* a member of a religious sect founded in India

silage *n* animal fodder made from green crops and stored in a silo as winter food for cattle

silence *n* the absence of sound

silent *adj* not making any sound

silhouette *n* a picture or portrait like a black shadow

silk *n* fine, soft cloth made from the thread of silk worms

sill *n* a ledge below a window or door

silo *n* a tall, round tower that is used to store farm crops

silt *n* sand or mud left by rivers etc.

silver *n* a precious, shiny, soft, white metal

similar *adj* nearly the same

simmer *v* to cook at heat that is just less than boiling

simple *adj*
1 easy; not difficult
2 plain

simplify *v* to make simple and easy

sin *n* a wrong or bad deed; wickedness

sin *v* to do wrong

since *adv* from that time until now

since *conj* as; because

sincere *adj* honest and true

sincerely *adv* truly

sing *v* to make a tune with your voice, using sounds or words

silhouette

Ss

singe *v*		to burn slightly
singer *n*		someone who sings
single *adj*	*1*	one only
	2	unmarried
	3	for the use of one person only
singular *adj*		one person or thing; not plural
sinister *adj*		frightening, something that seems evil
sink *n*		a basin for washing in
sink *v*	*1*	to go under water
	2	to move slowly downwards
sip *n*		a small drink
sip *v*		to drink in small amounts
sir *n*	*1*	a title of respect given to men
	2	the title placed before the name of a knight or baronet
siren *n*		a machine that makes a loud screaming noise to warn people of danger
sister *n*		a woman or girl who has the same parents as you
sit *v*		to rest your bottom on a chair, stool etc.
site *n*		the place where something was built or will be built
situation *n*		a place or a position
size *n*	*1*	how big a thing is
	2	a particular measurement
skate *n*	*1*	a steel blade fixed to a boot for gliding on ice
	2	a kind of flat fish
skate *v*		to glide over ice with blades or to move on small wheels attached to footwear, on an even surface
skeleton *n*		the framework of bones in a body
sketch *n*	*1*	a quick drawing
	2	a short play
sketch *v*		to make a quick drawing
ski *n*		one of two long pieces of wood, metal, or plastic that curve up at the front for travelling on snow
skid *v*		to slip or slide on something slippery or very smooth
skill *n*		the power or ability to do something well
skim *v*	*1*	to remove something from the top of a liquid
	2	to glide; to pass lightly over
	3	to read very quickly
skin *n*		the outer covering of people, animals and of some fruits and vegetables
skinny *adj*		very thin
skip *v*	*1*	to jump lightly from one leg to the other, often over a rope
	2	to miss out pieces when reading
skipper *n*		the captain of a ship or boat
skirt *n*		a garment that hangs from the waist, worn by women
skull *n*		the bony framework of the head
sky *n*		the space above the earth where you can see the sun, moon, stars, and clouds
skyscraper *n*		a very tall building with many floors
slab *n*		a flat, thick piece of wood, stone etc.
slack *adj*	*1*	not tight, loose
	2	careless; lazy
slam *v*		to shut with a loud bang
slant *v*		to tilt; to lean in a direction that is not straight up and down
slap *n*		to hit with an open hand
slash *v*		to make long cuts in; to slit

slate *n*		a rock that splits into smooth thin sheets, and used as a roofing material
slaughter *v*	*1*	to kill animals for food
	2	to kill many people cruelly
slave *n*		a person who is owned by another person
slay *v*		to kill
sledge *n*		a wooden frame on metal runners; it is used to carry people or things over snow
sleek *adj*		smooth and shiny
sleep *v*		to rest in a state of natural unconsciousness
sleepy *adj*		tired; ready for bed
sleet *n*		a mixture of rain and snow
sleeve *n*		the part of a garment that covers your arm
slender *adj*		thin, narrow
slice *n*		a thin piece cut off something
slide *n*	*1*	a smooth surface used for sliding
	2	a clip to hold the hair in place
	3	a piece of framed film for use in a projector
	4	a small piece of glass to put an object on for seeing under a microscope
slight *adj*		not big or not important
slim *adj*		slender, thin
slime *n*		soft, sticky mud etc.
sling *n*		a piece of cloth used to support an injured arm
sling *v*		to throw something
slip *n*	*1*	a loose garment worn under a dress or skirt
	2	a piece of paper
	3	a mistake
slip *v*		to slide suddenly, losing your balance

slipper *n*		a soft, light shoe to wear indoors
slit *n*		a long cut or narrow opening
slogan *n*		a word or group of words used by a group or business to describe itself
slope *n*		a surface higher at one end than the other
sloppy *adj*	*1*	wet and messy
	2	careless
slot *n*		a narrow hole or slit
slouch *v*		to walk with your shoulders drooping
slow *adj*		taking a long time; moving at less than normal speed
slug *n*		a kind of snail without a shell
slum *n*		an area with old, poor, unhealthy houses where too many people have to live
slump *n*		a heavy or sudden fall or loss; a decline in trade
slump *v*		to fall or drop heavily
slush *n*		partly melted snow
sly *adj*		clever at tricking people in secret; cunning
smack *n*	*1*	a hard hit with the open hand
	2	a small fishing boat
smack *v*		to hit hard with the flat part of your hand
small *adj*		little; tiny
smart *adj*	*1*	quick to understand
	2	neat and well-dressed
smart *v*		to feel a stinging pain
smash *v*		to break into pieces
smell *n*		the sense that tells you what scent something has
smell *v*		to give off an odour or scent
smile *v*		to look joyful or amused
smith *n*		someone who makes things from metal

smog	*n*	dense, smoky fog
smoke	*n*	a dark cloud from something burning
smooth	*adj*	having an even surface; gentle to the touch
smother	*v*	to stop someone breathing by covering the mouth and nose
smoulder	*v*	to burn slowly without a flame but a lot of smoke
smudge	*n*	a dirty mark, stain
smuggle	*v*	to take goods into or out of a country secretly, against the law
snack	*n*	a light meal that is easy to get ready
snail	*n*	a small, slow creature with a shell on its back
snake	*n*	a long, smooth reptile without legs
snap	*n*	a sudden sharp sound or break
snap	*v*	*1* to bite at someone suddenly *2* to break or crack
snare	*n*	a trap used to catch animals
snarl	*n*	a low, growling sound
sneak	*n*	a sly, dishonest person
sneak	*v*	to move, trying not to be seen or heard
sneer	*n*	a look showing hatred or scorn
sneeze	*n*	a loud noise made when air rushes out of your nose
sniff	*v*	to breathe air in quickly through your nose
snip	*v*	to cut a little bit off
snore	*v*	to breathe noisily when you are asleep
snorkel	*n*	a tube for breathing air through when you are under water
snout	*n*	an animal's nose
snow	*n*	soft, white flakes of ice crystals that fall in cold weather
snowball	*n*	a ball made of tightly packed snow
snowdrop	*n*	a small white flower which appears in the early spring
snowplough	*n*	a machine for moving snow off roads or railways
snowstorm	*n*	a heavy fall of snow with a high wind
so	*adv*	*1* in this way *2* to such an extent *3* very
so	*conj*	therefore; for that reason
soak	*v*	to wet through
soap	*n*	a washing material made from fats and oils
soar	*v*	to rise high in the sky
sob	*v*	to cry noisily
soccer	*n*	football played by the rules of Association Football
sociable	*adj*	friendly; enjoying the company of other people
society	*n*	*1* a group of people with the same interests *2* human beings living together in a group
sock	*n*	a short stocking
socket	*n*	an opening into which something fits
sofa	*n*	a soft seat for two or more people
soft	*adj*	*1* not hard; easily pressed into another shape *2* quiet and gentle
soil	*n*	ground in which plants grow
soil	*v*	to make or become dirty
solar	*adj*	having to do with, or coming from the sun
soldier	*n*	a member of an army

Ss

sole *n*	*1* the part underneath a foot, sock, or shoe
	2 a kind of flat fish living in the ocean
solemn *adj*	very serious
solicitor *n*	a lawyer; a legal adviser
solid *adj*	firm right through, not hollow
solo *n*	*1* a piece of music for one singer or player
	2 something undertaken by one person
solution *n*	*1* the answer to a puzzle, problem or mystery
	2 a liquid having something dissolved in it
solve *v*	to find an answer or explanation for
some *adj*	*1* a few
	2 an amount of
somebody *(pron)*	a person, particularly when you are not sure who it is
somehow *adv*	in a way not known
somersault *n*	a turn head over heels
something *pron*	a thing not known
sometimes *adv*	once in a while, now and then
somewhere *adv*	in a place not known
son *n*	a male child
sonar *n*	a way of using sounds and their echoes to find objects in deep water
song *n*	a piece of music with words for singing
sonic boom *n*	the bang heard when an aircraft travels faster than the speed of sound
soon *adv*	in a short time
soot *n*	black powder that comes from smoke
soothe *v*	*1* to make calm
	2 to reduce pain
sore *n*	a painful place on the body
sore *adj*	painful, tender when touched or used.
sorrow *n*	sadness, unhappiness
sorry *adj*	feeling unhappy at something that has happened, or something you have done
sort *n*	a kind; a class
sort *v*	to put things in groups of the same kind
soul *n*	the part of a person that is thought to live forever
sound *n*	a noise
soup *n*	a liquid food made by boiling meat, fish, or vegetables in water
sour *adj*	*1* sharp-tasting like lemons; not sweet
	2 bad-tempered
source *n*	the place where something comes from
south *n*	the direction opposite north on a compass
souvenir *n*	something you keep to remind you of a certain time, place etc.
sow *n*	a female pig
sow *v*	to plant seeds
space *n*	*1* the distance between things
	2 a place that is empty
	3 all the places beyond the earth's atmosphere
spaceship *n*	a vehicle that carries astronauts in space
spade *n*	a garden tool used for digging
spaghetti *n*	an Italian food made of pasta in long strings
span *n*	the length of something
spaniel *n*	a dog with long hair, drooping ears, and short legs

spank *v* to smack with the open hand

spare *adj* left over, not being used

spare *v* to give or lend something

spark *n*
1 a speck of something burning
2 a tiny electric flash

sparkle *v* to flash or glitter

sparrow *n* a small, common bird with brown, grey and white feathers

spawn *n* the eggs of fish, frogs, newts and other water animals

speak *v* to say in words

spear *n* a weapon with a long handle and a sharp point

special *adj* something not ordinary or usual

specialist *n* an expert in a particular subject or skill

speck *n* a tiny bit, a small spot

spectacles *n* a pair of lenses in a frame worn in front of your eyes to help you see better

spectacular *adj* very unusual

spectator *n* someone watching a game or other entertainment

speech *n*
1 the ability to speak
2 a talk given to an audience

speed *n* how quickly something moves or happens

speedometer *n* an instrument that shows the speed of a vehicle

spell *v* to write or say the letters of a word, in the corect order

spend *v*
1 to pay out money
2 to stay a period of time

sphere *n* a round object like a ball

spice *n* part of a plant used to flavour food

spider *n* a small creature with eight legs and no wings

spike *n* a long, sharp nail

spill *v* to let a liquid overflow

spin *v*
1 to turn round quickly in one place, like a top
2 to make thread by twisting fibres together

spinach *n* a dark green, leafy vegetable

spine *n* the long line of bones down the middle of your back; the backbone

spiral *n* a curve that keeps on winding, like the thread of a screw

spirit *n*
1 a person's soul
2 a ghost
3 a liquid containing much alcohol

spit *v* to force liquid from your mouth

spite *n* a wish to hurt someone by cruel behaviour

splash *n* the noise made when someone or something heavy falls into water

splash *v* to throw liquid about

splendid *adj* magnificent, wonderful

splinter *n* a thin, sharp piece of wood, glass or metal

split *n* a crack; a long thin break

split *v* to crack; to break open from end to end

spoil *v* to make or become damaged or useless

spoke *n* one of the rods or bars that connect the rim of a wheel to the centre

sponge *n*
1 a sea animal with a very light, soft body
2 a soft pad, full of holes, that soaks up liquid

sponsor *n* a person or company who pays for a show, broadcast, sports event etc., usually in return for advertising

Ss

spoon *n* a small, shallow bowl at the end of a handle

sport *n* games and pastimes such as football, tennis, snooker, darts etc.

spot *n*
1 a small mark
2 a special place

spot *v* to see, to notice

spotlight *n* a strong beam of light that can be moved around

spout *n* the narrow part of a container through which liquid flows

spout *v* to gush out with force

sprain *v* to damage a joint in your body by sudden twisting

sprawl *v* to sit or lie with arms and legs spread out

spray *n*
1 liquid carried through the air in tiny drops
2 a bunch of flowers

spray *v* to scatter fine drops of liquid

spread *v*
1 to open out
2 to cover a surface

spring *n*
1 the season after winter
2 a place where water flows out of the ground
3 a coil of metal or wire

spring *v* to jump up suddenly

sprinkle *v* to scatter powder or drops of liquid

sprint *v* to run very quickly for a short distance

sprout *v* to begin to grow

spruce *n* an evergreen tree with cones, and leaves that look like green needles

spur *n* a spiked wheel on a rider's boot, sometimes used to make the horse go faster

spurt *n* a short, sudden, extra effort

spurt *v* to gush out suddenly

spy *n* someone who tries secretly to find out things about a person or an enemy country

spy *v*
1 to watch secretly
2 to catch sight of

squabble *v* to quarrel noisily about small things

squad *n* a small group of trained people

square *n*
1 a flat shape with four equal sides and four equal angles
2 an open space with buildings on all sides

square 1

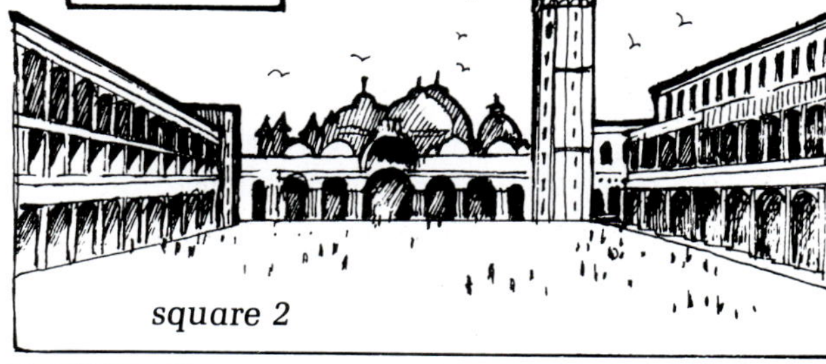

square 2

squash *n*
1 a game played in a four-walled court with rackets and a hollow, rubber ball
2 a crushed-fruit drink

squash *v* to squeeze or crush

squat *v* to sit on the floor or the ground with legs bent in front of your body

squat *adj* short and thick

squeak *n* a short, high sound

squeal *n* a long, high cry

squeeze *v* to press something hard

squirrel *n* a small grey or red animal with a bushy tail

squirt *v* to shoot out a jet of liquid

stab *v* to wound someone with a pointed object

stable *n* a building in which horses are kept

stack *n* a large pile; a heap

stack *v* to pile up

stadium *n* a sports ground with seats and standing room for spectators

staff *n*
1 a stick or pole
2 a group of people who work together

stage *n*
1 the raised platform in a theatre on which people perform
2 the point someone has reached in doing something

stagecoach *n* a large, closed coach pulled by a team of horses

stagger *v* to walk in an unsteady way

stain *n*
1 a dirty mark or patch
2 a paint or dye

stain *v* to mark; to change the colour of something

staircase *n* a set of steps with a handrail

stairs *n* a set of steps leading from one floor of a building to another

stake *n* a thick post, pointed at one end and hammered into the ground

stalactite *n* a sharp downward-pointing part of a cave roof, shaped like an icicle, caused by the dripping of water containing lime

stalagmite *n* an upward-pointing part of a cave floor

stale *adj* not fresh; old

stalk *n* a stem of a flower or plant

stalk *v* to hunt quietly, keeping out of sight

stall *n*
1 a stand for displaying goods
2 a place for a cow or horse to stand in a barn or stable

stall *v* to lose flying speed in an aircraft and fall out of control

stallion *n* a male horse

stamen *n* the part of the flower which produces pollen

stamina *n* staying power; strength

stammer *v* to speak with pauses and repeated sounds

stamp *v*
1 to bang your foot on the ground
2 to make a mark by pressure

stamp *n* a small label bought at a post office which has to go on letters and packages

stampede *n* a sudden rush of frightened people and animals

stand *n* something on which things can be displayed

stand *v*
1 to be on your feet or rise to your feet
2 to bear, to put up with

star *n*
1 a heavenly body that looks like a speck of light at night
2 an outstanding actress, actor, musician, sports player etc.

star *v* to have a leading part in a play, film etc.

starboard *n* the right-hand side of a ship or aircraft

starch *n* an important food substance formed in plants

stare *v* to look in a fixed way with wide-open eyes

starfish *n* a small sea creature that has a star-shaped body

starling *n* a common bird with greenish-black speckled plumage

start *n*
1 a beginning
2 a sudden movement of surprise

Ss

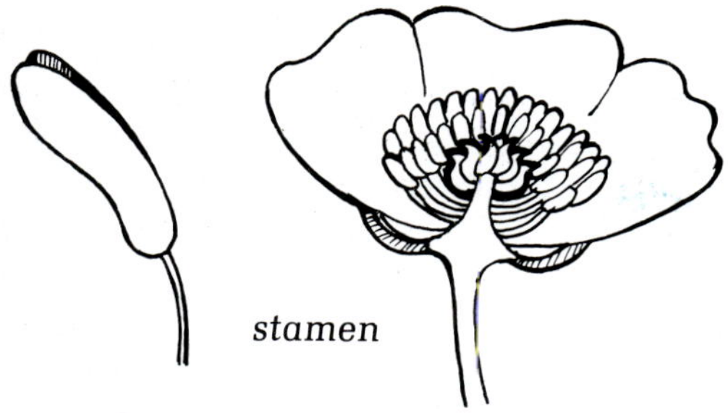
stamen

start *v*
1 to begin
2 to move suddenly

startle *v* to surprise or frighten

starve *v* to suffer or die from hunger

state *n*
1 how someone or something is
2 a nation

state *v* to say firmly

statement *n* something said or written

station *n*
1 a stopping place for trains and buses
2 a building used for firemen, police etc.

stationary *adv* not moving

stationery *n* writing paper, envelopes etc.

statistics *n* facts and figures collected and arranged for information

statue *n* a figure carved from stone or cast in metal

stay *v*
1 to remain behind
2 to live somewhere for a short time

steady *adj*
1 firm; not wobbling
2 not changing

steak *n* a slice of meat or fish for cooking

steal *v* to take something that is not yours, and keep it

steam *n* water in the form of gas or vapour

steel *n* a strong metal, made from iron

steep *adj* sloping sharply

steeple *n* a church tower with a top part rising to a point

steer *n* a young bull

steer *v* to make a ship or vehicle go where you want

stem *n* the stalk of a plant

step *n*
1 the part of a staircase on which you walk
2 a movement made when you walk

step *v* to move your feet when walking or dancing

stereo *n* sound that is put through two or more loudspeakers

sterling *n* the money of Great Britain

stern *n* the back part of a ship

stern *adj* strict; harsh

stew *n* meat and vegetables cooked gently together in water

steward *n* a person who looks after passengers on an aircraft, ship etc. (fem. stewardess)

stick *n* a thin piece of wood

stick *v* to glue or fix things together

stiff *adj* not easy to move or bend

still *adj* quiet and with no movement

stilts *n* two poles, each with a step part way up, for walking high above the ground

sting *n* a sharp-pointed weapon in some insects, animals and plants

stingy *adj* not willing to spend money or share something

stink *n* a bad smell

stir *v* to mix soft or liquid things with an object such as a spoon

stirrups *n* a rider's footrests hanging from each side of a horse's saddle

stitch *n*
1 a loop of thread made in sewing or knitting
2 a sudden pain in your side

stoat *n* a small slim brown mammal of the weasel family with reddish-brown fur

stock *n*
1 a supply of things kept to be used or sold
2 animals on a farm

stocking *n* a long, close-fitting cover for your leg and foot

stomach *n* the part of your body that receives food and begins to digest it

stone *n*
1 a small piece of rock
2 the hard seed of some fruits

stool *n* a small seat with no back or arms

stoop *v* to bend your body forward

stop *v*
1 to come to a halt
2 to prevent

stop *n*
1 a place where a bus or train halts for passengers
2 a short stay

store *n* a large shop

store *v* to keep things until they are needed

storey *n* a floor in a building with all its rooms

Ss

stork *n* a large, white bird with a long beak, neck and legs

storm *n* bad weather with heavy rain or snow, strong winds, and sometimes thunder

story *n* an account of real or imagined happenings

stout *adj* thick and heavy

stove *n* an apparatus used for cooking or heating

stowaway *n* someone who hides in a ship or plane without paying the fare

straight *adj*
1 not bent or curved
2 true and honest

strain *n* an injury caused by too much effort

strain *v*
1 to stretch, pull, push or try too much
2 to pass liquid through a net or cloth of tiny holes

strait *n* a narrow channel of water connecting two seas

strand *n* one of many threads or wires twisted together to make a rope or wire

strand *v* to leave in a dangerous or difficult situation

strange *adj* unusual; odd

stranger *n* someone you do not know

strangle *v* to kill by pressing hard on the throat

strap *n* a strip of leather or some other material

strategy *n* a plan for achieving something

straw *n*
1 the dried stems of corn or other cereals
2 a thin tube for drinking through

strawberry *n* the juicy red fruit of a plant that grows close to the ground

stray *n* a lost person or animal

stray *v* to wander about and get lost

streak *n* a line or stripe of contrasting colour

streak *v*
1 to mark with stripes
2 to move quickly

stream *n*
1 a small river
2 a movement of water, air, light, traffic, people etc.

street *n* a road with buildings on each side

strength *n* how strong something or someone is; power

stretch *v* to make something longer by pulling it
2 to reach
stretcher *n* a movable bed for carrying sick or injured people
strict *adj* firm; severe
strike *n* a stopping of work because of a dispute
strike *v* *1* to hit with a lot of force
2 to refuse to work because of a dispute
string *n* *1* a thin cord for tying things
2 a cord or wire on a musical instrument
strip *n* a long, narrow piece
strip *v* *1* to tear off e.g. wallpaper from a wall
2 to undress
stripe *n* a long, narrow streak of colour
stroke *n* *1* a blow
2 a swimming movement
3 a mark made by a brush, pen, or crayon
stroke *v* to rub gently
stroll *v* to walk slowly and easily
strong *adj* powerful, having strength
structure *n* anything that is built
struggle *n* a hard fight or effort
struggle *v* to make a great effort; to fight
stubborn *adj* not willing to change or to do what other people want
student *n* someone who is studying at a place of education or training
stud *n* a number of horses kept for breeding
studio *n* *1* a workroom for an artist or photographer
2 a place where films, radio and television programmes, or records are made
study *v* to spend time in learning
stuff *n* the material from which something is made
stuff *v* to pack full
stuffing *n* *1* a filling used to stuff a chicken, turkey etc., before cooking it
2 padding or filling in a pillow or cushion
stumble *v* to trip over something and nearly fall
stump *n* the part of a tree left in the ground after the trunk has been cut down
stump *n* to puzzle or confuse
stun *v* *1* to knock unconscious or nearly so
2 to astonish
stunt *n* something done to attract attention or gain publicity
stunt *v* to slow down the growth
stupid *adj* silly; not clever
sturdy *adj* strong and healthy
sty *n* a place where pigs are kept
style *n* the way something is done or made
sub a prefix meaning 'under'
submarine *n* a ship that can travel underwater
submerge *v* to go beneath the surface of a liquid
submit *v* to give in, to surrender
substance *n* anything that can be seen or touched
substitute *v* to put someone or something in place of another
subtract *v* to take away
suburb *n* an area of houses on the edge of a town or city
subway *n* an underground passage for pedestrians

succeed *v*	*1*	to manage to do what you are trying to do
	2	to come after; to take the place of
success *n*		a favourable ending or result
such *adj*	*1*	of the same kind
	2	so great
suck *v*		to draw something into your mouth
sudden *adj*		quick; unexpected
sue *v*		to use the law when you feel you have been unfairly treated
suffer *v*		to feel great pain or sorrow
sufficient *adj*		enough
suffix *n*		a syllable or syllables added at the end of a word to make another word e.g. water and proof = waterproof
suffocate *v*		to ckoke, to keep from breathing
sugar *n*		a sweet substance used in cooking and put in drinks
suggest *v*		to offer an idea to other people
suggestion *n*		an idea, plan or thought
suit *n*	*1*	a set of clothes to be worn together
	2	one of the four sets in a pack of playing-cards
suit *v*		to be right for
suitcase *n*		a flat bag for carrying clothes
sulk *v*		to be in a funny mood and silent
sum *n*		the total obtained when adding numbers, quantities or items
summary *n*		a short description giving the main points
summer *n*		the season after spring
summit *n*		the top, the highest point
sun *n*		the bright star we see during the day; it sends us heat and light
sunbeam *n*		a ray of sunshine
sunburn *n*		the burning of your skin by the sun
sunflower *n*		a large yellow flower that grows on a tall plant
sunrise *n*		the time when the sun comes up
sunset *n*		the time when the sun goes down
sunshine *n*		the sun's heat and rays
super		a prefix meaning 'a lot of', 'great', 'above'
superb *adj*		excellent, splendid
superior *adj*		better than
supermarket *n*		a very large, self-service store that sells food and household goods
supernatural *adj*		something that does not have an ordinary explanation
supersonic *adj*		travelling faster than sound
superstition *n*		a belief in magic and supernatural powers
supervise *v*		to oversee, watch over, control
supervisor **n**		a person who is in charge
supper *n*		a meal eaten at the end of the day
supply *v*		to provide what is needed
support *v*	*1*	to hold up
	2	to provide what is needed
suppose *v*	*1*	to imagine; to pretend
	2	to think something is likely to happen
sure *adj*	*1*	certain
	2	safe; reliable
surf *n*		waves breaking on the seashore
surface *n*		the outside or top part of anything

surgeon *n* — a doctor who does operations

surgery *n*
1 the treatment of illness and injury by operations to the body
2 a room where a doctor or dentist sees patients

surname *n* — your family name

surprise *n* — something unexpected

surprise *v* — to catch unawares

surrender *v* — to give in to

surround *v* — to enclose; to be all around

survive *v* — to remain alive

suspect *n* — someone thought to be guilty of a crime

suspect *v* — to be doubtful of; to think there is something wrong

suspend *v*
1 to hang something so that it can swing
2 to stop, cancel or postpone

suspense *n* — the feeling of being uncertain and worried that something may happen

suspicious *adj* — feeling that something is wrong, not trusting

swallow *n* — a small bird with long, slim wings and a forked tail; it flies to northern countries in summer

swallow *v* — to pass food and drink down your throat

swamp *n* — an area of soft, very wet ground

swan *n* — a very large waterbird with a long neck

swarm *n* — a large group of insects

sway *v* — to swing from side to side

swear *v*
1 to use bad language
2 to make a promise or take an oath

sweat *n* — the moisture from your skin when you are very hot or ill

sweater *n* — a knitted piece of clothing worn on the top part of your body

swede *n* — a variety of turnip

sweep *n* — to clean with a brush

sweet *adj*
1 tasting like sugar
2 pleasant to smell, taste or hear

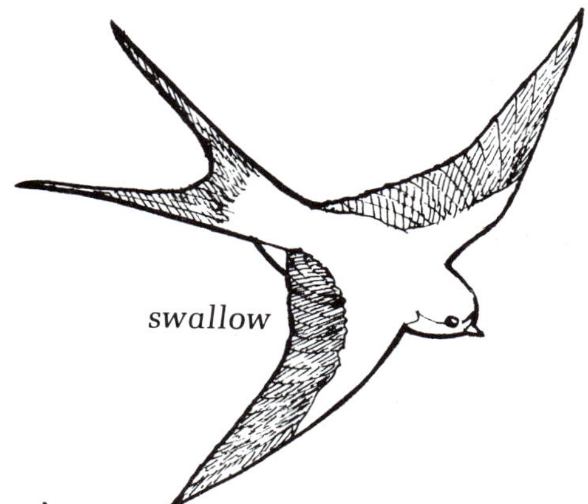

swallow

swamp

swarm

Ss

swell *v* to keep growing bigger
swerve *v* to change direction quickly
swift *adj* fast, speedy, quick
swim *v* to move through the water using your arms and legs
swindle *v* to cheat, usually over money
swing *n* a seat hanging on ropes or chains on which you can move back and forth
swing *v* *1* to move back and forth
2 to turn quickly
swirl *v* to move around and around
switch *n* a little knob or button used to turn something on or off
switch *v* *1* to change from one thing to another
2 to turn on or off with an electrical switch
swoop *v* to move down quickly
sword *n* a weapon with a long steel blade and a handle
sycamore *n* a large, broad-leaved tree of the maple family
syllable *n* one section or part of a word that can be said by itself.
syllabus *n* a programme for a course of study
symbol *n* something that stands for or represents something else; an emblem
symmetry an exact likeness between the opposite sides of something
sympathy *n* a feeling for another person's illness, loss, unhappiness etc.
synagogue *n* a building for Jewish worship and teaching
syringe *n* an instrument for squirting or injecting liquids
syrup *n* a thick, sweet liquid
system *n* a way of doing things

Ss
Tt

Tt

tab *n* a label; a small flap
tabby *n* a cat whose fur has dark stripes
table *n* *1* a piece of furniture with a flat top and legs
2 a list of facts and figures
table-cloth *n* a piece of cloth spread over a table to cover it
tablespoon *n* a large spoon used for serving food
tablet *n* *1* a small, round, hard piece of medicine which you swallow
2 a piece of soap
table tennis *n* a game played on a table, using bats and a small, white, celluloid ball
tack *n* *1* a small nail
2 a long, loose stitch
tack *v* *1* to stitch loosely
2 to sail a boat on a zig-zag course into the wind
tackle *n* the things you need for some kind of sports or jobs
tackle *v* *1* to try to do a job that needs doing
2 in rugby, to bring an opponent down
3 in soccer, to try to get the ball from an opponent
tadpole *n* a very young frog or toad, at the stage between the egg and the adult

tail *n*
1 the movable back end of an animal, fish, or bird
2 end or back part of something, such as the tail of an aeroplane

tailor *n* a person who makes clothes

take *v*
1 to get hold of something or someone
2 to carry something
3 to remove something
4 to steal

take-away *n* a shop or restaurant that sells hot food that you buy and take it out with you

tale *n* a story, true or made-up

talent *n* the ability to do something very well

talk *v* to speak to other people

talkative *adj* fond of talking

tall *adj* measuring more than usual from top to bottom

talon *n* a long claw of a bird of prey, such as a hawk

tambourine *n* a small, shallow drum with jingling cymbals around it

tame *adj* not wild or fierce; not dangerous to humans

tamper *v* to meddle with; to interfere

tan *n*
1 skin that has gone brown because of the sun
2 a light brown colour

tan *v* to make animal skins into leather

tapestry

tandem *n* a bicycle for two riders

tandoori *n* a kind of Indian cookery

tang *n* a sharp taste

tangerine *n* a small, juicy fruit that is similar to an orange

tangle *v* to mix threads, string etc., so that it is difficult to undo

tank *n*
1 a large container that holds liquid or gas
2 an armoured fighting vehicle with guns, which moves on tracks instead of wheels

tanker *n*
1 a large ship for carrying oil
2 a large lorry for carrying liquids such as oil, milk etc.

tantrum *n* a sudden fit of bad temper

tap *n* a device for turning on and off the flow of water, gas etc.

tap *v* to hit something quickly and lightly

tape *n*
1 a long, narrow strip of cloth, paper, or plastic
2 a thin, narrow strip with one sticky side
3 a narrow strip of plastic coated with a magnetic substance used to make sound or video recordings

tape measure *n* a long narrow tape marked out in centimetres or inches

tape-recorder *n* a machine that records sounds on special tape, which can be played back later

tapestry *n* a picture on cloth, made by sewing or weaving in coloured threads

tar *n* a thick, black, sticky substance used in road-making

tarantula *n* a large, hairy spider

target *n* something that people aim at and try to hit

tarnish *v* to become dull; to lose its shine

tart *n* a piece of pastry with fruit or jam on it

tart *adj* very sour

tartan *n* a woollen cloth with a check pattern, made in Scotland and used for making kilts

task *n* a job to be done

tassel *n* a bundle of hanging threads

taste *n* the sense by which you can tell the flavour of food and drink

taste *v* to eat a little bit of food or sip a drink to see what it is like

tasty *adj* good to eat; having a good flavour

tattered *adj* torn, ragged

tattoo *n*
1 a coloured picture or design put on someone's skin with a needle and dyes
2 a military display at night

tax *n* money that is paid to a government to help pay for education, health, roads etc.

taxi *n* a car with a driver that can be hired for short journeys

taxi *v* to move along the ground before or after flying

Tt

tea *n*
1 a drink made by pouring boiling water over dried leaves of a plant
2 an afternoon meal

teach *v* to show people how to do things, to give lessons

teacher *n* someone who gives lessons

teak *n* a very hard wood grown in Burma, India and Thailand

team *n* a group of people who work together or play together on the same side in a game

tea-bag *n* a small bag containing tea-leaves

teapot *n* a container in which tea is made; it has a handle, a spout and a lid

tear *n* a drop of salty water coming from your eye

tear *v* to pull something apart so that you damage it

tease *v* to bother or annoy someone for fun

teaspoon *n* a small spoon used for eating, stirring and measuring

teem *v*
1 to swarm, to be present in large numbers
2 to rain very hard

teenager *n* a person who is between 13 and 19 years of age

tee-shirt *n* a short-sleeved shirt, like a vest, with no collar or buttons

teeth *n* plural of 'tooth'

teetotal *adj* never drinking alcohol

telegram *n* a short message that is sent quickly along electric wires or by radio

telephone *n* an instrument connected by wires to other apparatus which enables people to speak to each other over long distances

telescope *n* a tube with glass lenses that make distant things look larger and nearer

television *n* an apparatus that receives certain kinds of radio signals and turns them into pictures and sound

tell *v* to give information to somebody

temper *n* the mood someone is in; it can be good or bad

temperature *n* how hot or cold something is

temple *n* a building for prayer and worship

tempo *n* the speed at which a piece of music is played

temporary *adj* lasting for a short time; not permanent

tempt *v* to try to make someone do something, usually something that is foolish or wrong

tenant *n* a person who rents somewhere to live or work

tend *v*
1 to look after
2 to be likely to do something

tender *adj*
1 delicate, soft, easily hurt
2 sore

tennis *n* a game played by two or four people with rackets and a ball on a court with a net across the middle

tent *n* a canvas or nylon shelter, held up by poles

tentacle *n* a leg or feeler of some animals

term *n* a period of time during which a school or college is open

terminal *n*
1 the building where you start or finish a journey by plane etc.
2 one of the two places on a battery for wires to be attached

terminate *v* to end

terminus *n* the end of a railway line or bus route

termite *n* a small, ant-like insect that eats wood

terrace *n*
1 a level area cut out of a slope
2 a raised, level place in front of a building
3 a row of houses built as a single block

terrapin *n* a type of small turtle that lives in warm seas

terrible *adj* very bad, frightening, awful

terrier *n* a kind of small dog

terrific *adj*
1 very great
2 very good

terrify *v* to cause great fear

territory *n* an area of land

terror *n* great fear, panic

test *n* an examination

test *v*
1 to find out how much someone knows
2 to try out

testament *n* one of the two main parts of the Bible — the Old Testament and the New Testament

test match *n* an international match in cricket and some other games

test-pilot *n* someone who flies a new aircraft to see whether it works

test-tube *n* a long, narrow glass bottle used for experiments

tether *n* a rope for tying up an animal

text *n* the words in a book

textbook *n* a book giving information for study in a school or a college

texture *n* the feel or look of something

than *conj* compared with another person or thing

thank *v* to tell people you are grateful for something given to you or done for you
thatch *n* a roof covering made from reeds or straw
thaw *n* the melting of snow or ice
theatre *n* a place where people go to see plays, concerts etc.
theft *n* the act of stealing
their *adj* belonging to them
theirs *pron* thing that belongs to them
them *pron* word that you say when you speak about other people or things
theme *n* the main subject or topic
themselves *pron* they and no one else
then *adv* *1* at that time
2 therefore, for that reason
3 after that; next
there *adv* in that place; to that place
therefore *adv* for that reason; and so
thermometer *n* an instrument that measures temperature
Thermos *n* the trade name for a container that keeps hot drinks, soup etc. hot
thermostat *n* an automatic device for controlling temperature
thick *adj* *1* measuring a lot from one side to the other
2 flowing stiffly
3 crowded together
thicken *v* to make or become thick
thief *n* someone who steals
thigh *n* the part of your leg between the knee and hip
thimble *n* a metal or plastic cap, worn to protect the end of your finger when sewing
thin *adj* lean, slim; not thick
thing *n* anything that can be seen or touched
think *v* *1* to use your mind
2 to have an idea, an opinion
third *adj* next after second
third *n* one of the three parts that make the whole thing
thirst *n* a strong desire or need to drink
thirsty *adj* wanting a drink
this *adj, pron* the one here, not a different one
thistle *n* a wild plant with prickly leaves
thorn *n* a sharp point on a stem or branch
thorough *adj* *1* done properly
2 complete
though *conj* even so; even if; although
thought *n* what is in your mind when thinking
thoughtful *adj* *1* thinking deeply
2 thinking of others; kind
thoughtless *adj* careless, not thinking about other people or things
thread *n* a length of spun fibre such as cotton, wool, or nylon, used in sewing or weaving cloth
thread *v* to put thread through the eye of a needle
threat *n* a warning that harm or punishment may be coming
thrifty *adj* careful about the way you use money
thrill *n* an excited feeling
thriller *n* a scary book, play or film
thrilling *n* very exciting
throat *n* the inside of the neck, used for swallowing food and breathing
throb *v* to beat with a steady rhythm
throne *n* a special chair for a king or queen
throng *n* a large number of people

through *prep* from end to end; from the beginning to the end of

through *adv* all the way

throw *v* to make something move through the air

thrush *n* a brown song-bird often seen in gardens

thrust *v* to push hard and suddenly

thud *n* a dull, heavy sound

thug *n* someone who attacks and harms other people

thumb *n* the short, thick finger on your hand

thump *v* to hit something heavily

thunder *n* the loud noise that follows lightning in a storm

thunderstorm *n* a rainstorm with thunder and lightning

tick *n*
1 the sound that a clock or watch makes
2 a small mark (✓)

ticket *n* a piece of printed card or paper that allows travel on a bus or train, or entry into a cinema, theatre etc.

tickle *v* to touch a person's skin lightly, often causing laughter

tide *n* the regular rise and fall of the sea

tidy *adj* neat, with everything in order

tie *n* a thin piece of cloth worn knotted around the neck of a shirt

tie *v* to fasten something with string or rope

tiger *n* a large, striped animal belonging to the cat family

tight *adj* fitting very closely

tights *n (pl)* a piece of clothing that fits closely over the feet, legs, and lower part of the body

tile *n* a thin piece of baked clay or other material for covering roofs, walls or floors

till *n* a drawer for money on the counter of a shop

till *v* to plough and cultivate the land

till *prep* up to; as late as

tiller *n* a handle or lever for turning a boat's rudder from side to side

tilt *v* to lean to one side

timber *n* the sawn and prepared wood from trees, ready for use in building etc.

time *n*
1 a movement shown on a clock or watch
2 seconds, minutes, hours, days, weeks, months, and years
3 the speed and rhythm of a piece of music

timid *adj* shy, nervous, afraid

tin *n*
1 a soft, white metal
2 a metal container for keeping foods etc.

tingle *v* to have a slight prickly feeling on the skin

tinkle *v* to make a light, ringing sound, such as a small bell makes

tinsel *n* glittering and sparkling strips used for decoration, particularly at Christmas

tint *n* a shade of colour

tiny *adj* very small

tip *n*
1 the point or the end of something
2 extra money given to someone who has done a service for you
3 a place where rubbish is left
4 a piece of advice

tip *v* 1 to tilt or overturn
2 to give extra money for a service

tiptoe *v* to walk quietly on the tip of your toes

tired *adj* feeling that you need to rest or sleep

tissue *n* very thin, soft paper

title *n* 1 the name of a book, song, film etc.
2 a word like Sir, Lady, Dr. etc. that is put in front of a person's name

titter *v* to laugh in a silly way

toad *n* an animal that lives on land and in water: it looks like a frog, but has rougher skin

toadstool *n* a kind of fungus which looks like a mushroom, but is often poisonous

toast *n* bread that is made crisp and brown by heating it

toaster *n* an electrical device that toasts bread

tobacco *n* a plant whose leaves are dried and used for smoking in pipes, cigars, or cigarettes

toboggan *n* a long, flat sledge for sliding down snowy hills

today *n* this day

toddler *n* a small child just learning to walk

toe *n* one of the five end parts of your foot

toffee *n* a sticky kind of sweet

together *adv* 1 in company with someone or something
2 at the same time

toil *v* to work very hard

toilet *n* a bowl containing water, used for flushing away body wastes; a lavatory

token *n* a sign, mark, or symbol

tolerate *v* to allow to happen; to put up with

toll *n* a charge made for using some roads and bridges

toll *v* to ring a bell slowly

tomahawk *n* a small axe, once used by North American Indians as a tool or weapon

tomato *n* a round, red, juicy fruit eaten as a vegetable

tomb *n* a place where a dead person's body is buried

tom-cat *n* a male cat

tomorrow *n* the day after today

ton *n* a unit of weight equal to 1016kg

tone *n* 1 a musical sound
2 a shade of a colour

tongue *n* the soft, fleshy part your mouth, used for licking and tasting

tonight *n* this evening or night

tonne *n* a metric unit of weight, 1000kg

tonsils *n (pl)* the two soft, small organs at the back of the throat

too *adv* 1 also; as well as
2 more than is needed

tool *n* something that helps you to do a job, such as a hammer, screwdriver etc.

tooth *n* one of the bonelike parts in your mouth, used for chewing and biting

toothache *n* a pain in a tooth

toothbrush *n* a small brush on a long handle, used to clean teeth

toothpaste *n* a paste for cleaning the teeth

top *n* 1 the highest point
2 the upper side
3 a toy which can be made to spin

Tt

topic *n* something interesting that you are writing or talking about

topple *v* to fall down

torch *n* an electric light that you can carry about with you

torment *v* to tease; to annoy; to cause distress

tornado *n* a violent storm with winds that whirl around at high speed

torpedo *n* a weapon which travels under water to destroy ships

torrent *n* a very fast stream of water

tortoise *n* a slow-moving land reptile with a hard shell

torture *n* great pain

torture *v* to cause horrible pain

toss *v* to throw up into the air

total *n* the full amount

totem pole *n* a tall pole with many carvings on it, made by the Pacific Coast Indians of North America

totter *v* to walk unsteadily

toucan *n* a large bird with an enormous orange beak

touch *v*
1 to feel with your fingers or some other part of your body
2 to be so close to something else that there is no space in between

touchdown *n* a score made in American and Canadian football by getting the ball across the other team's goal

tough *adj*
1 tough; not easily broken or bent
2 hard to chew

tour *n* a journey on which a number of places are visited

tour *v* to travel about from place to place

tourist *n* a person on holiday who travels about to see different places and things

tournament *n* a series of games or contests

tow *v* to pull along with a rope or chain

toward, towards *prep* in the direction of

towel *n* a piece of cloth for drying yourself after washing or swimming

tower *n* a tall or narrow building, or part of a building

town *n* an area with a large number of houses, shops, offices, factories etc.

towpath *n* a path beside a canal or river

toy *n* something to play with

trace *v*
1 to copy something by placing transparent paper on top of it and drawing over the lines
2 to search for and find someone or something

track *n*
1 the set of metal rails a train travels along
2 marks left on the ground by something moving
3 a kind of path

tractor *n* a machine with wheels and a powerful engine that is used on farms to pull farm machinery

trade *n* buying and selling

tradition *n* something done over and over, and passed on from parents to their children

traffic *n* the movement of cars, buses, lorries and other vehicles along the roads

traffic jam *n* when a road is so full of vehicles none of them can move

traffic lights *n (pl)* electric lights that change from green to amber and red to control vehicles

traffic warden *n* a person who controls the movement and parking of vehicles in a town

tragedy *n* a very sad happening

tragic *adj* very sad, terrible

trail *n* 1 marks on the ground showing which way some animal or person has gone
2 a rough path

trail *v* 1 to pull something along behind
2 to follow behind

trailer *n* a vehicle that is pulled by another vehicle

train *n* railway coaches or wagons joined together and pulled by a locomotive

train *v* 1 to practise for something
2 to teach a person or animal to do something

trainer *n* 1 a person who teaches people a sport
2 someone who teaches animals to do something

traitor *n* someone who betrays country or friends

tram *n* a kind of bus that runs on rails like a train; a streetcar

tramp *n* a homeless person who wanders, or tramps, from place to place

tramp *v* to walk heavily

trample *v* to tread heavily on something and so spoil it

trampoline *n* a large piece of canvas held to a frame by strong springs for bouncing up and down on

trance *n* a kind of sleep

transfer *v* to move somebody or something to another place

transistor *n* 1 a very small electronic device that is used in radios, televisions, calculators, and other electrical equipment
2 a radio that uses transistors and is easy to carry from place to place

translate *v* to put into another language

transparent *adj* something that is clear enough to see through

transplant *v* 1 to move a plant from one place and put it to grow somewhere else
2 to move an organ, such as a heart or a kidney, from one person's body to another

transport *v* to carry people or goods from one place to another

transport *n* vehicles, ships or planes used to carry people and goods

trap *n* something for catching animals etc.

trapdoor *n* a kind of door in the floor or ceiling

trapeze *n* a swinging bar held by two ropes, used by acrobats

travel *v* to go from one place to another

traveller *n* a person who travels

trawler *n* a fishing boat that drags (or trawls) its nets along the bottom of the sea to catch fish

tray *n* a flat piece of wood, metal, or plastic used for carrying things

treacle *n* a thick, sticky liquid made from sugar

tread *v* to walk on something

tread *n* the part of a tyre with a pattern cut into it that touches the road

treason *n* helping the enemy of your country

treasure *n* something very valuable such as gold, precious stones etc.

treasure *v* to value very highly

treasurer *n* the person in charge of the money of a business or a club

treat *n* something that pleases you very much

treat *v*
1 to behave in a certain way towards somebody or something
2 to pay for another person's food and drink
3 to try to cure a sick person

treaty *n* an agreement with nations

tree *n* a large plant with leaves, branches, and a woody trunk

trek *n* a long and tiring journey

tremble *v* to shake or shiver with fear, excitement, or cold

tremendous *adj* of great size or power

trench *n* a long, narrow ditch dug in the ground

trespass *v* to go on somebody else's land or property without permission

trial *n* the hearing in court to decide whether a person is innocent or guilty of doing wrong

triangle *n*
1 a flat shape with three straight edges and three corners
2 a musical instrument made from a steel rod bent to the shape of a triangle

tribe *n* a group of people who have the same customs and language

trick *n*
1 something done to deceive someone or make someone look foolish
2 a piece of 'magic' done by a conjuror

trick *v* to fool; to cheat

trickle *n* a small flow of something

trickle *v* to flow or fall in drops or a small stream

tricycle *n* a three-wheeled cycle

trifle *n* a sweet pudding made from pieces of sponge cake, custard, fruit, cream, and other ingredients

trigger *n* the small lever on a gun or pistol that is pulled to make it fire

trim *adj* neat and tidy

trim *v* to cut something so as to make it neat and tidy

trio *n* a group of three

trip *n* a short journey

trip *v* to stumble, to catch your foot on something

tripe *n* part of the stomach of an ox or a cow eaten as food

triple *adj*
1 having three parts
2 three times as much or as many

triple *v* to multiply by three

triplet *n* one of three children born to the same mother at one time

triumph *n* a great victory or success

troll *n* a goblin or dwarf, usually evil, in Scandinavian legends

trolley *n*
1 a kind of basket on wheels used in supermarkets
2 a small table on wheels

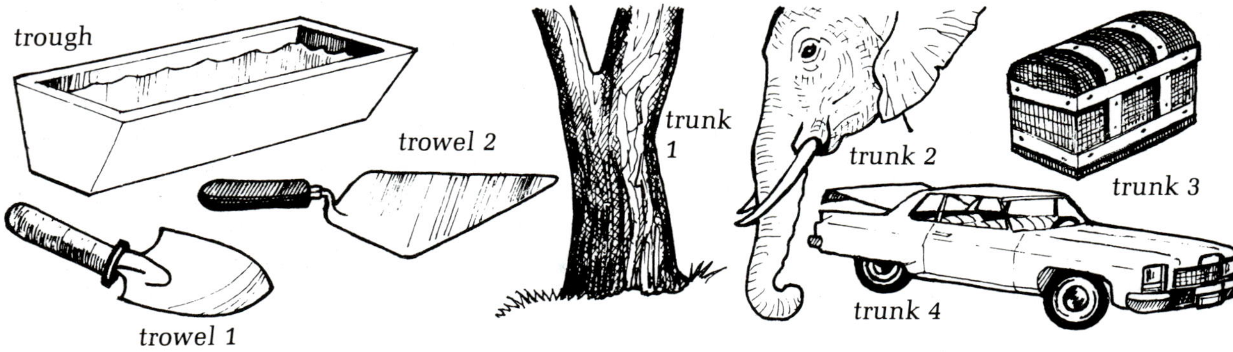

trombone *n* — a large, brass instrument made up of two long tubes

troop *n* — an organized group of soldiers, scouts etc.

trophy *n* — a cup, shield, or other object given to the winner of a contest

tropical *adj* — having to do with the warmest parts of the world

trot *v* — to run with short steps like the slow run of a horse

trouble *n* — anything that bothers or disturbs you

trough *n* — a long, narrow, open box that holds water or food for animals

trousers *n (pl)* — an article of clothing for the lower half of the body, divided into two sections, one for each leg

Tt

trousseau *n* — a bride's outfit 0f clothes

trout *n* — a fish that lives in rivers and lakes

trowel *n*
1 a garden tool like an small spade
2 a flat-bladed tool for spreading mortar

truant *n* — a pupil who stays away from school without permission

truck *n*
1 a kind of lorry
2 a railway wagon

trudge *v* — to walk in a tired way

true *adj*
1 correct, exactly right
2 loyal, to be relied on

truly *adv* — in a true or honest way

trumpet *n* — a brass wind musical instrument, played by pressing valves

trunk *n*
1 the main part of a tree
2 an elephant's long nose
3 a large box or chest, used for storing or carrying personal belongings
4 the boot of a car, in USA and Canada

trust *v* — to believe that someone is honest and loyal

truth *n* — something that is true

try *v*
1 to aim at doing something; to attempt
2 to judge someone in a court of law
3 to test something to see if it works well

tub *n* — a round container

tube *n*
1 a long, thin pipe of metal, glass, rubber or plastic
2 a soft container used for holding toothpaste or other products

tuck *v* — to tidy away the loose ends of something

tug *n*	*1*	a sharp pull
	2	a small, powerful boat used for pulling and pushing large ships
tug of war *n*		a contest between two teams pulling a pope
tulip *n*		a colourful, spring flower that grows from an bulb and is shaped like a cup
tumble *v*		to fall suddenly
tumble drier *n*		a machine that tosses washing in warm air to dry it
tumbler *n*		a drinking glass
tuna *n*		a large ocean fish that is caught for food
tundra *n*		a large area of flat, treeless land in the Arctic
tune *n*		a series of notes that make a piece of music
tunnel *n*		an underground passage
turban *n*		a covering for the head made by wrapping a long strip of cloth around it in a special way
turbine *n*		an engine which is operated by a jet of gas, steam or air
turf *n*		short grass and the soil it is growing in
turkey *n*		a large bird that is raised for food
turn *v*	*1*	to make something go around
	2	to change direction
	3	to become
turnip *n*		a plant with a large, round root that is used as a vegetable
turnstile *n*		a kind of gate which turns and allows one person through at a time
turntable *n*		the part of a record-player that you put the record on

turpentine *n*		an oil from pine trees, used for thinning paint and cleaning brushes
turquoise *n*		a greenish-blue colour
turtle *n*		an animal that lives on land or in the sea; it has a hard shell and moves very slowly
tusk *n*		one of the two very long teeth that stick out from the mouth of an elephant, walrus etc.
tweed *n*		warm cloth woven from wool
tweezers *n (pl)*		a small tool for picking up or gripping small objects
twice *adv*		two times
twig *n*		a small branch on a tree or bush
twilight *n*		the dim light at the end of the day before it gets completely dark
twin *n*		one of two children born at the same time to the same mother
twinkle *v*		to sparkle; to send out little flashes of light
twirl *v*		to spin round quickly
twist *v*	*1*	to turn something round
	2	to wrap things round each other
	3	to bend something and change its shape
type *n*	*1*	a kind
	2	printed letters
type *v*		to use a typewriter
typewriter *n*		a machine with a keyboard for printing letters on paper
typhoon *n*		a violent, windy storm, much like a hurricane
typist *n*		someone who uses a typewriter
tyre *n*		an air-filled rubber tube round a wheel

udder *n*	the bag-like part of a cow, goat or sheep from which milk comes
ugly *adj*	not pleasant to look at
ukulele *n*	a small guitar with four strings
ulcer *n*	an open sore
ultrasonic *adj*	sounding so high that you cannot hear it
umbrella *n*	a folding frame covered with material, to give shelter from sun or rain
umpire *n*	someone who sees that the rules of a game, such as tennis, cricket etc., are followed
un-	a prefix meaning 'not' or 'the opposite of': **unable** means not able; **unkind** means not kind
unbelievable *adj*	difficult to believe; amazing
uncertain *adj*	not sure; doubtful
uncle *n*	your aunt's husband or the brother of your father or mother
uncomfortable *adj*	not comfortable
unconscious *adj*	in a very deep sleep
uncover *v*	*1* to take the cover or wrapping off *2* to make known
under *prep*	below; beneath
under *adv*	in a lower position or place
undercarriage *n*	the wheels and landing gear of an aeroplane
underground *adj*	below the ground
undergrowth *n*	shrubs, bushes etc., growing beneath tall trees
underline *v*	to draw a line under some writing
underneath *adv, prep*	beneath; below
underpants *n (pl)*	underclothing for men and boys, worn on the lower half of the body
underpass *n*	a place where one road passes under another one
understand *v*	to know what something means or how it works
undertaker *n*	a person whose job is to arrange funerals
underwear *n*	clothes you wear next to your skin under a shirt and trousers, or under a dress, etc.
undo *v*	to loosen, untie or unfasten something
undress *v*	to take off your clothes
unemployed *adj*	out of work
uneven *adj*	not even or level
unexpected *adj*	not expected, coming as a surprise
unfair *adj*	not fair; not treating people in the right way
unfortunate *adj*	not lucky
ungrateful *adj*	not grateful or thankful
unhealthy *adj*	not healthy; ill
unicorn *n*	an imaginary animal that looks like a horse with a long horn on its head
uniform *n*	special clothes worn to show that people belong to the same group
union *n*	*1* a joining together *2* a group of workers in the same occupation who have joined together to make sure they are treated fairly by the people who employ them
unit *n*	*1* a single thing, person, or group *2* an amount used for measuring
unite *v*	to join together, to make or become one

universal *adj*		concerning everybody and everything
universe *n*		everything that exists, including all the planets and all of space
university *n*		a place where people go on studying when they have left school
unkind *adj*		not kind; cruel
unknown *adj*		not known; strange
unless *conj*	*1*	if not
	2	except when
unlike *prep*		different from
unlikely *adj*		probably not going to happen
unload *v*	*1*	to take off a load from something
	2	to take the bullets out of a gun
unlock *v*		to open a lock by using a key or combination number
unlucky *adj*		not lucky; unfortunate
unnecessary *adj*		not necessary; not needed
unpleasant *adj*		not pleasant; that you do not enjoy
untidy *adj*		not neat; not in good order
untie *v*		to undo something that has been tied
until *conj*		up to the time when
until *prep*		up to a certain time
unusual *adj*		not usual, strange
unwell *adj*		ill; not in good health
unwrap *v*		to take something out of the paper it is wrapped in
upon *prep*		on; on top of
upper *adj*		higher
upright *adj*		standing straight up; vertical
uproar *n*		loud shouting; disturbance
upset *v*	*1*	to knock something over
	2	to make someone unhappy
upside-down *adj*	*1*	the wrong way up
	2	untidy, in disorder
upstairs *adv*		to or on a higher floor of a building
up-to-date *adj*		modern
uranium *n*		a vauable, radioactive metal used as a source of atomic energy
urban *adj*		having to do with a city or large town
urge *v*		to encourage, to try to get someone to do something
urge *n*		a strong wish to do something
urgent *adj*		so important it has to be seen to at once
use *v*		to put to some purpose
useful *adj*	*1*	helpful
	2	able to be used a lot
useless *adj*		not good for anything; not useful
usual *adj*		normal; happening often
utensil *n*		a piece of equipment, especially one that is used in cooking
utter *v*		to speak

utensils

Uu

Vv

vacant *adj* empty; unoccupied

vacation *n* a holiday

vaccination *n* an injection that stops you getting an illness

vacuum *n* totally empty space; a space without any air in it

vacuum cleaner *n* an electric machine that sucks up dirt and dust from carpets, floors, etc.

vague *adj* not clear or certain

vain *adj* proud, having too high an opinion of yourself

Valentine *n* a love greeting sent on St. Valentine's Day (February 14th)

valley *n* an area of lowland between hills or mountains

valuable *adj* having great value; worth much money

value *n*
1 the amount of money something could be sold for
2 how useful or important something is to you

valve *n* a device that controls the flow of liquid or gas

van *n* a vehicle for carrying goods

vandal *n* someone who deliberately spoils or damages things

vanilla *n* a flavouring used for ice cream and other foods

vanish *v* to disappear, to go out of sight

vanity *n* thinking too well of your looks, etc.

vapour *n* a substance such as gas, mist, steam or smoke

variety *n*
1 a number of different kinds of things
2 a certain sort or kind

various *adj*
1 different
2 several

varnish *n* a clear liquid which gives a hard, glossy surface

vary *v* to change; to be different

vase *n* a glass, china or pottery container, used to hold flowers

vast *adj* very large in size

vat *n* a large container for holding liquids

vault *n* a room, underground, for keeping valuable or important things

vault *v* to jump over onto something with hands or a pole

veal *n* the meat of a calf

vegetable *n* a plant or part of a plant used for food

vegetarian *n* a person who does not eat meat or fish

vehicle *n* anything on wheels that carries people or goods from one place to another on land

veil *n* a thin piece of material used to hide or protect the face

vein *n* one of the thin, long tubes in the body carrying blood to the heart

velvet *n* a kind of cloth that feels soft and thick on one side

venom *n* the poison of some snakes and spiders

ventilator *n* a kind of opening in a room which allows air freely in and out

ventriloquist *n* someone who can make his or her voice appear to come from some other person, puppet or place

verandah *n* an open space with a floor and a roof along one side of a house

verb *n* the word in a sentence that tells you what someone or something is doing

Vv

verdict *n*	what a jury decides at the end of a case in a law court
verse *n*	part of a poem or song
vertebrae *n (pl)*	the small bones which make up the backbone
vertical *adj*	straight up and down; upright
very *adv*	to a great extent; extremely
vessel *n*	*1* a ship or boat *2* a container for holding liquids
vest *n*	a piece of underwear worn on the top half of the body
vet *n*	a highly trained person who looks after sick animals
vex *v*	to annoy or irritate someone
viaduct *n*	a long bridge built on a series of arches or supports, to carry a road or railway across a valley
vibrate *v*	to tremble, to shake
vicar *n*	a clergyman in charge of a parish
vicious *adj*	cruel; nasty; wicked
victim *n*	someone who has been killed, injured, robbed or swindled
victory *n*	a win in a battle, game or contest
video recorder *n*	an electronic machine for recording and playing back TV pictures and films
view *n*	*1* everything you can see from one place *2* what a person thinks about something
vigour *n*	strength, energy
vile *adj*	horrible, unpleasant
village *n*	a group of houses in a country area
villain *n*	a wicked or evil person
vine *n*	a climbing plant that bears grapes
vinegar *n*	a sour liquid used for giving flavouring and preserving food
vineyard *n*	a large piece of land where grapes are grown
vinyl *n*	a hard plastic used for making records, floor polishes, and other things
viola *n*	a stringed, musical instrument like a large violin
violent *adj*	very strong and rough, and usually dangerous
violet *n*	a small purple or white flower
violin *n*	a musical instrument that has four strings and is played with a bow
virus *n*	an extremely tiny living thing which can cause disease
visible *adj*	able to be seen
vision *n*	*1* being able to see *2* a kind of dream
visit *v*	*1* to pay a call on someone *2* to stay somewhere for a while
visitor *n*	someone who visits you; a guest
vitamins *n (pl)*	chemical substances, found in certain kinds of food, needed for good health
vivid *adj*	bright, lively, clear
vixen *n*	a female fox
vocabulary *n*	*1* all the words in a language *2* all the words a person knows
voice *n*	the sound from your mouth when you are speaking or singing
volcano *n*	a mountain with a hole in the top where fire, hot rock, ash, and gas come out

vole *n* a small, mouse-like rodent with short ears and a long tail

volley *n* in ball games, the return of the ball before it touches the ground

volleyball *n* a game in which two teams, standing on either side of a net, hit a large ball back and forth

volume *n*
1 the amount of space filled by something
2 how loud a sound is
3 a book, or one of a set of books

volunteer *n* someone who offers to do something that he or she does not have to do

vomit *v* to be sick

vote *v* to say which idea or person you think should be chosen

voucher *n* a kind of ticket, coupon, receipt etc.

vow *n* a solemn promise

vowel *n* any of the five letters a,e,i,o,u

voyage *n* a journey by sea

vulture *n* a large bird that has dark feathers and a bald head and feeds largely on dead animals

vulture

Ww

waddle *v* to walk like a duck

wade *v* to walk through shallow water

wafer *n* a thin, crisp biscuit, often eaten with ice cream

waffle *n* a small, crisp kind of pancake

wag *v* to move quickly from side to side

wage *n* money people are paid for doing work

wagon *n*
1 an open cart with four wheels pulled by horses or oxen
2 an open railway truck

wagtail *n* a small bird with a long tail

wail *v* to cry or moan loudly

waist *n* the part of your body between the ribs and the hips

waistcoat *n* a sleeveless jacket, sometimes worn as part of a suit

wait *v* to stay in one place until something happens or someone comes

waiter (fem. waitress) *n* someone who serves food in a café, hotel, restaurant etc.

wake *v*
1 to stop sleeping
2 to arouse somebody from sleep

walk *v* to travel on foot

walkie-talkie *n* a kind of radio-telephone that can be carried

wall *n*
1 the side of a building or room
2 a barrier made of bricks or stone put round a field or garden

wallet *n* a flat, folding case in which money, cards and pictures etc., are kept

wallpaper *n* special paper used to cover the walls of rooms

walnut *n* a hard, round nut with a crinkled shell

walrus *n* a large sea animal, something like a seal, that has two long tusks

waltz *n* a graceful dance done with a partner

wand *n* a slender stick used in stories by fairies and wizards

wander *v* to move from one place to another, not sure of where you want to go

want *v*
1 to desire or wish for something
2 to need or require

war *n* fighting between countries

ward *n* a room for patients in a hospital

warden *n* a prison officer

wardrobe *n* a large cupboard in which clothes are hung

warehouse *n* a large building where goods are stored

warm *adj* fairly hot, between hot and cold

warn *v* to tell someone about possible danger or trouble

warning *n* something that tells you about danger

warp *v* to bend or twist out of shape

warren *n* a place where a group of rabbits live together in burrows

warrior *n* someone who fights in battles

wart *n* a small, hard lump on the skin

wash *v* to clean with soap and water

washer *n*
1 a small, flat ring used to make a joint tight, such as on a tap
2 a washing-machine

washing-machine *n* machine for washing clothes, bedding, towels etc.

washing-powder *n* a soap powder or detergent for washing clothes etc.

wasp *n* a stinging insect that has a narrow waist and black and yellow stripes

waste *v* to use more of something than you need to

waste *n*
1 things you get rid of because you do not need them anymore
2 a poor use of something

watch *n* a small clock, usually worn on the wrist

watch *v*
1 to look at closely
2 to guard

water *n* the clear liquid in seas, rivers and lakes; it falls from the sky as rain

watercress *n* a small, green plant used in salads

waterfall *n* the place where a river falls from a high place to a lower place

watering-can *n* a container for watering plants

watermelon *n* a large, juicy fruit that is pink inside and has a thick, green skin

water-polo *n* a ball game played by swimmers

waterproof *adj* not allowing water to pass through

water-skiing *n* a sport on water, in which the person on skis is towed along at high speeds by a motor boat

wave *n*	*1*	one of the ridges of water you can see moving on the surface of the sea
	2	a curve or curl in your hair
wave *v*		to move your hand or arm as a way of saying hello or goodbye
wax *n*		soft stuff for making candles
way *n*	*1*	a road, path, track or route
	2	how to do something
weak *adj*		not strong
wealth *n*		a lot of money or valuable things
wealthy *adj*		rich
weapon *adj*		anything used for fighting or hunting
wear *v*	*1*	to be dressed in something
	2	to become damaged or weak through much use
weary *adj*		very tired
weasel *n*		a small, fierce animal with a long, slender body
weather *n*		the conditions of rain, sunshine, wind etc. at a certain time
weave *v*		to make cloth by putting threads over and under one another
web *n*		a nest of sticky threads spun by a spider to catch insects
web-foot *n*		a foot, like the ones on frogs and ducks, which have skin joining the toes together
wedding *n*		the time when a man and a woman become husband and wife
wedge *n*		a piece of wood or metal that is very thin at one end and wider at the other
weed *n*		any wild plant that grows in places where it is not wanted
weed *v*		to remove weeds
week *n*		the seven days from Sunday to the next Saturday
weekend *n*		Saturday and Sunday
weekly *adv*		once a week
weekly *adj*		coming out or happening every week
weep *v*		to cry, to sob
weigh *v*		to find the mass or heaviness of a person or thing
weight *n*	*1*	the amount of heaviness of a person or thing
	2	a heavy piece of metal put on scales when something is being weighed
weird *adj*		very strange
welcome *n*		a friendly greeting
welcome *v*		to greet someone in a friendly way
welfare *n*		the health and happiness of people
well *n*		a deep hole in the ground with water or oil at the bottom
well *adj*		in good health
well *adv*		in a good way
wellingtons *n (pl)*		knee length rubber boots that you wear in rain, mud etc.
well-off *adj*		rich; wealthy
west *n*		in the direction of the setting sun; one of the points of the compass
western *n*		a film or book about the American Wild West
wet *adj*	*1*	covered or saturated with water or other liquid
	2	rainy; showery
whale *n*		a huge sea animal
wharf *n*		a place where ships are loaded and unloaded
what *adj*		which; how much

what *pron*		that which; whatever
wheat *n*		a plant with grain that is made into flour
wheel *n*		a circular frame or disc fixed in the middle so that it can keep turning
wheel *v*		to move something on wheels
wheelbarrow *n*		a small cart with one wheel at the front and two handles
wheel-chair *n*		a chair on wheels for a person not able to walk
when *adv*	*1*	at what time
	2	how long ago
	3	as soon as
when *conj*		at the time; although
where *adv*	*1*	in what place
	2	in the place which
whether *conj*		if
which *adj*		word that you say when you ask about a person or thing
which *pron*		a word showing the one you are talking about, such as: "This is the record which you asked for."
while *n*		a period of time
while *conj*		during the time that
whimper *n*		a soft cry of fear or pain
whine *v*		to make a long cry or sound, as a dog does when it is unhappy or injured
whip *n*		a long piece of rope or leather joined to a handle and used for hitting things
whip *v*		to beat cream or other liquids very hard until they are thick
whirl *v*		to spin round quickly
whirlpool *n*		a place in a sea or river where the water whirls round
whirlwind *n*		a very fierce wind that blows in circles
whisk *v*		to stir eggs or other other foods
whiskers *n (pl)*		hair or bristles that grow on the face
whisky *n*		a strong alcoholic drink made from barley or other grain
whisper *v*		to speak very softly
whistle *n*	*1*	a high, sharp sound
	2	a small instrument that makes a shrill sound when blown
white *n*		a colour; the colour of fresh snow
who *pron*	*1*	which person or persons
	2	the person or persons that
whole *adj*		all of something, a complete thing
whooping-cough *n*		an illness that causes you to keep coughing and breathing in heavily
whose *pron*		of whom; of which
why *adv*		for what reason
wick *n*		the thread or material put into a candle or lamp which is lit with a flame
wicked *adj*		very bad; evil
wicket *n*		the three stumps which are bowled at in cricket
wide *adj*		measuring a lot from one side to the other
widen *v*		to make or become wider
widow *n*		a woman whose husband is dead
widower *n*		a man whose wife is dead
width *n*		how wide something is
wife *n*		a married woman
wig *n*		a covering of false hair worn on the head
wiggle *v*		to move with short, quick movements from side to side

wigwam

wigwam *n* — a hut or tent that some North American Indians used to live in

wild *adj* — not tame; living in the free and natural way

wilderness *n* — a desert or other wild place where no one lives

will *n*
1 the power of your mind to choose what to do
2 a written paper saying who is to have someone's money and things when he or she is dead

willing *adj* — glad and ready to do what is wanted

willow *n* — a tree that often grows near water and has thin branches that bend easily

wilt *v* — to droop like a plant without water; to be limp

wily *adj* — crafty, cunning

win *v* — to come first in a contest or game

wind *n* — air moving along quickly

windmill *n* — a building with sails that the wind blows round so that the machinery inside can grind flour etc.

windmill

Ww

window *n* — an opening in the wall of a building, filled with glass, to let in light

windpipe *n* — a tube in the body from the mouth to the lungs

windscreen *n* — the front window of a car or other vehicle

windsurfing *n* — the sport of riding on a kind of surf-board with a sail

wine *n* — a strong drink made from grapes or other fruit

wing *n*
1 one of the parts of a bird, bat, or insect used for flying
2 one of the flat surfaces that support an aircraft in the air

wink *v* — to close and open an eyelid quickly

winner *n* — a team, person, or animal, that wins

winter *n* — the season after autumn; the coldest part of the year

wipe *v* — to rub something with a cloth to make it clean or dry

wire *n* — a long thread of metal that can be bent or twisted

wireless *n* — a radio

wiring *n* — a system of wires carrying electricity

wise *adj* — able to understand many things; having plenty of sense

wish *v* — to want; to say or think what you would like to happen

witch *n* — a bad woman in fairy tales who is thought to have magic powers

with *prep*
1 having or possessing
2 in the company of
3 because of

withdraw *v* — to pull back from something; to take back

wither *v* — to become dry and smaller

within *prep* — inside

without *prep*		not having
witness *n*		someone who saw something happen
witty *adj*		clever and amusing
wizard *n*		a man in fairy tales who is thought to have magic powers
wobble *v*		to move unsteadily from side to side
wolf *n*		a wild animal usually grey, that looks like a dog
woman *n*		a grown-up female human being
wonder *n*	*1*	a surprising or unusual thing
	2	a feeling of amazement
wonder *v*		to ask yourself about something
wonderful *adj*		so good it surprises and pleases you very much
wood *n*	*1*	the hard part of the tree under the bark
	2	a lot of trees growing together
wooden *adj*		made of wood
woodpecker *n*		a tree-climbing bird that taps trees with its strong, pointed beak to find insects

woodpecker

woodwork *n*		making things out of wood
wool *n*	*1*	the thick hair of sheep and some other animals
	2	the thread made from this hair and used for making cloth and knitting
woollen *adj*		made of wool
word *n*		a sound or group of sounds that mean something when spoken, written, or read
work *n*		anything that requires effort; a job
worker *n*		someone who works for a living
workshop *n*		a place in which work is done by hand or by machine
world *n*	*1*	the earth, its countries and peoples
	2	the universe
worm *n*		a small, thin animal with a soft body and no legs
worry *n*		a troubled feeling
worry *v*		to feel upset about something bad that may happen or may have happened
worse *adj*		more than bad
worship *v*		to love and praise God or a god
worst *adj*		the most bad
worth *n*		the value or cost of something
worth *adj*	*1*	having a value of
	2	good enough for
worthless *adj*		something that has no value
wound *n*		an injury such as a cut
wound *v*		to hurt or injure
wrap *v*		to put paper or cloth around something
wreath *n*		an arrangement of flowers, leaves etc. tied together in a ring

Ww

wreck *n* — the broken remains of something destroyed, such as a ship on rocks or a crashed aircraft
wreck *v* — to ruin or destroy completely
wren *n* — a very small, brown songbird
wrench *v* — to pull or twist violently
wrench *n* — a kind of spanner
wrestle *v* — to struggle with someone and try to force him or her to the ground
wretched *adj* — very miserable; unhappy; ill
wriggle *v* — to twist and turn your body around
wring *v* — to twist and squeeze something wet to get the water out of it
wrinkle *n* — a small crease on the skin or other flat surfaces
wrist *n* — the joint between your hand and arm
write *v* — to make letters and words on paper or some other surface
writer *n* — 1 someone who writes
2 an author
wrong *adj* — not true or correct; not fair; not good

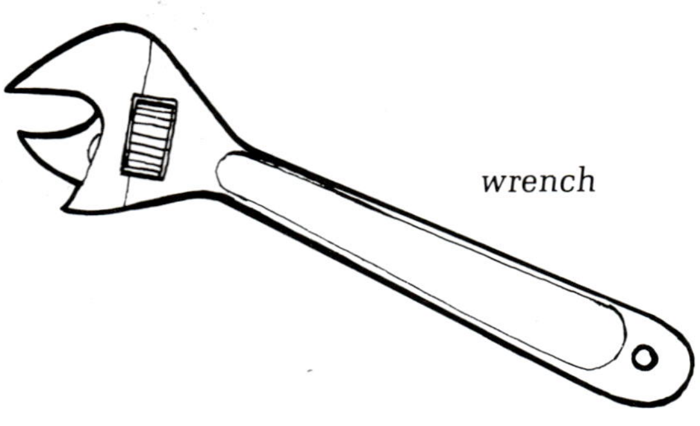

wrench

Xx

Xmas *n* — a short way of writing Christmas
X-ray *n* — an instrument with powerful rays that show parts inside the body and takes photographs of them
xylophone *n* — a musical instrument made of wooden or metal bars that are hit by small hammers

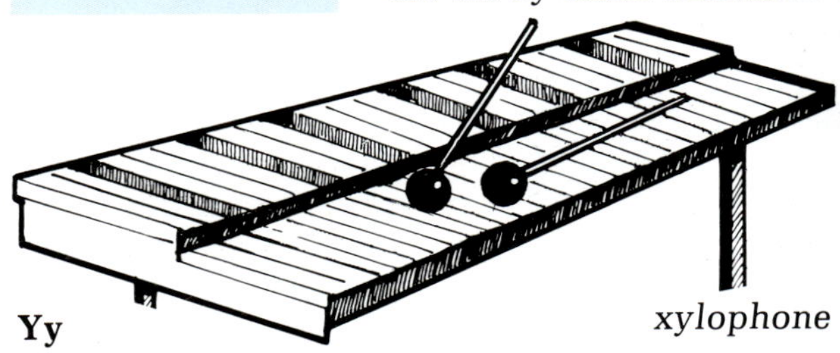

xylophone

Yy

yacht *n* — a sailing-boat built for racing or cruising
yap *v* — to make short barking sounds
yam *n* — a kind of sweet potato
yard *n* — 1 a measure of length equal to 36 inches or about 91cm
2 an open space surrounded by walls and buildings
yarn *n* — 1 a thick thread used in sewing, weaving, or knitting
2 a made-up story
yawn *v* — to open your mouth wide when you are bored or sleepy
year *n* — a measure of time lasting 365 days, 52 weeks, or 12 months
yearly *adj* — every year; once a year
yeast *n* — a substance used to make dough rise when making bread etc.
yell *v* — to shout loudly
yellow *n* — a colour; the colour of buttercups

Ww
Xx
Yy

yes *adv*	the opposite of no
yesterday *n*	the day before this one
yet *adv*	up to the present time
yet *conj*	but; however
yew *n*	a type of evergreen tree with small, dark green leaves and small red berries
yield *v*	to give way to someone or something
yield *n*	the amount of fruit or grain on a plant
yoghurt/yogurt *n*	a thick, creamy food made from milk
yolk *n*	the yellow part of an egg
Yom Kippur *n*	a Jewish fast day, observed in September or October
you *pron*	the person or people you are speaking or writing to
young *adj*	not old; in the early part of life
youngster *n*	a young boy or girl
your *adj*	belonging to you
yours *pron*	the one belonging to you
yourself *pron*	you alone
youth *n*	the time between being a child and an adult
yo-yo *n*	a small toy that is spun up and down on a string

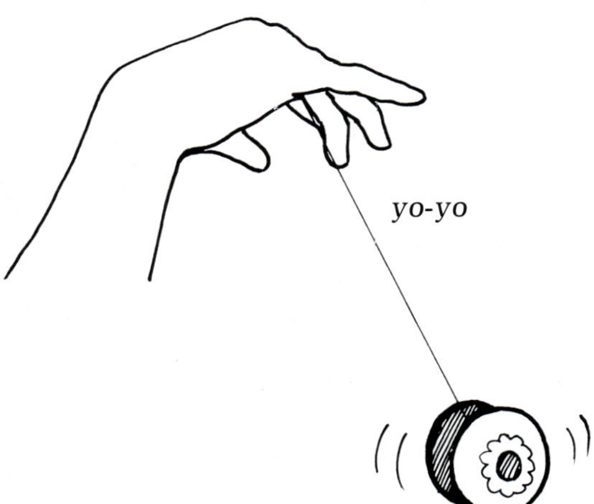

yo-yo

zebra

Zz

zebra *n*	an African horse-like animal that has dark stripes on a light body
zebra crossing *n*	a place marked with black and white stripes for pedestrians to cross the road
zero *n*	the figure or symbol 0; nothing; nought
zigzag *adj*	full of short, sharp turns from one side to the other
zinc *n*	a bluish-white metal
zip-fastener *n* or **zip** *(abbr)*	a fastener with a sliding tab, for joining together two edges of material
zone *n*	a part of a town, country, or the world that is special in some way
zoo *n*	a place where different kinds of wild animals are kept for people to look at them
zoom *v*	to move or climb suddenly

MATHEMATICS: USEFUL FORMULAE

Mathematical signs

+	plus - addition
−	minus - substraction
×	multiplication
÷	division
∴	therefore
=	equal
√	square root
∛	cube root
%	per cent
>	greater than
<	less than
‖	parallel
∠	angle
⊥	perpendicular

Roman Numerals

I	1	XIX	19
II	2	XX	20
III	3	XXX	30
IV	4	XL	40
V	5	L	50
VI	6	LX	60
VII	7	LXX	70
VIII	8	LXXX	80
IX	9	XC	90
X	10	C	100
XI	11	CC	200
XII	12	CCC	300
XIII	13	CD	400
XIV	14	D	500
XV	15	DC	600
XVI	16	DCC	700
XVII	17	DCCC	800
XVIII	18	CM	900
		M	1000

Ordinal Numbers

1st	First	15th	Fifteenth
2nd	Second	16th	Sixteenth
3rd	Third	17th	Seventeenth
4th	Fourth	18th	Eighteenth
5th	Fifth	19th	Nineteenth
6th	Sixth	20th	Twentieth
7th	Seventh	30th	Thirtieth
8th	Eighth	40th	Fortieth
9th	Ninth	50th	Fiftieth
10th	Tenth	60th	Sixtieth
11th	Eleventh	70th	Seventieth
12th	Twelfth	80th	Eightieth
13th	Thirteenth	90th	Ninetieth
14th	Fourteenth	100th	Hundreth

Angles

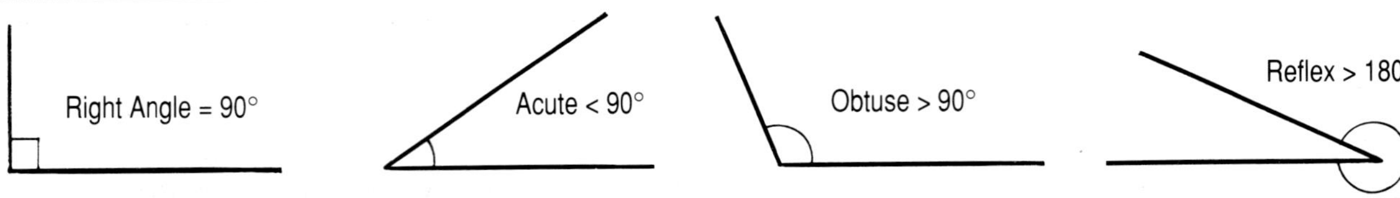

Area

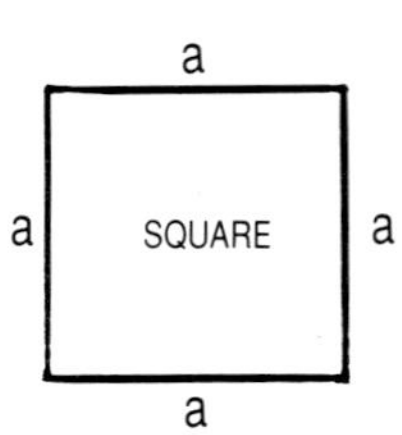

All sides equal

Perimeter = 4a Area = $a \times a = a^2$

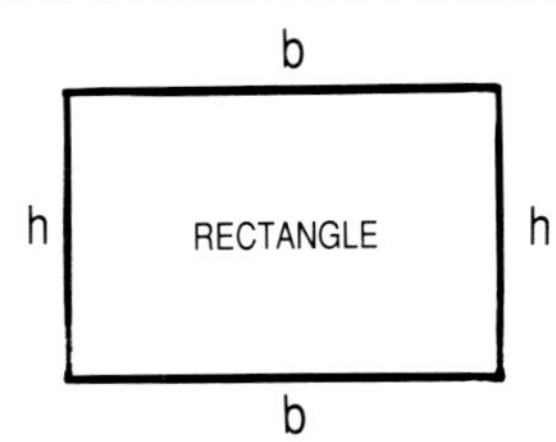

Opposite sides equal

Perimeter = 2(b+h) Area = $b \times h$

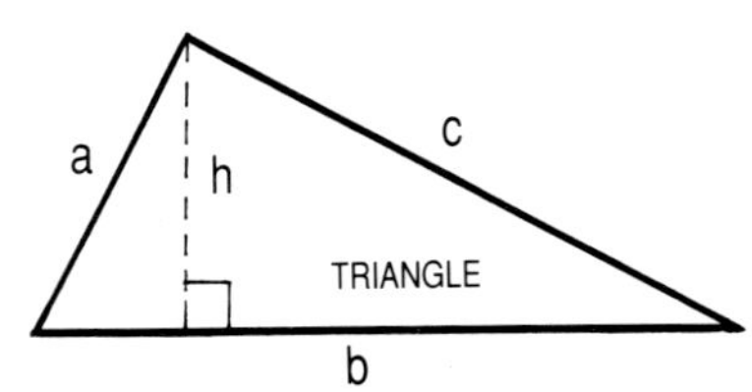

Perimeter = a + b + c Area = $\frac{1}{2} b \times h$

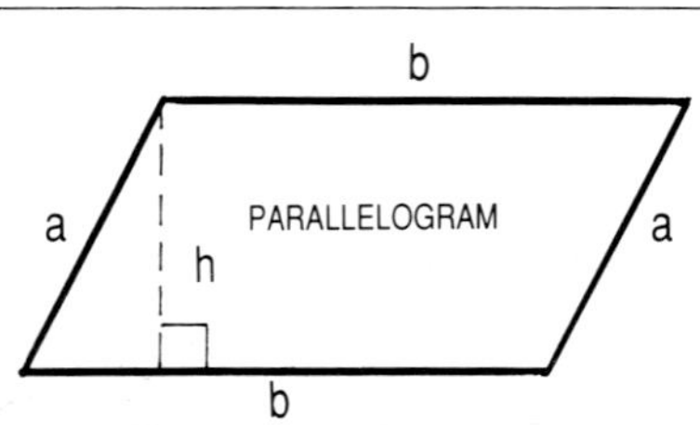

Perimeter = 2 (a + b) Area = $b \times h$

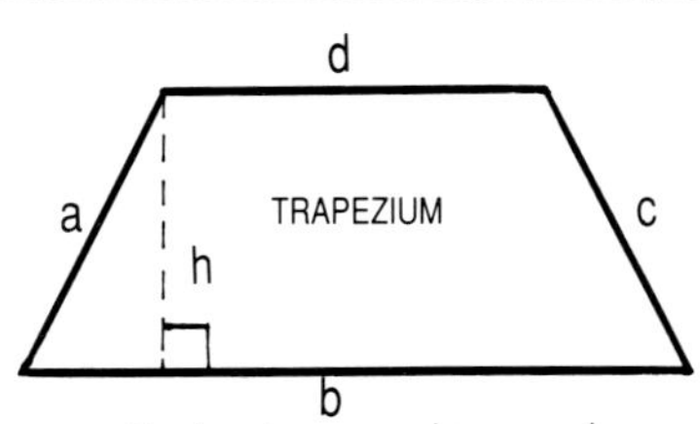

Perimeter = a + b + c + d

Area = $\frac{1}{2}(a + b) \times h$

Circumference = $2\pi r$ or πD (Perimeter)

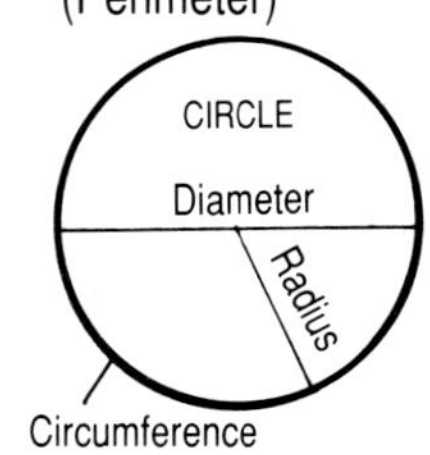

Area = πr^2

π (pi) $\frac{22}{7}$

(3.142)

Volume

CUBE

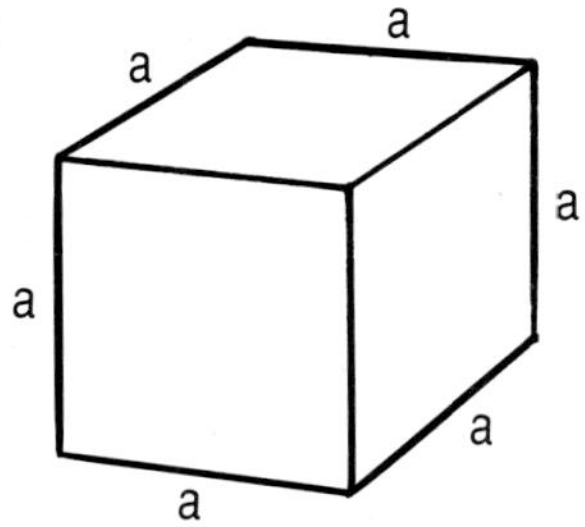

Volume of cube = $a \times a \times a = a^3$

CUBOID

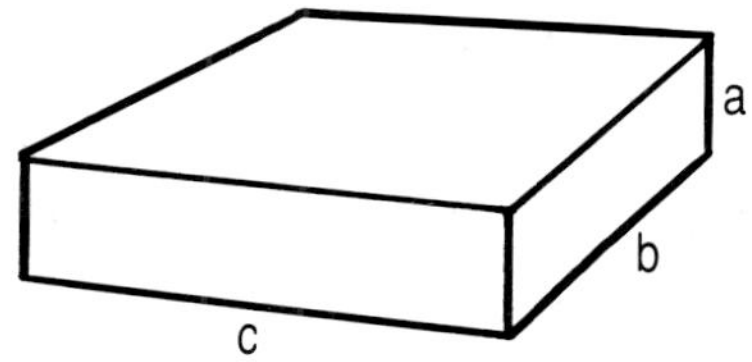

Volume of cuboid = $a \times b \times c$

PRISM

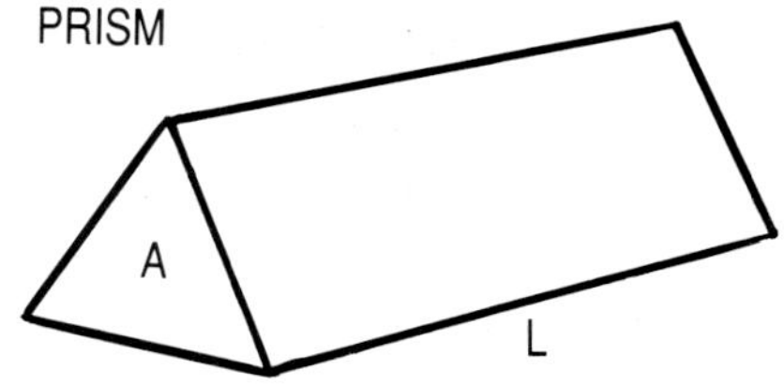

Volume of prism = Area of end × Length
= $A \times L$

CYLINDER

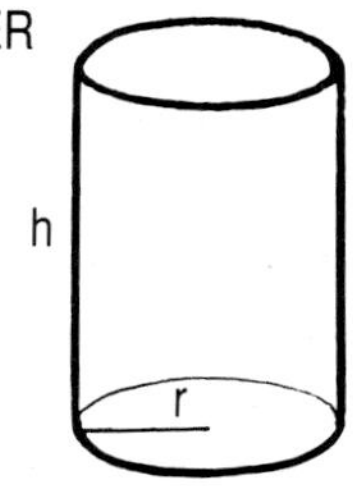

Volume = area of base × height
= $\pi r^2 \times h$

SPHERE

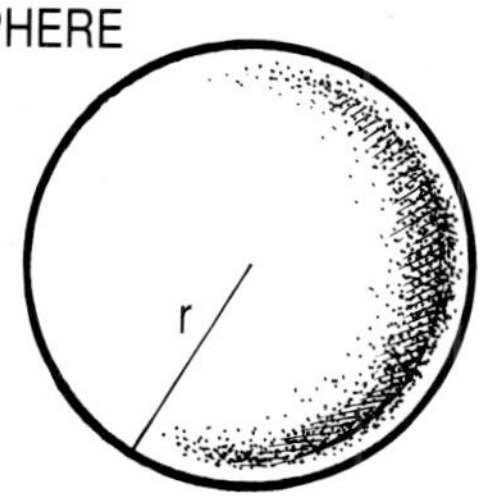

Volume = $\frac{4}{3} \pi r^3$

CONE

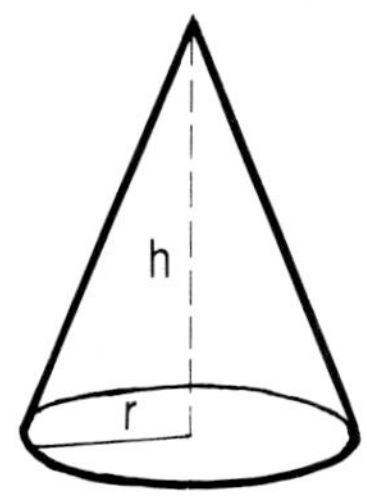

Volume = $\frac{1}{3} \pi r^2 h$

PYRAMID

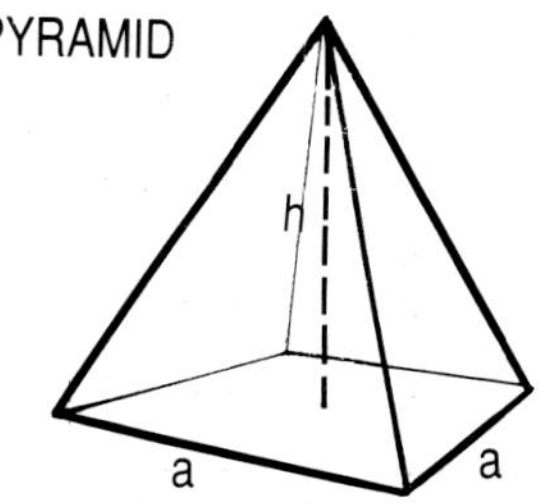

Volume = $\frac{1}{3}$ area of base × perp. height = $\frac{1}{3} a^2 \times h$

Pythagoras Theorem

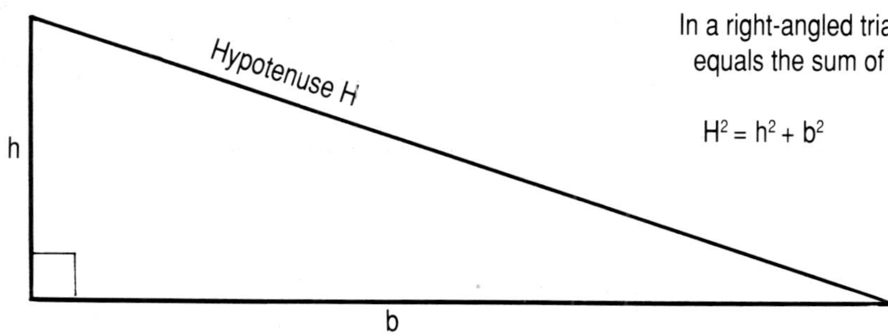

In a right-angled triangle the square of the hypotenuse equals the sum of the squares of the other two sides.

$$H^2 = h^2 + b^2$$

Trigonometry: ratios

Sine (SIN) Cosine (COS) Tangent (TAN)

$$\text{SIN A} = \frac{\text{opposite}}{\text{hypotenuse}} = \frac{BC}{AC}$$

$$\text{COS} = \frac{\text{adjacent}}{\text{hypotenuse}} = \frac{AB}{AC}$$

$$\text{TAN} = \frac{\text{opposite}}{\text{adjacent}} = \frac{CB}{AB}$$

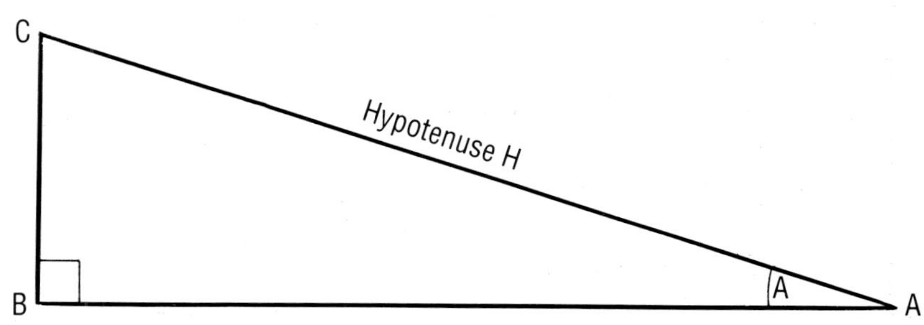

CLASSIFICATION: WHAT ARE?

Plants
Living things which produce their own food by PHOTOSYNTHESIS are called PLANTS.

Animals
Animals cannot make their own food, they must feed on plants or other animal

Vertebrates
These are animals with backbones.

Insects
Animals with three parts to their body and six legs are INSECTS. Many have wings.

Fish
Cold blooded vertebrates which live in water and have fins and scales are calle FISH.

Mammals
MAMMALS are warm blooded vertebrates with four limbs. They give birth to liv young, for which they produce milk. Most have hairy skin.

Amphibians
Cold blooded vertebrates which live on land and in water are called AMPHIBIANS. They have four limbs and soft moist skin.

Reptiles
Cold blooded vertebrates with dry skin of scales or plates which have lungs an lay eggs are called REPTILES.

Birds
Birds are warm blooded vertebrates. They have feathers and four limbs. Their front limbs are wings and their back limbs are legs. They lay eggs.

Marsupials
Mammals with pouches for rearing their young are called MARSUPIALS.

RELIGIONS

St. George

Patron Saints

St. Agatha	Nurses
St. Andrew	Scotland (November 30)
St. Anthony	Gravediggers
St. Augustine of Hippo	Brewers
St. Benedict	Speleologists
St. Cecilia	Musicians
St. Christopher	Sailors
St. Crispin	Shoemakers
St. David	Wales (March 1)
St. Dunstan	Goldsmiths and Silversmiths
St. George	England (April 23)
St. Hubert	Hunters
St. Jerome	Librarians
St. John of God	Booksellers
St. Lawrence	Cooks
St. Luke	Physicians
St. Martha	Dieticians
St. Matthew	Tax Collectors
St. Michael	Policemen
St. Nicholas	Children
St. Patrick	Ireland (March 17)
St. Paul	Carpet weavers, tent makers
St. Peter	Blacksmiths and fishermen
St. Valentine	Sweethearts
St. Vincent	Wine Growers
St. Vitus	Dancers and Comedians
St. William	Hatters
St. Winifred	Bakers

Major Religions

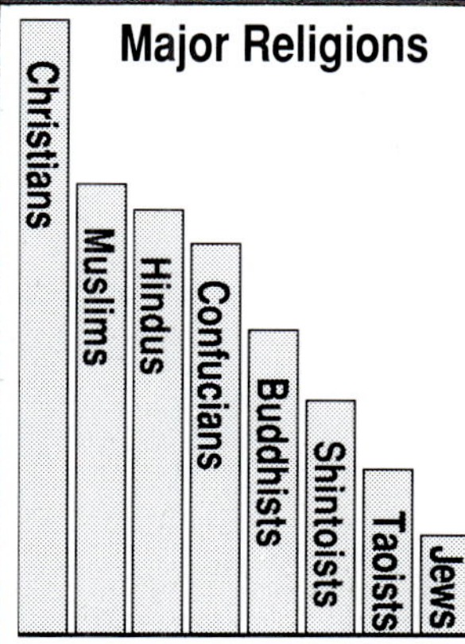

Religious Symbols

Christian symbols, Cross, crucifix

Celtic cross

Russian cross (Russian Orthodox Church)

Greek cross (Greek Orthodox Church)

Menorah (Ancient Judaism)

Star of David (Modern Judaism and the Jewish people)

Ankh (Ancient Egyptian)

Yin Yang (Ancient Chinese)

Shinto

Swastika (form of cross used by early Christians and Indian Buddhists)

THE SEVEN WONDERS OF THE WORLD

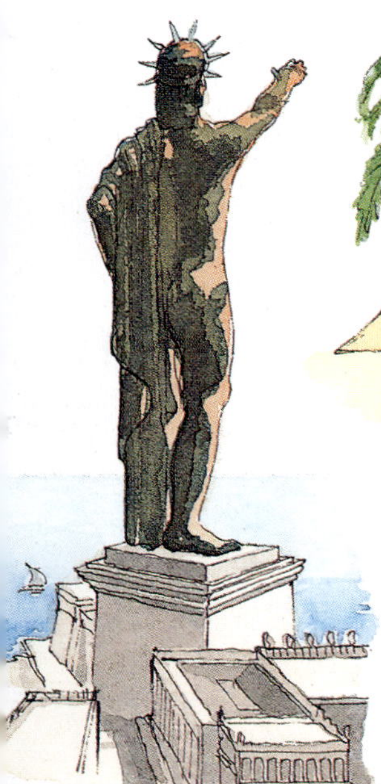
The Colossus of Rhodes

ThePyramids of Egypt

The Hanging Gardens of Babylon

The Statue of Zeus at Olympia

TheTemple of Diana at Ephesus

The Pharos Lighthouse of Alexandria

The Tomb of Mausolus at Halicarnassus

FLAGS OF THE NATIONS: UNITED NATIONS AND EEC

Yugoslavia

Malaysia

Mexico

Ghana (W. Africa)

Japan

Canada

New Zealand

India

America

United Nations (founded 1945) : Member Nations

Afghanistan
Albania
Algeria
Angola
Antigua & Barbuda
Argentina
Australia
Austria
Bahamas
Bahrain
Bangladesh
Barbados
Belgium
Belize
Benin
Bhutan
Bolivia
Botswana
Brazil
Bulgaria
Burma
Burundi
Cameroon
Canada
Cape Verde
Central African Rep.
Chad
Chile
China
Colombia
Comoros
Congo
Costa Rica
Cuba
Cyprus
Czechoslovakia
Denmark
Djibouti
Dominica
Dominican Republic
Ecuador
Egypt
El Salvador
Equatorial Guinea
Ethiopia
Fiji
Finland
France
Gabon
Gambia
Germany, East
Germany, West
Ghana
Greece
Grenada
Guatemala
Guinea
Guinea Bissau
Guyana
Haiti
Honduras
Hungary
Iceland
India
Indonesia
Iran
Iraq
Ireland, Republic of
Israel
Italy
Ivory Coast
Jamaica
Japan
Jordan
Kampuchea
Kenya
Kuwait
Laos
Lebanon
Lesotho
Liberia
Libya
Luxemburg
Madagascar
Malawi
Malaysia
Maldives, Republic of
Mali
Mauritania
Mauritius
Mexico
Mongolian People Rep.
Morocco
Mozambique
Nepal
Netherlands
New Zealand
Nicaragua
Niger
Norway
Oman
Pakistan
Panama
Papua New Guinea
Paraguay
Peru
Philippines
Poland
Portugal
Qatar
Romania
Rwanda
St. Vincent & the Grenadines
St. Lucia
Samoa
Sao Tome & Principe
Saudi Arabia
Senegal
Seychelles
Sierra Leone
Singapore
Solomon Islands
Somali Republic
South Africa
Spain
Sri Lanka
Sudan
Surinam
Swaziland
Sweden
Syria
Tanzania
Thailand
Togo
Trinidad & Tobago
Tunisia
Turkey
Uganda
USSR
United Arab Emirates
United Kingdom
United States
Upper Volta
Uruguay
Vanuatu
Venezuela
Vietnam
Yemen P D R
Yugoslavia
Zaire
Zambia
Zimbabwe

ustralia

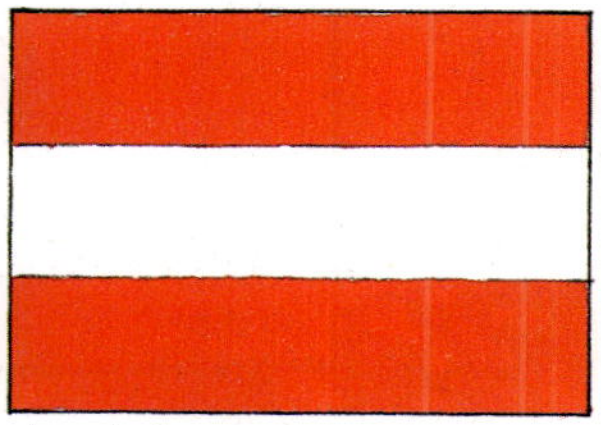

Austria

United Arab Emirates

China

Norway

Singapore

Pakistan

USSR

Belgium

Denmark

France

West Germany

ce

Ireland

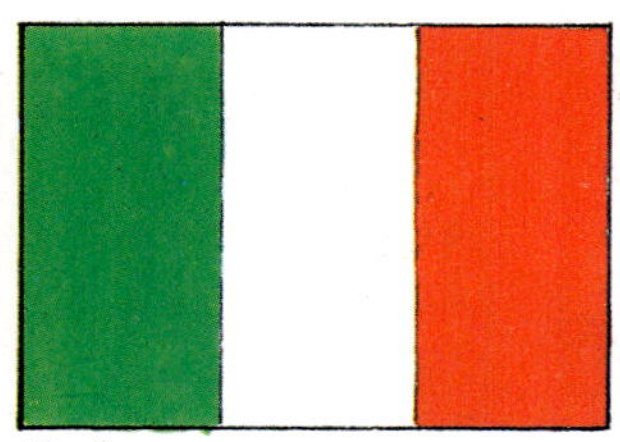

Italy

Luxemburg

Netherlands

EEC Member Countries

France
West Germany
Italy
Netherlands
Luxemburg
Belgium
Denmark
United Kingdom
Ireland
Greece
Spain
Portugal

Spain

Portugal

United Kingdom

THE CONTINENTS

Oceans

	Sq. miles	Sq. kilometres
Pacific	63 855 000	165 384 000
Atlantic	31 744 000	82 217 000
Indian	28 371 000	73 481 000
Arctic	5 427 000	14 056 000

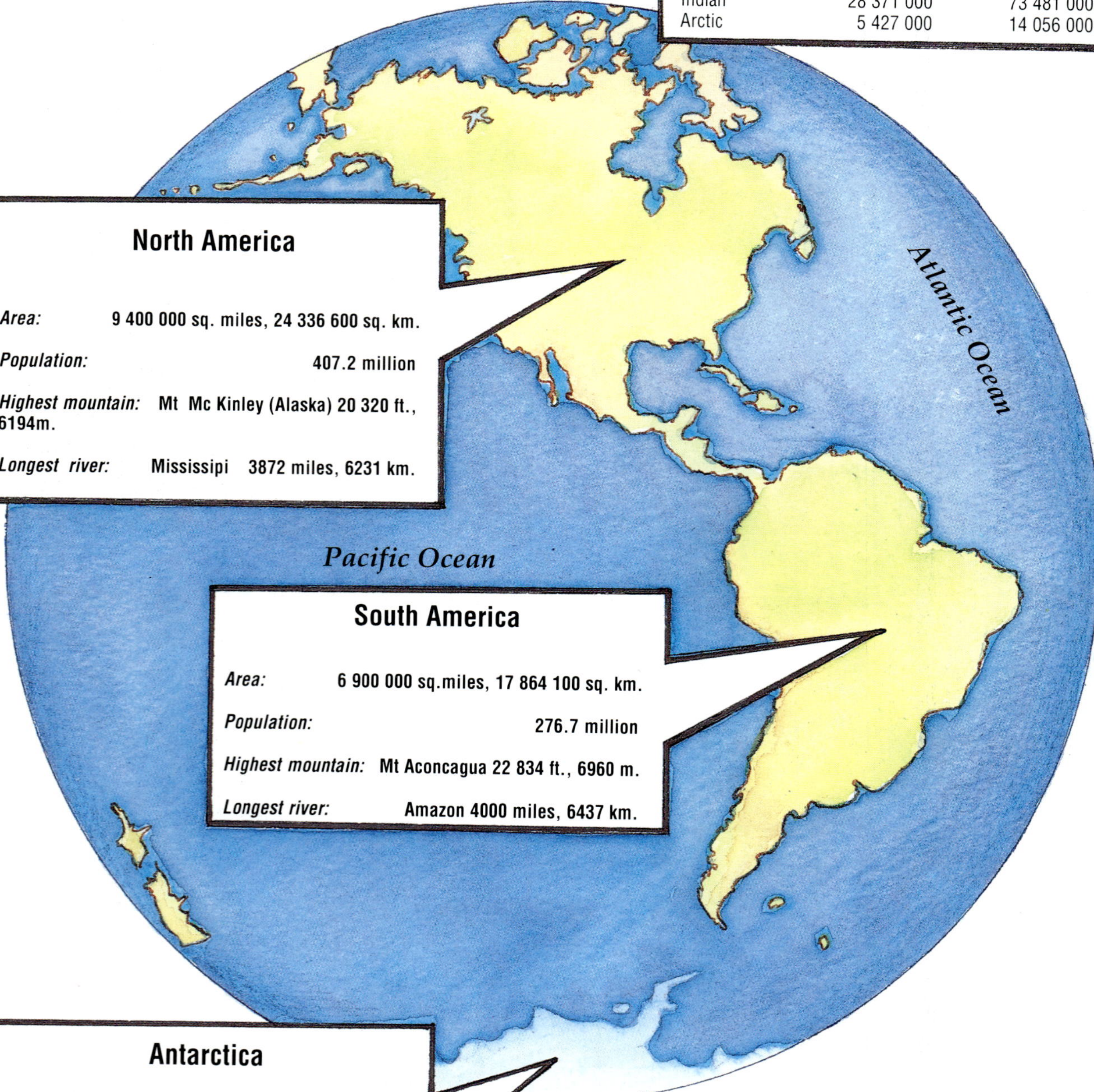

North America

Area: 9 400 000 sq. miles, 24 336 600 sq. km.

Population: 407.2 million

Highest mountain: Mt Mc Kinley (Alaska) 20 320 ft., 6194m.

Longest river: Mississipi 3872 miles, 6231 km.

South America

Area: 6 900 000 sq.miles, 17 864 100 sq. km.

Population: 276.7 million

Highest mountain: Mt Aconcagua 22 834 ft., 6960 m.

Longest river: Amazon 4000 miles, 6437 km.

Antarctica

Area: 5 100 000 sq. miles, 13 203 900 sq. km.
Population: -
Highest mountain: Vinson Massif 16 864 ft., 5140 m.
Longest river: -

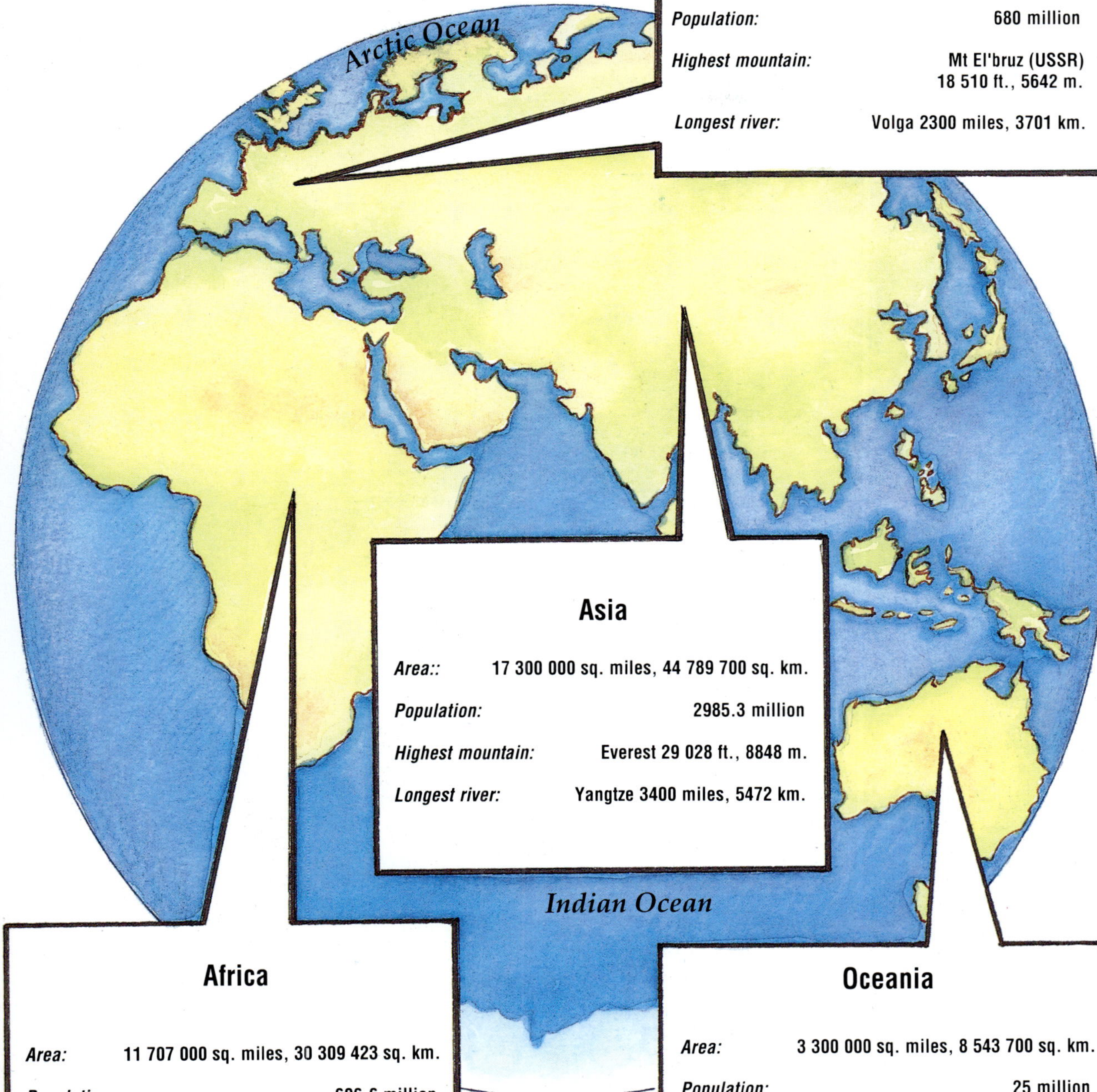

Europe

Area: 3 800 000 Sq. miles, 9 838 200 sq. km.

Population: 680 million

Highest mountain: Mt El'bruz (USSR) 18 510 ft., 5642 m.

Longest river: Volga 2300 miles, 3701 km.

Asia

Area:: 17 300 000 sq. miles, 44 789 700 sq. km.

Population: 2985.3 million

Highest mountain: Everest 29 028 ft., 8848 m.

Longest river: Yangtze 3400 miles, 5472 km.

Africa

Area: 11 707 000 sq. miles, 30 309 423 sq. km.

Population: 606.6 million

Highest mountain: Mt. Kilimanjaro 19 340 ft., 5895 m.

Longest river: Nile 4160 miles, 6695 km.

Oceania

Area: 3 300 000 sq. miles, 8 543 700 sq. km.

Population: 25 million

Highest mountain: Mt Jaya (Papua New Guinea) 16 500 ft., 5029 m.

Longest river: Darling 1702 miles, 2740 km.

COUNTRIES OF THE WORLD

Country	*Population (millions)*	*Capital*	*Currency*	*Language*
Afghanistan	15.43	**Kabul**	Afghani (100 Puls)	Pashtu, Dari
Algeria	22.50	**Algiers**	Dinar (100 Centimes)	Arabic, French
Argentina	32.10	**Buenos Aires**	Austral (100 Centavos)	Spanish
Australia	16.10	**Canberra**	Dollar (100 Cents)	English
Austria	7.61	**Vienna**	Schilling (100 Groschen)	German
Bahamas	0.23	**Nassau**	Dollar (100 Cents)	English
Bahrain	0.43	**Manama**	Dinar (1000 Fils)	Arabic
Bangladesh	101.20	**Dhaka**	Taka (100 Paisas)	Bangla
Barbados	0.25	**Bridgetown**	Dollar (100 Cents)	English
Belgium	9.91	**Brussels**	Belgian Franc (100 Centimes)	French, Flemish
Benin	4.25	**Cotonou/Porto Novo**	Franc C.F.A.	French
Bolivia	6.85	**La Paz**	Peso (100 Cents)	Spanish,Quechua, Aymara
Botswana	1.15	**Gaborone**	Pula (100 Thebe)	Setswana
Brazil	137.20	**Brasilia**	Cruzeiro (100 Centavos)	Portuguese
Bulgaria	8.98	**Sofia**	Lev (100 Stotinko)	Bulgarian
Burkina Faso	6.75	**Ouagadougou**	Franc C.F.A. (100 Centimes)	French, More, Dioula
Cameroon	10.10	**Yaoundé**	Franc C.F.A.	French, English
Canada	25.70	**Ottawa**	Dollar (100 Cents)	English, French
Chile	12.70	**Santiago**	New Peso (1000 Old Escudos)	Spanish
China	1060.00	**Beijing**	Yuan (100 Fen)	Chinese Mandarin
Colombia	29.50	**Bogotá**	Peso (100 Centavos)	Spanish
Costa Rica	2.82	**San José**	Colon (100 Centimos)	Spanish
Cote d'Ivoire	10.10	**Yamoussoukro**	Franc C.F.A.	French
Cuba	10.50	**Havana**	Peso (100 Cents)	Spanish
Cyprus	0.68	**Nicosia**	Cyprus Pound (100 Cents)	Greek, Turkish
Czechoslovakia	15.80	**Prague**	Crown (100 Heller)	Czech, Slovak
Denmark	5.14	**Copenhagen**	Kroner (100 Ore)	Danish
Dominican Rep.	6.35	**Santo Domingo**	Peso (100 Centavos)	Spanish
Ecuador Rep.	9.85	**Quito**	Sucre (100 Centavos)	Spanish
Egypt	49.95	**Cairo**	Pound (100 Piastres)	Arabic, French, English
El Salvador	5.80	**San Salvador**	Colon (100 Centavos)	Spanish
Ethiopia	34.00	**Addis Ababa**	Birr (100 Cents)	Amharic
Fiji	0.74	**Suva**	Dollar(100 Cents)	Fijian, Hindu, English
Finland	4.97	**Helsinki**	Markka (100 Pennia)	Finnish, Swedish
France	55.83	**Paris**	Franc (100 Centimes)	French
Gambia	0.65	**Banjul**	Dalasi (100 Bututs)	Mandinka, Fula, Wolof
Germany, East	16.80	**East Berlin**	Mark (100 Pfennige)	German
Germany, West	61.08	**Bonn**	Mark (100 Pfennige)	German
Ghana	12.80	**Accra**	Cedi (100 Pesewas)	English
Greece	10.10	**Athens**	Drachma (100 Lepta)	Greek
Grenada	0.13	**St. George's**	Eastern Caribbean Dollars	English
Guyana	0.97	**Georgetown**	Guyana Dollar (100 Cents)	English
Haiti	5.70	**Port au Prince**	Gourde (100 Centimes)	French, Creole
Honduras	4.60	**Tegucigalpa**	Lempira (100 Centavos)	Spanish
Hong Kong	5.59	**Victoria**	HK Dollar (100 Cents)	Chinese, English
Hungary	10.70	**Budapest**	Forint (100 Fillers)	Hungarian
Iceland	0.25	**Reykjavik**	Kroner (100 Aurar)	Icelandic
India	758.00	**New Delhi**	Rupee (100 Paise)	Hindi
Indonesia	171.50	**Jakarta**	Rupiah (100 Sen)	Indonesian, Bahasa
Iran	46.80	**Tehran**	Rial (100 Dinars)	Persian (Farsi)
Iraq	16.40	**Baghdad**	Dinar (1000 Fils)	Arabic
Ireland	3.57	**Dublin**	Irish Pound (100 Pence)	Irish, English
Israel	4.37	**Jerusalem**	New Shekel (100 Agorot)	Hebrew
Italy	57.40	**Rome**	Lira (100 Cents)	Italian
Jamaica	2.31	**Kingston**	Dollar (100 Cents)	English
Japan	122.00	**Tokyo**	Yen	Japanese
Jordan	3.60	**Amman**	Dinar (1000 Fils)	Arabic
Kenya	20.80	**Nairobi**	Shilling (100 Cents)	Kiswahili, English
Korea, Rep. of	42.25	**Seoul**	Won	Korean
Kuwait	1.99	**Kuwait City**	Dinar (1000 Fils)	Arabic
Lebanon	2.72	**Beirut**	Lebanese Pound (100 Piastres)	Arabic, French, English

Country	Population (millions)	Capital	Currency	Language
Lesotho	1.59	**Maseru**	Maloti (100 Lisente)	Arabic, French, English
Liberia	2.31	**Monrovia**	Dollar (100 Cents)	English
Luxemburg	0.37	**Luxemburg Ville**	Luxemburg Franc (100 Centimes)	French, German
Malawi	7.30	**Lilongwe**	Kwacha (100 Tambala)	Chichewa, English
Malaysia	16.05	**Kuala Lumpur**	M. Riggit (100 Sen)	Bahasa Malaysia
Malta	0.34	**Valletta**	Maltese Lira (100 Cents)	Maltese, English
Mauritius	1.05	**Port Louis**	Rupee (100 Cents)	English, French
Mexico	82.00	**Mexico City**	Peso (100 Centavos)	Spanish
Morocco	25.20	**Rabat**	Dirham (100 Centimes)	Arabic, French, Spanish
Nepal	17.15	**Kathmandu**	Rupee (100 Paise)	Nepali
Netherlands	14.56	**Amsterdam**	Guilder (100 Cents)	Dutch
New Zealand	3.30	**Wellington**	Dollar (100 Cents)	English, Maori
Nicaragua	3.43	**Managua**	Cordoba (100 Centavos)	Spanish, English, Miskito
Nigeria	96.20	**Lagos**	Naira (100 Kobo)	Hausa, Ibo, Yoruba
Norway	4.18	**Oslo**	Krone (100 Ore)	Norwegian
Oman	1.29	**Muscat**	Omani Riyal (1000 Baizas)	Arabic
Pakistan	99.22	**Islamabad**	Rupee (100 Paisa)	Urdu, English
Panama	2.40	**Panama City**	Balbao (100 Cents)	Spanish, English
Papua New Guinea	3.31	**Port Moresby**	Kina (100 Toca)	English, Motuy, Hiri
Paraguay	3.90	**Asuncion**	Guaranti (100 Centimos)	Spanish
Peru	20.50	**Lima**	Inti (1000 soles)	Spanish
Philippines	57.00	**Manila**	Philippine Peso (100 Centavos)	Philipino, English
Poland	37.64	**Warsaw**	Zloty (100 Groszy)	Polish
Portugal	10.36	**Lisboa (Lisbon)**	Escudo (100 Centavos)	Portuguese
Qatar	0.32	**Doha**	Qatar Riyal (100 Dirhams)	Arabic, English
Romania	22.90	**Bucharest**	Leu (100 Bani)	Romanian
Saudia Arabia	11.60	**Riyadh**	Riyal (100 Halalah)	Arabic
Senegal	6.48	**Dakar**	Franc C.F.A.	French, Wolof
Seychelles	0.06	**Port Victoria**	Rupee (100 Cents)	French, English, Creole
Sierra Leone	3.75	**Freetown**	Leone (100 Cents)	English
Singapore	2.61	**Singapore**	Dollar (100 Cents)	Malay, English, Chinese,Tamil
Somalia	4.70	**Mogadishu**	Shilling (100 Cents)	Somali, Arabic, Italian, English
South Africa	33.00	**Cape Town/Pretoria**	Rand (100 Cents)	Afrikaans, English
Spain	39.10	**Madrid**	Peseta (100 Cents)	Spanish
Sri Lanka	16.05	**Colombo**	Rupee (100 Cents)	Sinhala, Tamil, English
Sudan	22.00	**Khartoum**	Pound (100 Piastres)	Arabic, English
Swaziland	6.53	**Mbabane**	Lilangeni (100 Cents)	Siswati, English
Sweden	8.39	**Stockholm**	Krona (100 Ore)	Swedish
Switzerland	6.53	**Berne**	Swiss Franc (100 Centimes)	German, French, Italian
Taiwan	19.49	**Taipei**	New Taiwan Dollar (100 Cents)	Mandarin
Tanzania	21.60	**Dar-es Salaam**	Shilling (100 Cents)	Swahili, English
Thailand	59.10	**Bangkok**	Baht (100 Satang)	Thai, English
Togo	3.05	**Lome**	Franc C.F.A.	French, Kabye, Ewe
Tonga	0.10	**Nuku'alofa**	Tongan Pa'anga (100 Seniti)	Tongan, English
Trinidad and Tobago	1.25	**Port of Spain**	Dollar (100 Cents)	English
Tunisia	7.45	**Tunis**	Dinar (100 Millimes)	Arabic, French, English
Turkey	59.50	**Ankara**	Turkish Lira	Turkish
Uganda	15.65	**Kampala**	Shilling (100 Cents)	English, Kiswahili
United Arab Emirates	1.62	**Abu Dhabi**	Dirham (100 Fils)	Arabic
United Kingdom	55.00	**London**	Pound (100 Pence)	English
U.S. of America	242.40	**Washington D.C.**	Dollar (100 Cents)	English
U.S.S.R.	283.25	**Moscow**	Rouble (100 Kopecks)	Russian
Uruguay	3.09	**Montevideo**	Peso (100 Centavos)	Spanish
Venezuela	18.10	**Caracas**	Bolivar (20 Centimos)	Spanish
Yemen Arab Rep.	6.92	**Sana'a**	Rial (100 Fils)	Arabic
Yemen People's Dem. Rep.	2.32	**Aden**	Dinar (1000 Fils)	Arabic, English,
Yugoslavia	23.45	**Belgrade**	Dinar (100 Paras)	Serbocroat, Slovene, Macedonian
Zaire	31.22	**Kinshasa**	Zaire (100 Makutas)	French
Zambia	6.86	**Lusaka**	Kwacha (100 Ngwee)	English
Zimbabwe	8.75	**Harare**	Dollar (100 Cents)	English, Shona, Ndebele

THE WORLD: GEOGRAPHICAL FACTS

Largest Islands

	Sq. miles	Sq. km.
Greenland (N. Atlantic)	840 050	2 175 600
New Guinea (S.W. Pacific)	306 600	794 090
Borneo (S.W. Pacific)	280 100	725 179
Madagascar (Indian Ocean)	226 658	586 818
Baffin Island (Canadian Arctic)	195 928	507258
Sumatra (Indian Ocean)	165 000	427 185
Honshu (N.W. Pacific)	87 805	227 327
Great Britain (N. Atlantic)	84 200	217 994
Victoria Is. (Canadian Arctic)	83 896	217 206
Ellesmere Is. (Canadian Arctic)	75 767	196 109

Longest Rivers

	Miles	Km.
Nile (Africa)	4160	6695
Amazon (S. America)	4000	6437
Mississippi, Missouri, Red Rock (N. America)	3872	6231
Yangtze (China)	3400	5472
Ob Yrtysh (USSR)	3362	5410
Zaire (Africa)	3000	4828
Hwang Ho (China)	2903	4672
Amur (Asia)	2744	4416
Lena (USSR)	2734	4400
Mekong (S. Asia)	2600	4184
Yenisei (USSR)	2543	4092

Largest Lakes

	Sq. miles	Sq. km
Caspian Sea (USSR/Iran)	143 244	370 859
Superior (USA/Canada)	31 700	82 071
Victoria Nyanza (Africa)	26 828	69 457
Aral (USSR)	24 904	64 476
Huron (USA/Canada)	23 000	59 547
Michigan (USA)	22 300	57 735
Tanganyika (Africa)	12 700	32 880
Baykal (USSR)	12 162	31 487
Great Bear	12 096	31 317
Malawi (Africa)	11 150	28 867

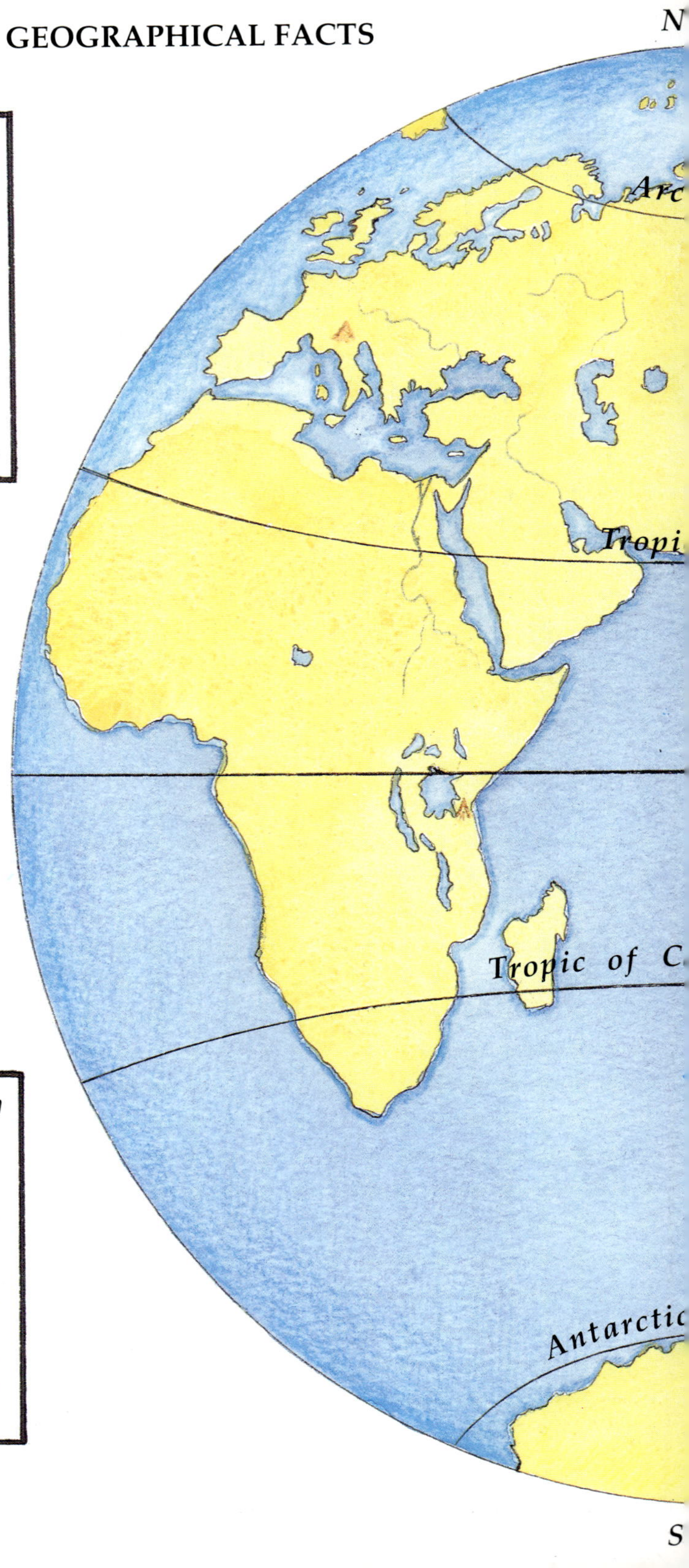

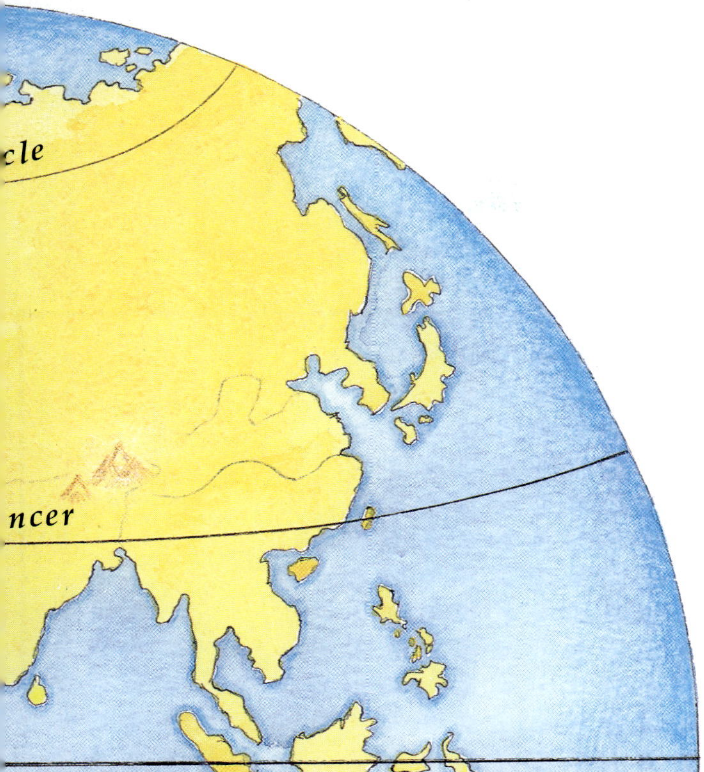

Highest Mountains

	Feet	Metres
ASIA		
Everest (Himalaya)	29 028	8848
Godwin Austen (India/Pakistan)	28 250	8611
Kanchenjunga (Himalaya)	28 146	8579
Makalu (Himalaya)	27 805	8475
Dhaulagiri (Himalaya)	26 810	8172
Nanga Parbat (Himalaya)	26 660	8126
Annapurna (Himalaya)	26 504	8078
Gasherbrum (Karakoram India)	26 470	8068
Gosainthan (Himalaya)	26 291	8013
Nanda Devi (Himalaya)	25 645	7817
SOUTH AMERICA		
Aconcagua (Andes)	22 834	6960
NORTH AMERICA		
McKinley (Alaska, USA)	20 320	6194
AFRICA		
Kilimanjaro (Tanzania)	19 340	5895
EUROPE		
El'bruz (USSR)	18 510	5642
Mont Blanc (Alps)	15 781	4810
ANTARTICA		
Vinson Massif	16 864	5140
OCEANIA		
Mt Jaya (New Guinea)	16 500	5029

International Time Zones

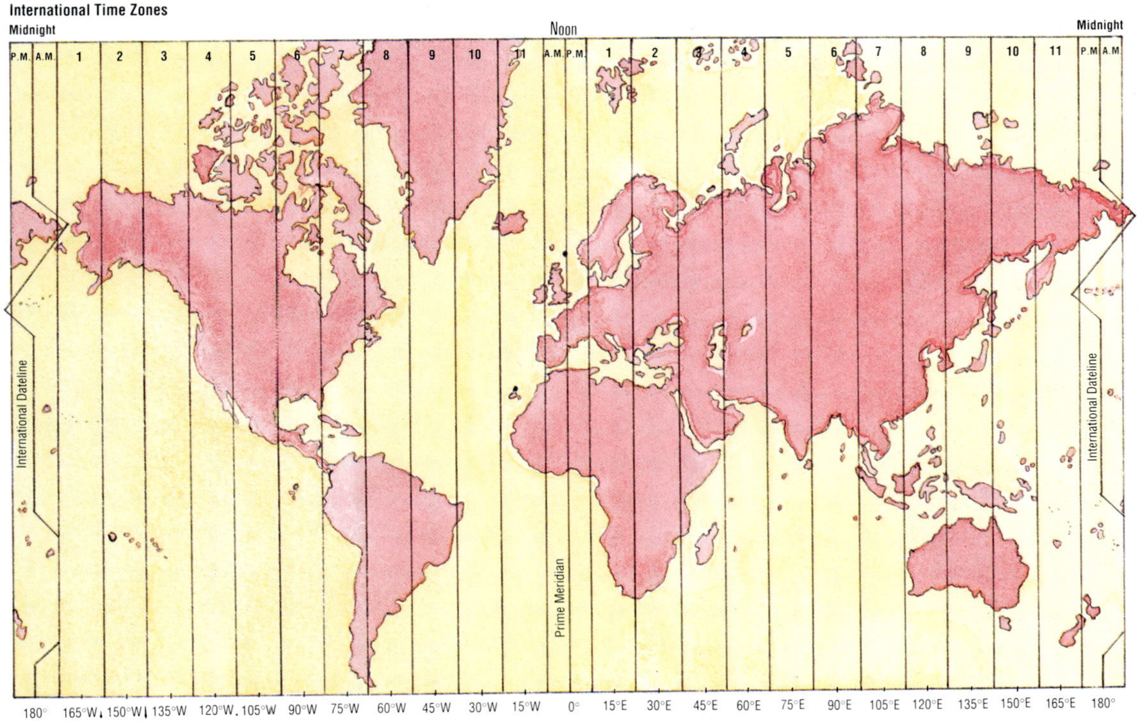

INTERNATIONAL AIRLINES

Air Portugal-Tap (Portugal)

Lufthansa (West Germany)

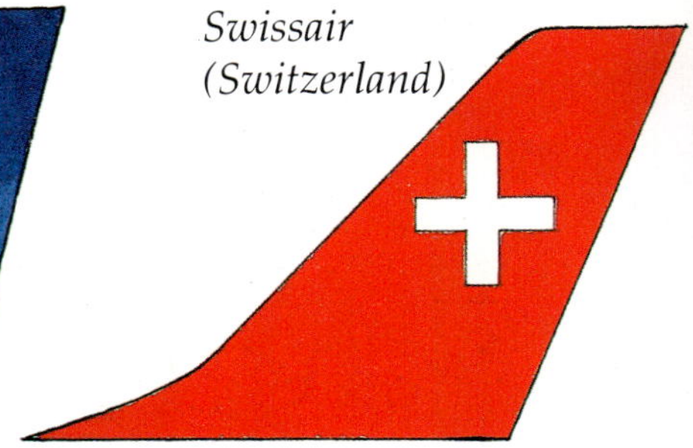

Swissair (Switzerland)

Pan American World Airways (USA)

Air Canada (Canada)

British Airways (UK) Concorde

British Airways (UK)

Civil Aircraft Markings: International Prefixes

AP	Pakistan
A2	Botswana
A3	Tonga
A6	United Arab Emirates
A7	Qatar
A9C	Bahrain
A40	Oman
B	China
C,CF	Canada
CC	Chile
CCCP	USSR
CN	Morocco
CP	Bolivia
CR, CS	Portugal
CU	Cuba
CX	Uruguay
C5	The Gambia
C6	Bahamas
C9	Mozambique
D	Germany, FR
DDR	Germany, DR
DQ	Fiji
D2	Angola
EC	Spain
EI, EJ	Ireland
EL	Liberia
EP	Iran
ET	Ethiopia
F	France
G	United Kingdom
HA	Hungary
HB (plus national emblem)	Switzerland
HB (plus national emblem)	Liechtenstein
HC	Ecuador
HH	Haiti
HI	Dominican Republic
HK	Colombia
HL	Republic of Korea
HP	Panama
HR	Honduras
HS	Thailand
HZ	Saudi Arabia
H4	Solomon Islands
I	Italy
JA	Japan
JY	Jordan
LN	Norway
LQ, LV	Argentina

LX	Luxembourg
LZ	Bulgaria
N	USA
OB	Peru
OD	Lebanon
OE	Austria
OH	Finland
OK	Czechoslovakia
OO	Belgium
OY	Denmark
P	Korea, PDR
PH	Netherlands
PJ	Netherlands Antilles
PK	Indonesia
PP, PT	Brazil
PZ	Suriname
P2	Papua New Guinea
RP	Philippines
SE	Sweden
SP	Poland
ST	Sudan
SU	Egypt
SX	Greece
S2	Bangladesh
S7	Seychelles
TC	Turkey
TF	Iceland
TG	Guatemala
TI	Costa Rica
TJ	Cameroon
TL	Central African Republic
TN	Congo
TR	Gabon
TS	Tunisia
TT	Chad
TU	Ivory Coast
VH	Australia
VP,VQ,VR	United Kingdom Colonies & Protectorates
VT	India
V3	Belize
V8	Brunei
XA,XB,XC	Mexico
XU	Democratic Kampuchea
XV	Vietnam
XY, XZ	Burma
YA	Afghanistan
YI	Iraq
YK	Syria
YN	Nicaragua

YR	Romania
YS	El Salvador
YU	Yugoslavia
YV	Venezuela
Z	Zimbabwe
ZK,ZL,ZM	New Zealand
ZP	Paraguay
ZS,ZT,ZU	South Africa
3A	Monaco
3B	Mauritius
3C	Equatorial Guinea
3D	Swaziland
3X	Guinea
4R	Sri Lanka
4W	Yemen
4X	Israel
5A	Libyan Arab Jamahiriya
5B	Cyprus
5H	Tanzania
5N	Nigeria
5R	Madagascar
5T	Mauritania
5U	Niger
5V	Togo
5W	Samoa
5X	Uganda
5Y	Kenya
6O	Somalia
6V,6W	Senegal
6Y	Jamaica
7O	Democratic Yemen
7P	Lesotho
7QY	Malawi
7T	Algeria
8P	Barbados
8Q	Maldives
8R	Guyana
9G	Ghana
9H	Malta
9J	Zambia
9K	Kuwait
9L	Sierra Leone
9M	Malaysia
9N	Nepal
9Q	Zaire
9U	Burundi
9V	Singapore
9XR	Rwanda
9Y	Trinidad and Tobago

Alitalia (Italy)
Aer Lingus (Eire)
Aeroflot (USSR)
Air France (France)
PIA (Pakistan)
PIA
Austrian Airlines (Austria)
Sabena (Belgium)
Iraqi Airways (Iraq)
Iraqi
Iberia (Spain)
Egyptair (Egypt)
Japan Air Lines (Japan)
JAL
KLM (Netherlands)
KLM
Air-India (India)
AIR-INDIA
Singapore Airlines (Singapore)
Cathay Pacific (Hong Kong)
Air New Zealand (New Zealand)
Quantas Airways (Australia)

RULERS

Elizabeth II

Richard III

Henry VIII

Robert the Bruce

Alfred the Great

Elizabeth I

Charles I

BRITISH RULERS

RULERS OF ENGLAND (827 to 1603)

Saxons

Egbert	827-839
Ethelwulf	839-858
Ethelbald	858-860
Ethelbert	860-865
Ethelred I	865-871
Alfred the Great	871-899
Edward the Elder	899-924
Athelstan	924-939
Edmund	939-946
Edred	946-955
Edwy	955-959
Edgar	959-975
Edward the Martyr	975-978
Ethelred II (the Unready)	978-1016
Edmund Ironside	1016

Danes

Canute	1016-1035
Harold I (Harefoot)	1035-1040
Hardicanute	1040-1042

Saxons

Edward (the Confessor)	1042-1066
Harold II	1066

House of Normandy

William I (the Conqueror)	1066-1087
William II	1087-1100
Henry I	1100-1135
Stephen I	1135-1154

House of Plantagenet

Henry II	1154-1189
Richard I	1189-1199
John	1199-1216
Henry III	1216-1272
Edward I	1272-1307
Edward II	1307-1327
Edward III	1327-1377
Richard II	1377-1399

House of Lancaster

Henry IV	1399-1413
Henry V	1413-1422
Henry VI	1422-1461

House of York

Edward IV	1461-1483
Edward V	1483
Richard III	1483-1485

House of Tudor

Henry VII	1485-1509
Henry VIII	1509-1547
Edward VI	1547-1553
Mary I	1553-1558
Elizabeth I	1558-1603

RULERS OF SCOTLAND (1005 to 1603)

Malcolm II	1005-1034
Duncan I	1034-1040
Macbeth	1040-1058
Malcolm III (Canmore)	1058-1093
Donald Bane	1093-1094
Duncan II	1094
Donald Bane (restored)	1094-1097
Edgar	1097-1107
Alexander I	1107-1124
David I	1124-1153
Malcolm IV	1153-1165
William the Lion	1165-1214
Alexander II	1214-1249
Alexander III	1249-1286
Margaret of Norway	1286-1290
Interregnum	1290-1292
John Balliol	1292-1296
Interregnum	1296-1306
Robert I (Bruce)	1306-1329
David II	1329-1371

House of Stuart

Robert II	1371-1390
Robert III	1390-1406
James I	1406-1437
James II	1437-1460
James III	1460-1488
James IV	1488-1513
James V	1513-1542
Mary	1542-1567
James VI	1567-1625

(became James I of England in 1603)

RULERS OF BRITAIN

House of Stuart

James I	1603-1625
Charles I	1625-1649

Commonwealth 1649-1660

House of Stuart (restored)

Charles II	1660-1685
James II	1685-1688
William III	1689-1702
Mary II	1689-1694
Anne	1702-1714

House of Hanover

George I	1714-1727
George II	1727-1760
George III	1760-1820
George IV	1820-1830
William IV	1830-1837
Victoria	1837-1901

House of Saxe-Coburg

Edward VII	1901-1910

House of Windsor

George V	1910-1936
Edward VIII	1936
George VI	1936-1952
Elizabeth II	1952

BRITISH PRIME MINISTERS

Sir Robert Walpole	Whig	1721-42
Earl of Wilmington	Whig	1742-54
Henry Pelham	Whig	1743-54
Duke of Newcastle	Whig	1754-56
Duke of Devonshire	Whig	1756-57
Duke of Newcastle	Whig	1757-62
Earl of Bute	Tory	1762-63
George Grenville	Whig	1763-65
Marquess of Rockingham	Whig	1765-66
Earl of Chatham	Whig	1766-67
Duke of Grafton	Whig	1767-70
Lord North	Tory	1770-82
Marquess of Rockingham	Whig	1782
Earl of Shelburne	Whig	1782-83
Duke of Portland	Coalition	1783
William Pitt	Tory	1783-01
Henry Addington	Tory	1801-04
William Pitt	Tory	1804-06
Lord Grenville	Whig	1806-07
Duke of Portland	Tory	1807-09
Spencer Perceval	Tory	1809-12
Earl of Liverpool	Tory	1812-27
George Canning	Tory	1827
Viscount Goderich	Tory	1827-28
Duke of Wellington	Tory	1828-30
Earl Grey	Whig	1830-34
Viscount Melbourne	Whig	1834-41
Sir Robert Peel	Tory	1841-46
Lord John Russell	Whig	1846-52
Earl of Derby	Tory	1852
Earl of Aberdeen	Peelite	1852-55
Viscount Palmerston	Liberal	1855-58
Earl of Derby	Conservative	1858-59
Viscount Palmerston	Liberal	1859-65
Earl Russell	Liberal	1865-66

Earl of Derby	Conservative	1866-68
Benjamin Disraeli	Conservative	1868
William Gladstone	Liberal	1868-74
Benjamin Disraeli	Conservative	1874-80
William Gladstone	Liberal	1880-85
Marquess of Salisbury	Conservative	1885-86
William Gladstone	Liberal	1886
Marquess of Salisbury	Conservative	1886-92
William Gladstone	iberal	1892-94
Earl of Rosebery	Liberal	1894-95
Marquess of Salisbury	Conservative	1895-1902
Arthur Balfour	Conservative	1902-05
Sir H. Campbell-Bannerman	Liberal	1905-08
Herbert Asquith	Liberal	1908-15
Herbert Asquith	Coalition	1915-16
David Lloyd-George	Coalition	1916-22
Andrew Bonar Law	Conservative	1922-23
Stanley Baldwin	Conservative	1923-24
James Ramsay MacDonald	Labour	1924
Stanley Baldwin	Conservative	1924-29
James Ramsay MacDonald	Labour	1929-31
James Ramsay MacDonald	Coalition	1931-35
Stanley Baldwin	Coalition	1935-37
Neville Chamberlain	Coalition	1937-40
Winston Churchill	Coalition	1940-45
Winston Churchill	Conservative	1945
Clement Atlee	Labour	1945-51
Sir Winston Churchill	Conservative	1951-55
Sir Anthony Eden	Conservative	1955-57
Harold Macmillan	Conservative	1957-63
Sir Alec Douglas-Home	Conservative	1963-64
Harold Wilson	Labour	1964-70
Edward Heath	Conservative	1970-74
Harold Wilson	Labour	1974-76
James Callaghan	Labour	1976-79
Margaret Thatcher	Conservative	1979-

William Gladstone

William Pitt

Margaret Thatcher

AMERICAN PRESIDENTS

***Fed.**= Federalist* ***DR.**= Democratic Republican* ***Dem.**=Democratic* ***W**=Whig* ***U**=Union* ***Rep.**=Republican*

George Washington	Fed.	1789-1797
John Adams	Fed.	1797-1801
Thomas Jefferson	DR	1801-1809
James Madison	DR	1809-1817
James Monroe	DR	1817-1825
John Quincey Adams	DR	1825-1829
Andrew Jackson	Dem.	1829-1837
Martin Van Buren	Dem.	1837-1841
William H. Harrison	W	1841
Jonn Tyler	W	1841-1845
James Knox Polk	Dem.	1845-1849
Zachary Taylor	W	1849-1850
Millard Fillmore	W	1850-1853
Franklin Pierce	Dem.	1853-1857
James Buchanan	Dem.	1857-1861
Abraham Lincoln	Rep.	1861-1865
Andrew Johnson	U	1865-1869
Ulysses S. Grant	Rep.	1869-1877
Rutherford B. Hayes	Rep.	1877-1881
James A. Garfield	Rep.	1881
Chester A. Arthur	Rep.	1881-1885
Grover Cleveland	Dem.	1885-1889
Benjamin Harrison	Rep.	1889-1893
Grover Cleveland	Dem.	1893-1897
William McKinley	Rep.	1897-1901
Theodore Roosevelt	Rep.	1901-1909
William H. Taft	Rep.	1909-1913
Woodrow Wilson	Dem.	1913-1921

Warren G. Harding	Rep.	1921-1923
Calvin Coolidge	Rep.	1923-1929
Herbert C. Hoover	Rep.	1929-1933
Franklin Roosevelt	Dem.	1933-1945
Harry S. Truman	Dem.	1945-1953
Dwight D. Eisenhower	Rep.	1953-1961
John F. Kennedy	Dem.	1961-1963
Lyndon B. Johnson	Dem.	1963-1969
Richard Nixon	Rep.	1969-1974
Gerald R. Ford	Rep.	1974-1977
Jimmy Carter	Dem.	1977-1981
Ronald Reagan	Rep.	1981-1989
George H. W. Bush	Rep.	1989-

George Washington

Abraham Lincoln

Franklin D. Roosevelt

Ronald Reagan

SPACE

Northern Hemisphere Constellations

Southern Hemiphere Constellations

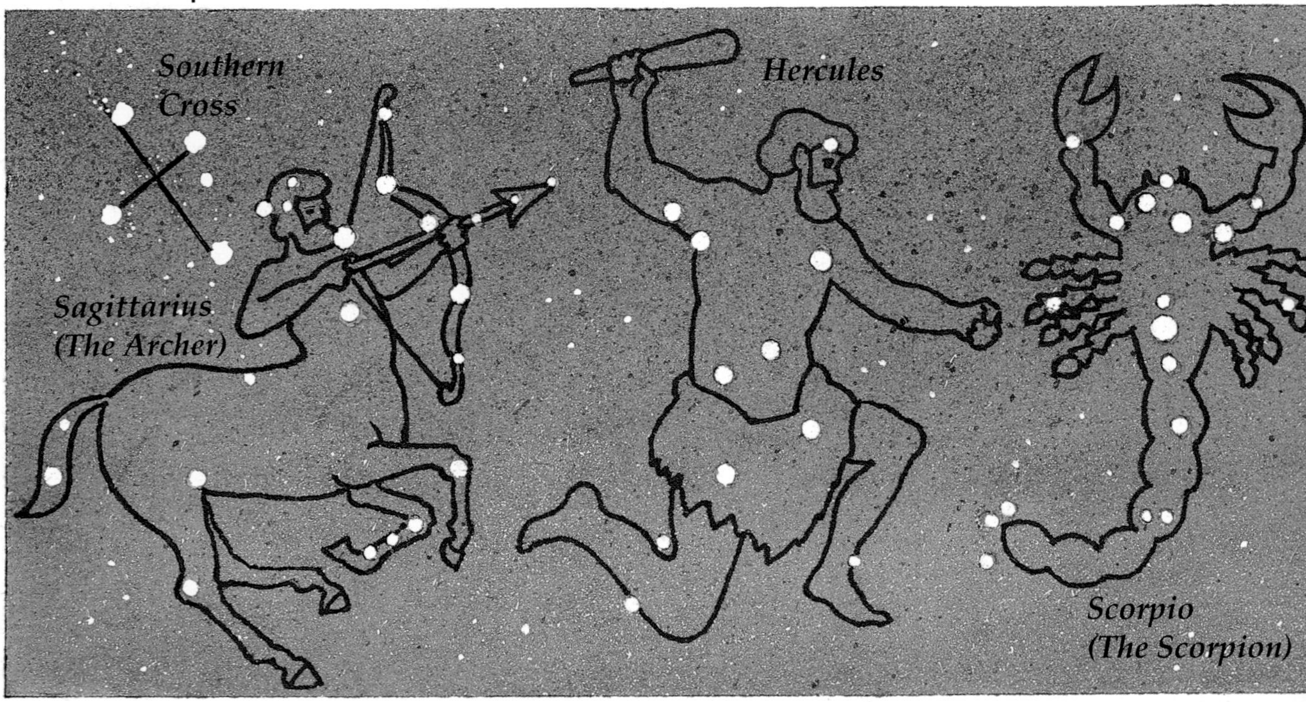

Space Shuttle (USA) 1981

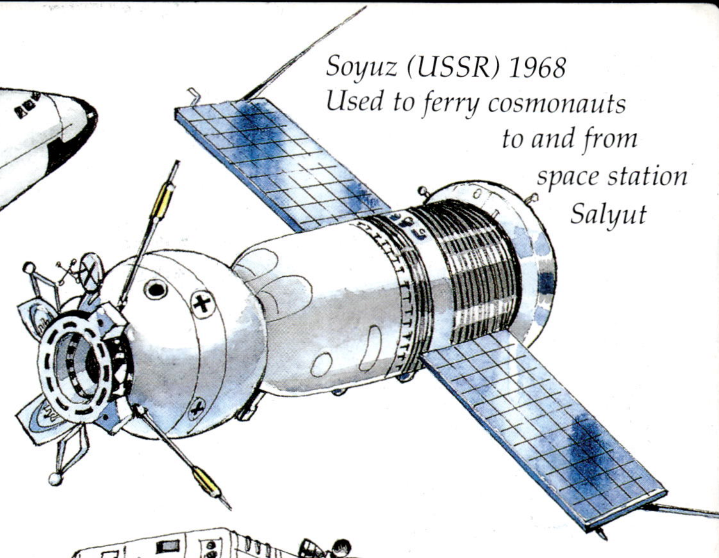

Soyuz (USSR) 1968
Used to ferry cosmonauts to and from space station Salyut

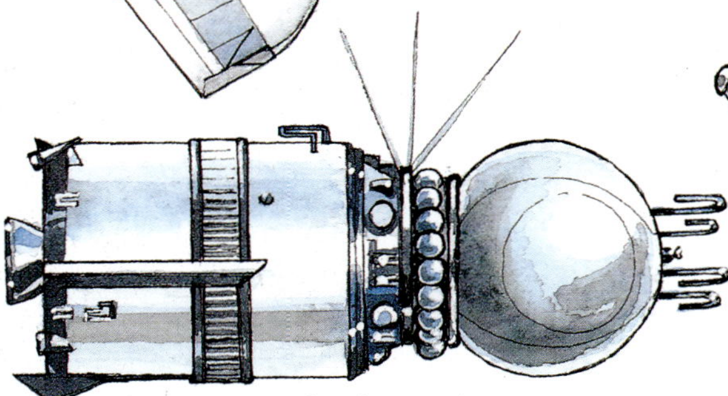

Vostok I (USSR) 1961
First manned space flight

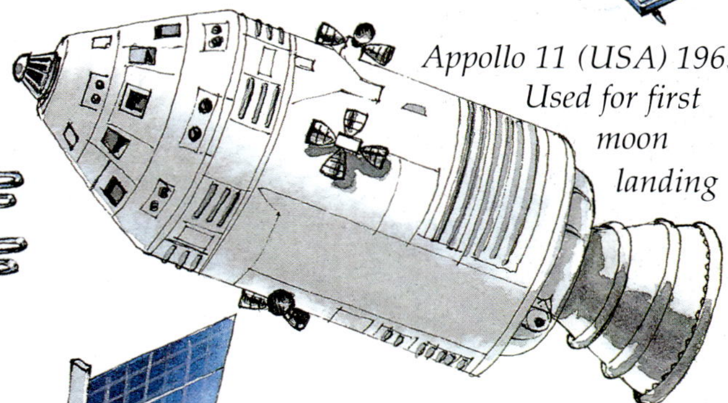

Appollo 11 (USA) 1969
Used for first moon landing

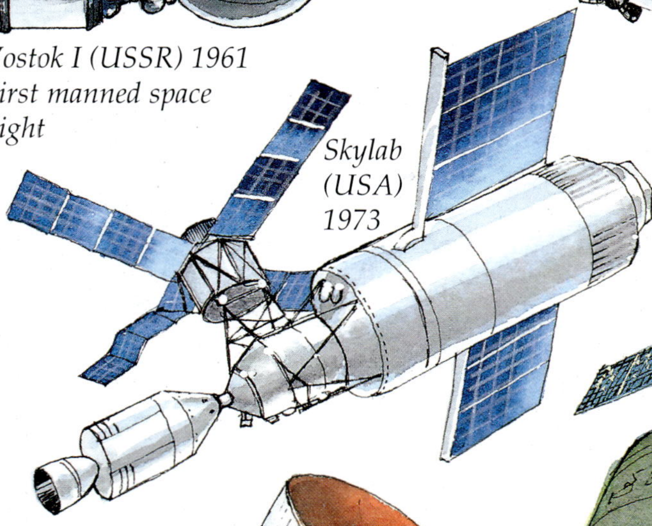

Skylab (USA) 1973

Saturn V(USA)
Used for the launch of Appollo 11 to the moon

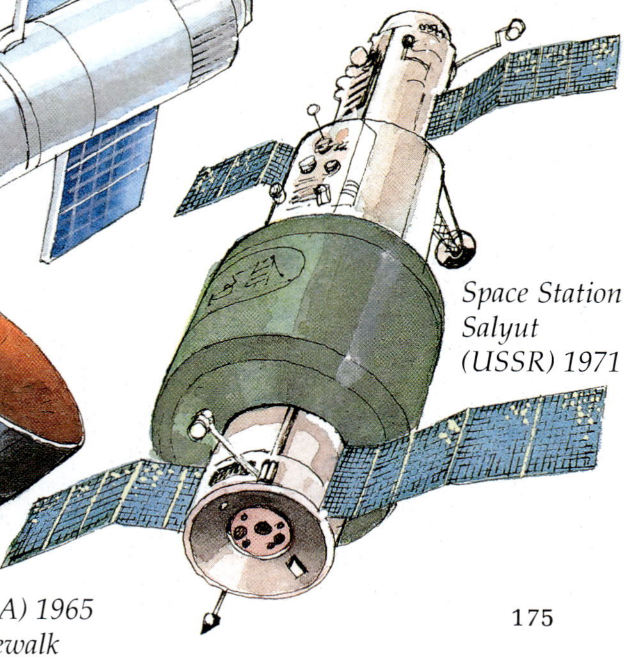

Space Station Salyut (USSR) 1971

Gemini 4 (USA) 1965
First US spacewalk

PRECIOUS STONES AND ANNIVERSARIES

Sapphire

Opal

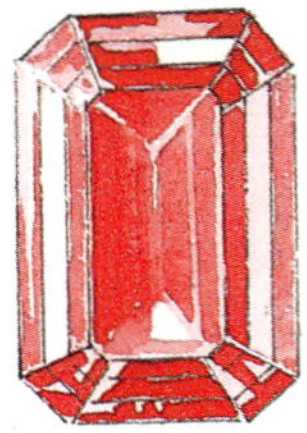

Ruby

Aquamarine

Peridot

Diamond

Amethyst

Emerald

Garnet

Pearl

Turquoise

Topaz

Gemstones

Agate	brown, red, blue, green, yellow
Amethyst	violet
Aquamarine	sky blue, greenish, blue
Beryl	green, blue, pink
Bloodstone	green with red spots
Citrine	yellow
Diamond	colourless, tints of various colours
Emerald	green
Garnet	red and other colours
Jade	green, whitish, mauve, brown
Lapis Lazuli	deep blue
Malachite	dark green banded
Moonstone	whitish with blue shimmer
Onyx	various colours with regular coloured bands
Opal	black, white, orange-red, rainbow coloured
Peridot	green
Ruby	red
Sapphire	blue and other colours
Serpentine	red and green
Topaz	blue, green, pink, yellow, colourless
Tourmaline	brown-black, blue, pink, red, violet
Turquoise	green and blue

Silver

Gold

Birthstones

January	garnet
February	amethyst
March	aquamarine
April	diamond
May	emerald
June	pearl
July	ruby
August	peridot
September	sapphire
October	opal
November	topaz
December	turquoise

Traditional Anniversary Names

Year	Name	Year	Name
1	paper	**13**	lace
2	cotton	**14**	ivory
3	leather	**15**	crystal
4	fruit or flowers	**20**	china
5	wood	**25**	silver
6	iron or sugar	**30**	pearl
7	wool or copper	**35**	coral
8	bronze	**40**	ruby
9	pottery	**45**	sapphire
10	tin or aluminium	**50**	golden
11	steel	**55**	emerald
12	silk or fine linen	**60**	diamond